Cyanide & Happiness™
PUNCHING ZOO

Kris, Rob, Matt & Dave

BOOM! BOX™

BOOM! Box Edition

Designer Scott Newman
Assistant Editor Jasmine Amiri
Editors Shannon Watters & Bryce Carlson

BOOM! BOX™

ROSS RICHIE CEO & Founder • MARK SMYLIE Founder of Archaia • MATT GAGNON Editor-in-Chief • STEPHEN CHRISTY President of Development • FILIP SABLIK VP of Publishing & Marketing
LANCE KREITER VP of Licensing & Merchandising • PHIL BARBARO VP of Finance • BRYCE CARLSON Managing Editor • MEL CAYLO Marketing Manager • SCOTT NEWMAN Production Design Manager
IRENE BRADISH Operations Manager • CHRISTINE DINH Brand Communications Manager • DAFNA PLEBAN Editor • SHANNON WATTERS Editor • ERIC HARBURN Editor • REBECCA TAYLOR Editor
IAN BRILL Editor • CHRIS ROSA Assistant Editor • ALEX GALER Assistant Editor • WHITNEY LEOPARD Assistant Editor • JASMINE AMIRI Assistant Editor • CAMERON CHITTOCK Assistant Editor
KELSEY DIETERICH Production Designer • EMI YONEMURA BROWN Production Designer • DEVIN FUNCHES E-Commerce & Inventory Coordinator • ANDY LIEGL Event Coordinator • BRIANNA HART Administrative Coordinator
AARON FERRARA Operations Assistant • JOSÉ MEZA Sales Assistant • MICHELLE ANKLEY Sales Assistant • ELIZABETH LOUGHRIDGE Accounting Assistant • STEPHANIE HOCUTT PR Assistant

A catalog record of this book is available from OCLC and from the BOOM! Studios website, www.boom-studios.com, on the Librarians Page.

For other Cyanide & Happiness comics, animated shorts, books, and merchandise, visit www.explosm.net

BOOM! Studios, 5670 Wilshire Boulevard, Suite 450, Los Angeles, CA 90036-5679. Printed in Korea. First Printing. ISBN: 978-1-60886-473-7, eISBN: 978-1-61398-327-0

Dedicated to Kris, Rob, Matt & Dave.

FOREWORD

Kris, Rob, Matt, and Dave asked me to do this foreword for Cyanide & Happiness, which was fitting because when Steve and I first launched reddit, our master plan was to ensure that four social deviants would become famous for crude doodles doing and saying offensive things. You're welcome, guys.

Hell, the creators worked together for years before even *meeting* each other in meatspace. The internet is amazing.

Sure, this book will likely offend people, but probably not the people who'd buy this book. In the event that you are that kind of easily-offended person — perhaps you were mistakenly gifted this comic, or your friend is a jerk — behold the splendor of the internet. Yes, it's in murdered tree form, but what you're holding is a tangible example of unfettered creativity. Seriously. It's unfettered.

How do I know this?

Imagine a world where the only comic strips are the ones that made it into the pages of the Sunday Comics section of the newspaper. Do you even remember newspapers? Their editors once determined which comics were worthy (and benign) enough to entertain (and not offend) *anyone* reading.

That's why no one's laughed at Family Circus since 1960.

Think of all the other minds as twisted (and creative) as the four behind C&H who never got a chance to share their genius—yes genius—with the world. Now imagine if Gary Larson had actually been able to write some of the jokes you know the censors never would've let him print.

Basically, the world is a lot less hilarious because of it.

Until now.

Well, OK, it's not like this book in particular was the turning point, but since they didn't ask me to write the foreword to their first two books I'm working with what I've got — sloppy thirds.

Really, three books? These guys are making a living off this? Only on the internet, folks.

Enjoy this book while I learn how to draw stick figures and work on my fart jokes.

-Alexis Ohanian
co-founder of reddit

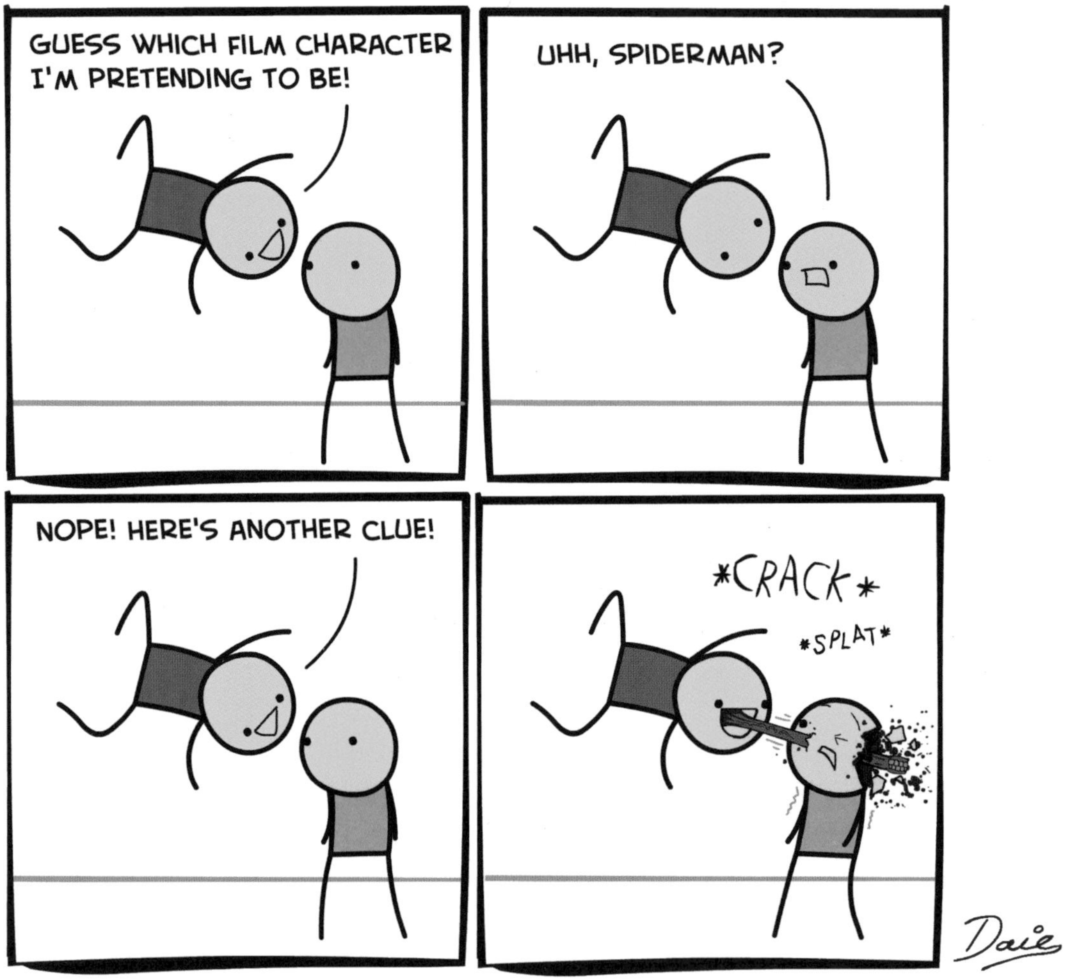
GUESS WHICH FILM CHARACTER I'M PRETENDING TO BE!
UHH, SPIDERMAN?
NOPE! HERE'S ANOTHER CLUE!
CRACK
SPLAT
Dave

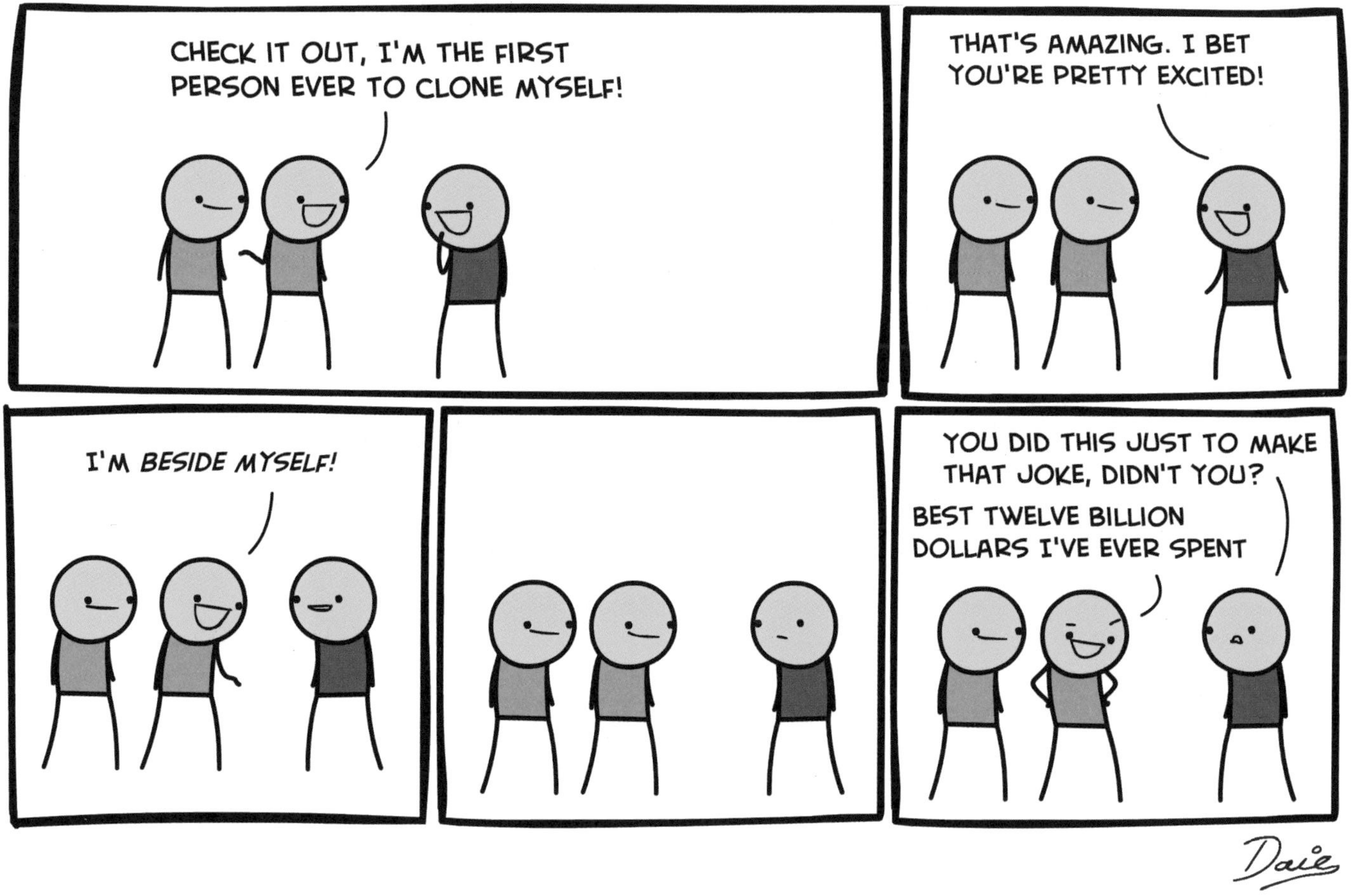
CHECK IT OUT, I'M THE FIRST PERSON EVER TO CLONE MYSELF!
THAT'S AMAZING. I BET YOU'RE PRETTY EXCITED!
I'M *BESIDE MYSELF!*
YOU DID THIS JUST TO MAKE THAT JOKE, DIDN'T YOU?
BEST TWELVE BILLION DOLLARS I'VE EVER SPENT

WHAT'S THIS, DAD? MY BIRTHDAY'S NOT UNTIL OCTOBER...
IT'S YOUR CONCEPTION DAY! WHEN YOUR MOTHER AND I FIRST PRODUCED YOU.
IN A MOMENT OF PURE ECSTASY, OUR SEX CELLS SLAMMED TOGETHER AND PRODUCED A ZYGOTE THAT WOULD, ONE DAY, BECOME YOU.
WHOOPS, FORGOT THE ICING.

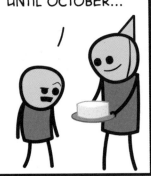

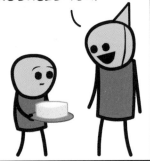

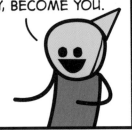

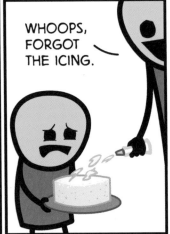

HEY MAN, I'M HEADING OVER TO THE PARTY. SEXT ME THE DIRECTIONS.
ONE SEC.
BZZT

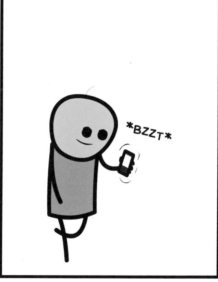

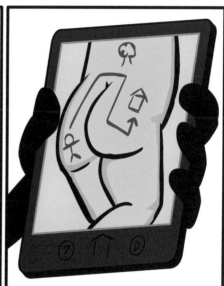

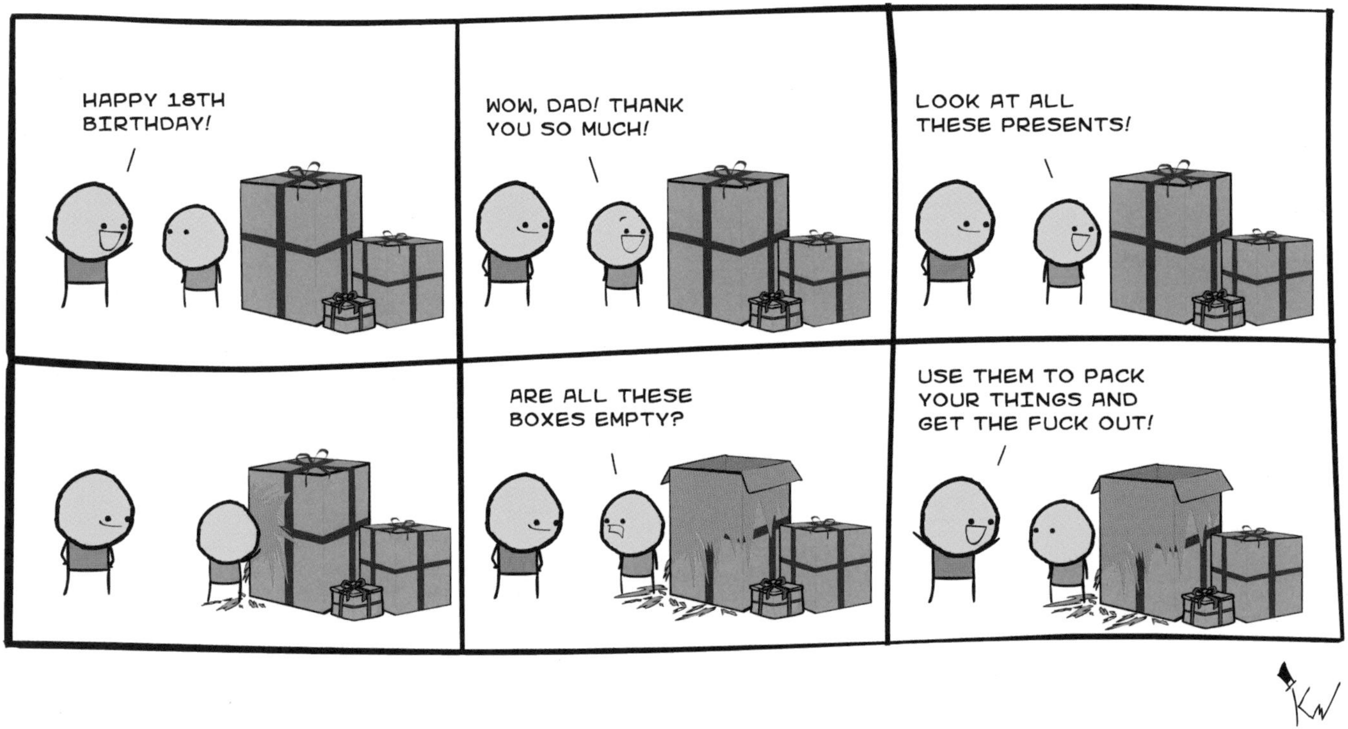
HAPPY 18TH BIRTHDAY!
WOW, DAD! THANK YOU SO MUCH!
LOOK AT ALL THESE PRESENTS!
ARE ALL THESE BOXES EMPTY?
USE THEM TO PACK YOUR THINGS AND GET THE FUCK OUT!

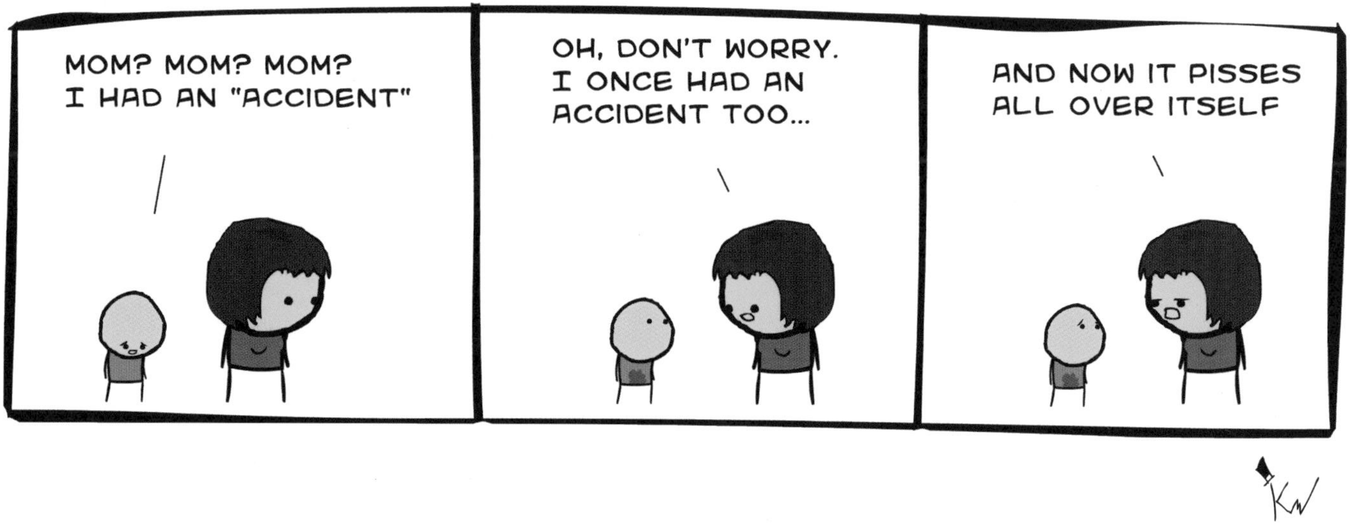
MOM? MOM? MOM?
I HAD AN "ACCIDENT"
OH, DON'T WORRY.
I ONCE HAD AN
ACCIDENT TOO...
AND NOW IT PISSES
ALL OVER ITSELF

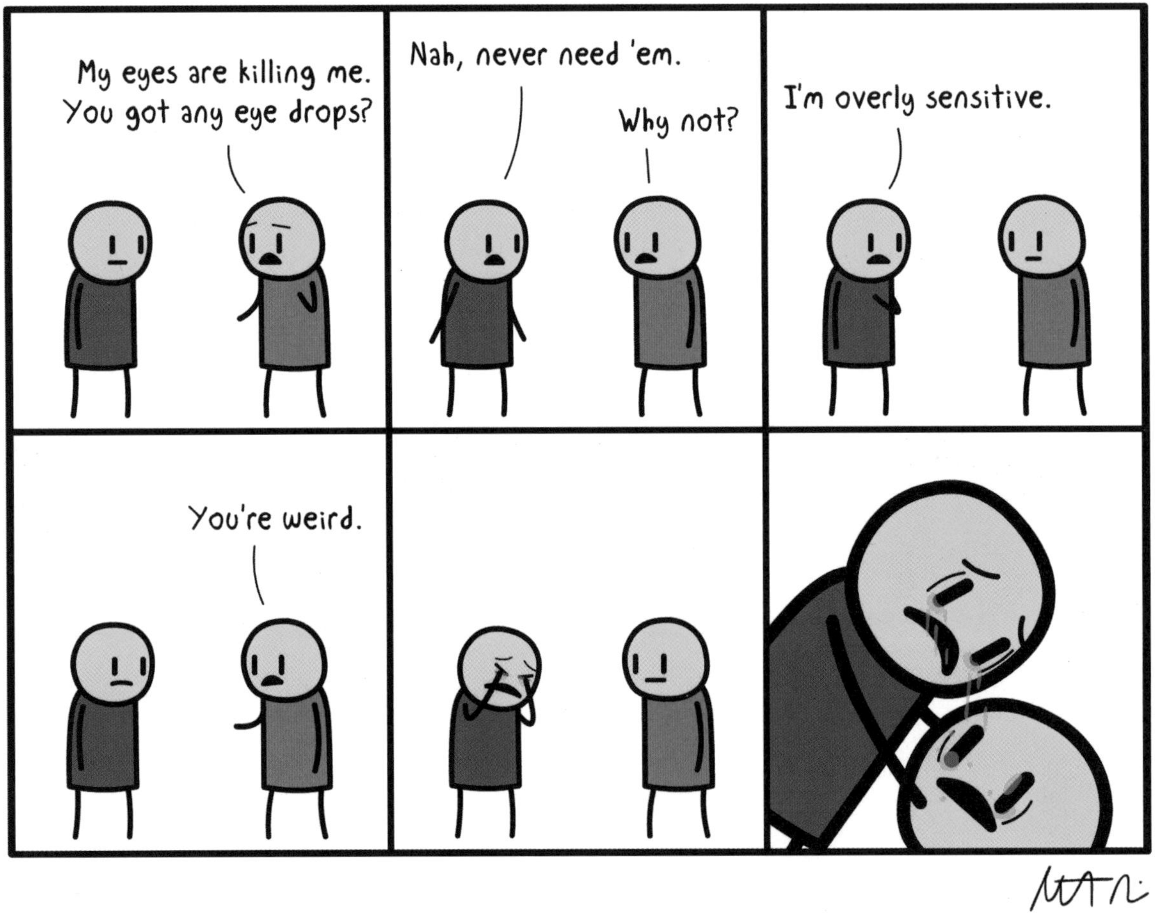
My eyes are killing me. You got any eye drops?
Nah, never need 'em.
Why not?
I'm overly sensitive.
You're weird.

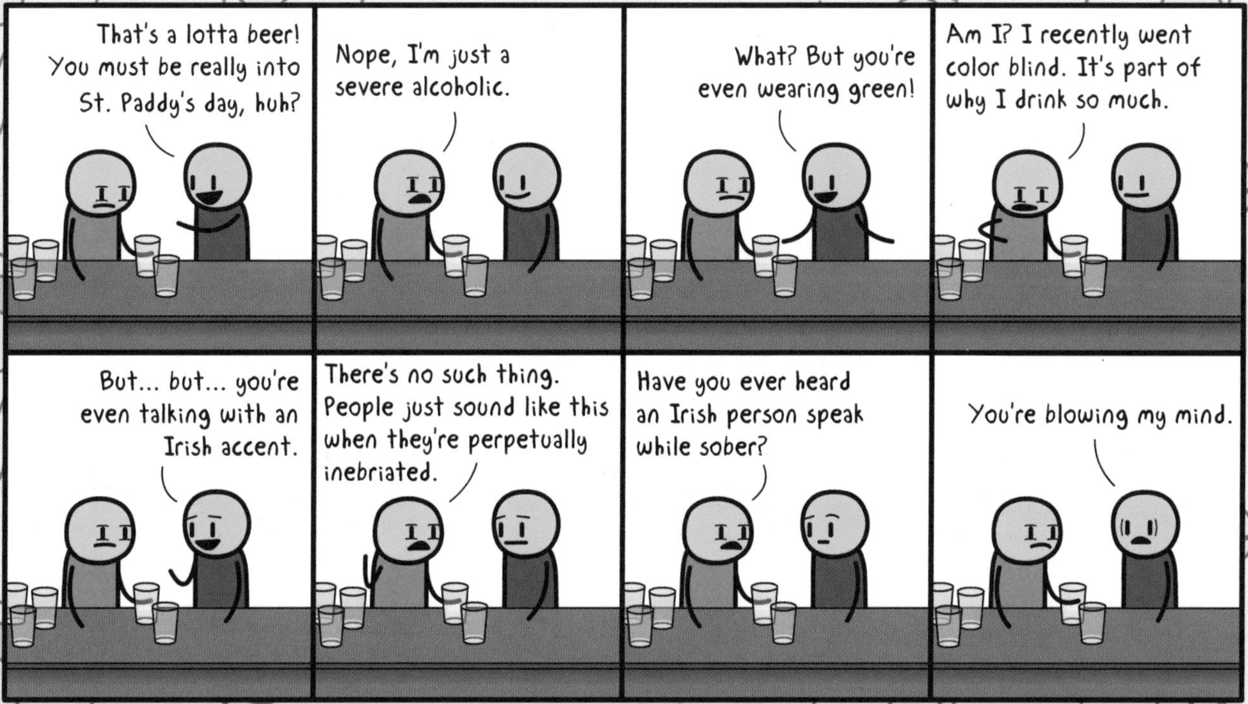
That's a lotta beer! You must be really into St. Paddy's day, huh?
Nope, I'm just a severe alcoholic.
What? But you're even wearing green!
Am I? I recently went color blind. It's part of why I drink so much.
But... but... you're even talking with an Irish accent.
There's no such thing. People just sound like this when they're perpetually inebriated.
Have you ever heard an Irish person speak while sober?
You're blowing my mind.

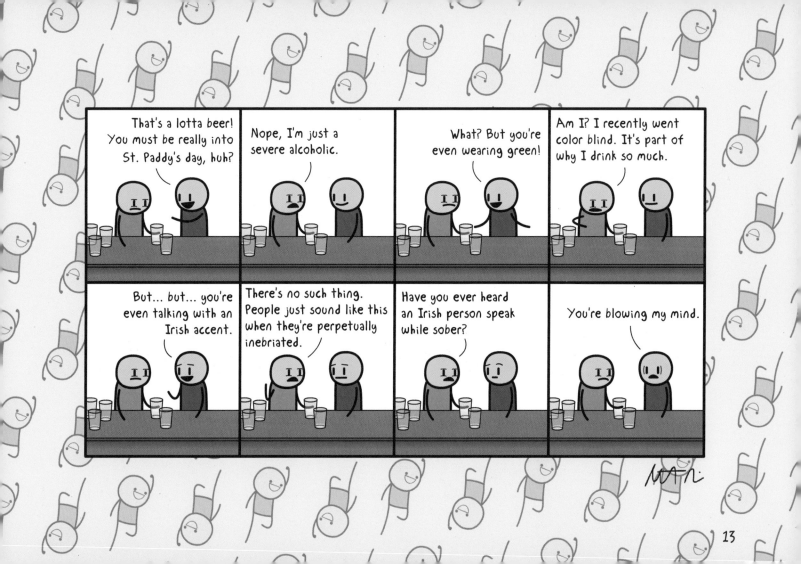

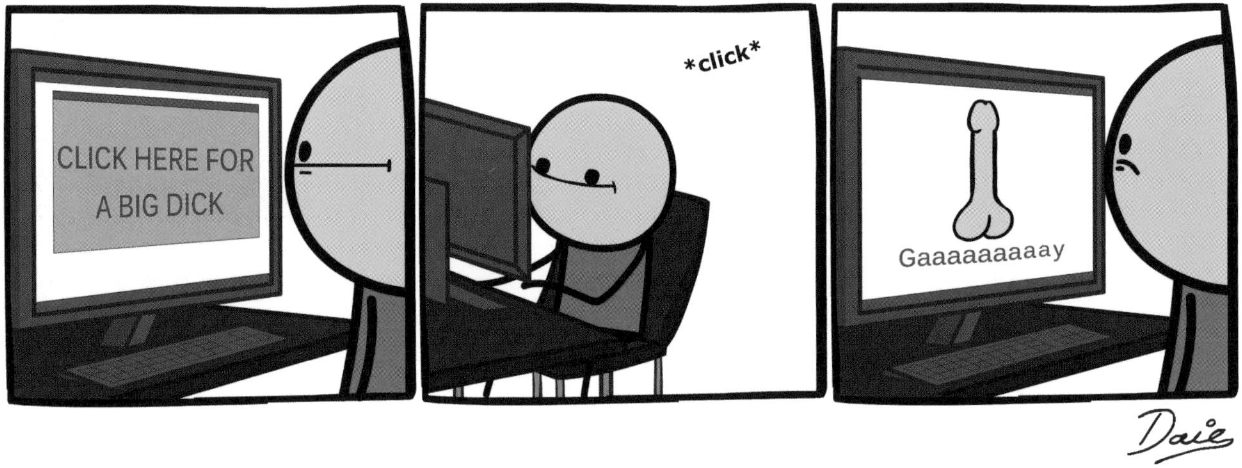
CLICK HERE FOR A BIG DICK
click
Gaaaaaaaaay

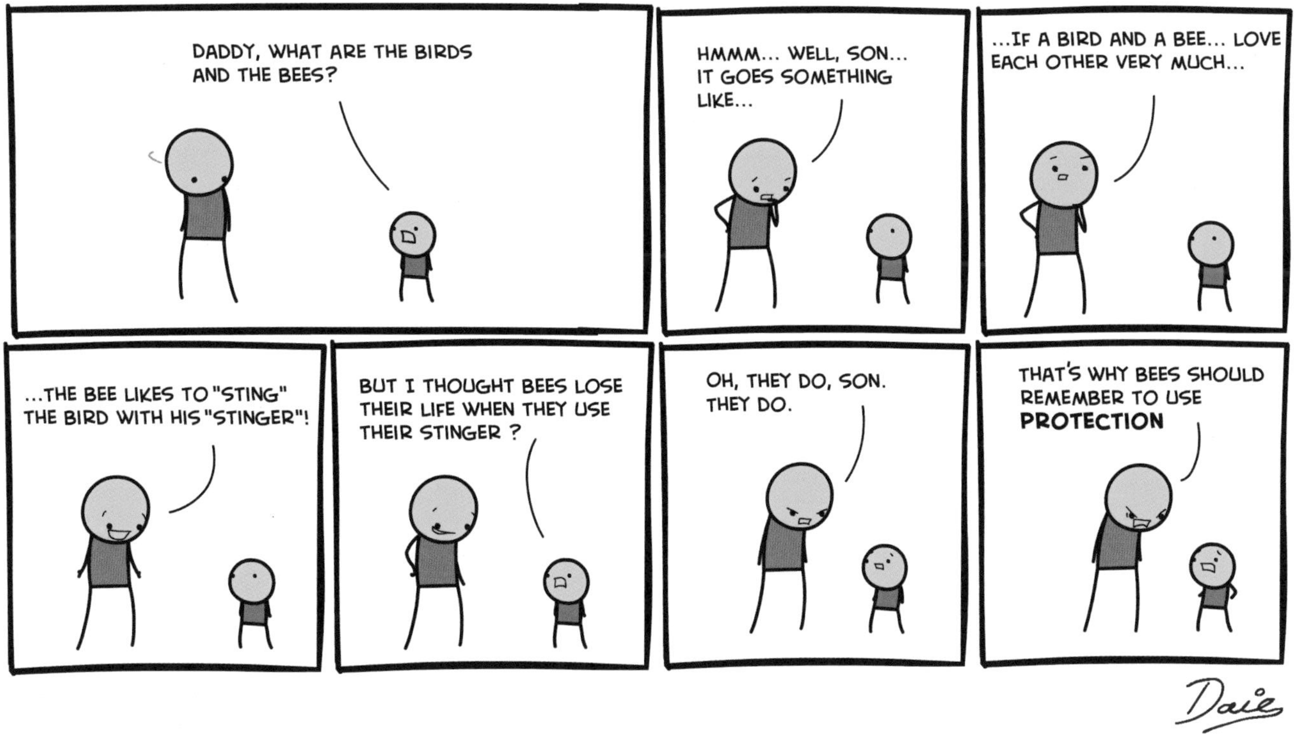
DADDY, WHAT ARE THE BIRDS AND THE BEES?
HMMM... WELL, SON... IT GOES SOMETHING LIKE...
...IF A BIRD AND A BEE... LOVE EACH OTHER VERY MUCH...
...THE BEE LIKES TO "STING" THE BIRD WITH HIS "STINGER"!
BUT I THOUGHT BEES LOSE THEIR LIFE WHEN THEY USE THEIR STINGER ?
OH, THEY DO, SON. THEY DO.
THAT'S WHY BEES SHOULD REMEMBER TO USE PROTECTION
Dave

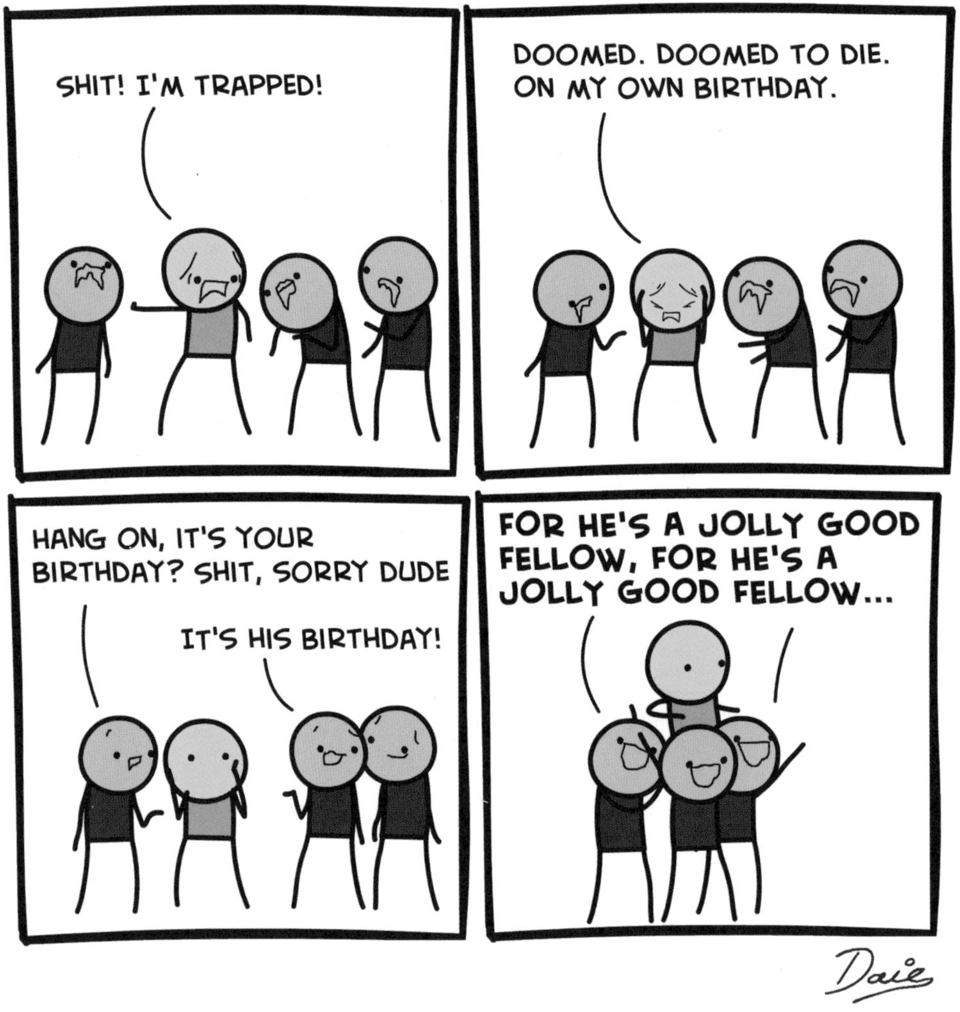
SHIT! I'M TRAPPED!
DOOMED. DOOMED TO DIE. ON MY OWN BIRTHDAY.
HANG ON, IT'S YOUR BIRTHDAY? SHIT, SORRY DUDE
IT'S HIS BIRTHDAY!
FOR HE'S A JOLLY GOOD FELLOW, FOR HE'S A JOLLY GOOD FELLOW...
Dave

THE COMIC SANS GAME! TRY IT!

Keep an eye out for everyone's favorite stylistically-awkward font in everyday life!
You'll notice it more often than you think!
If you see it, just raise your fist and shout "COMIC SAAAAAAAAAANNS!!!"

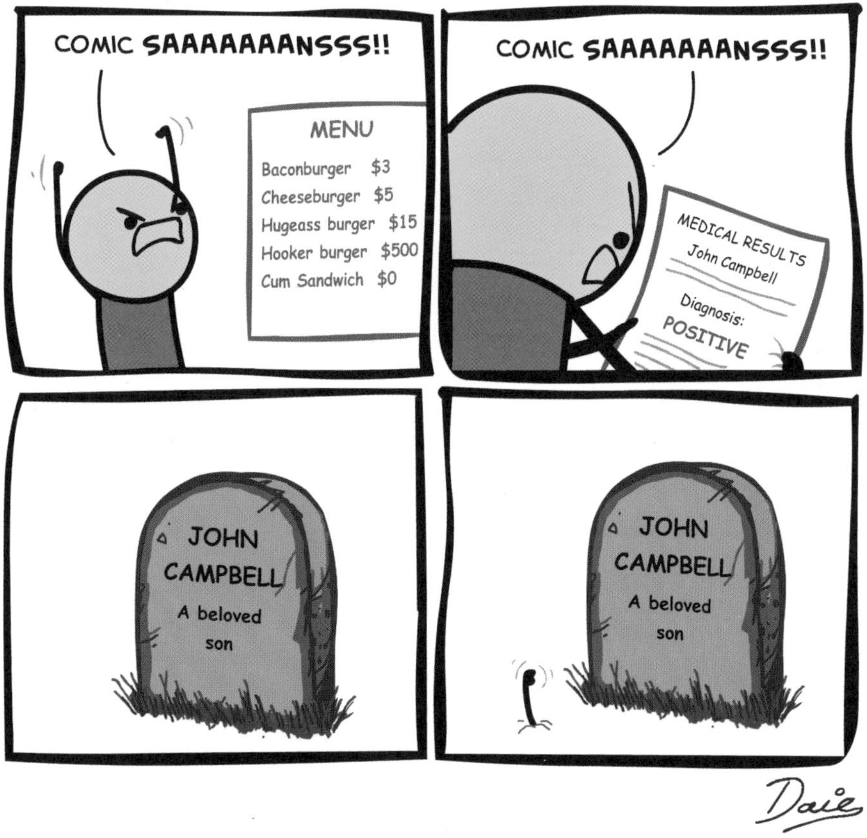

COMIC SAAAAAAANSSS!!
MENU
Baconburger $3
Cheeseburger $5
Hugeass burger $15
Hooker burger $500
Cum Sandwich $0
COMIC SAAAAAAANSSS!!
MEDICAL RESULTS
John Campbell
Diagnosis:
POSITIVE
JOHN CAMPBELL
A beloved son
JOHN CAMPBELL
A beloved son
Daie

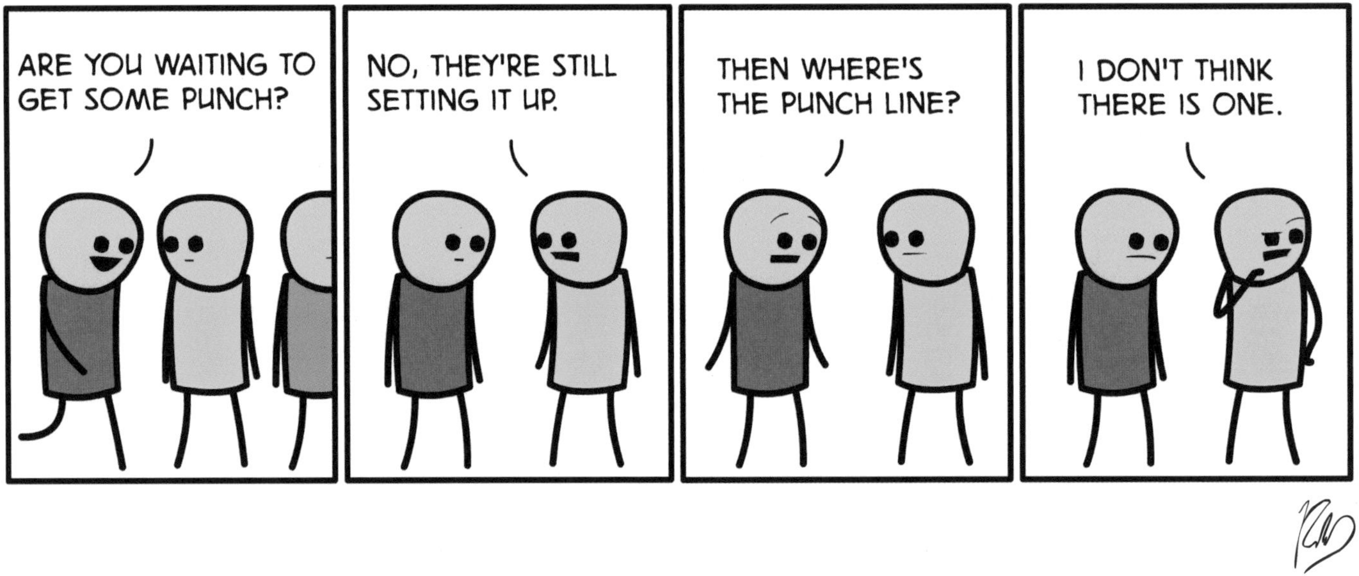
ARE YOU WAITING TO GET SOME PUNCH?
NO, THEY'RE STILL SETTING IT UP.
THEN WHERE'S THE PUNCH LINE?
I DON'T THINK THERE IS ONE.

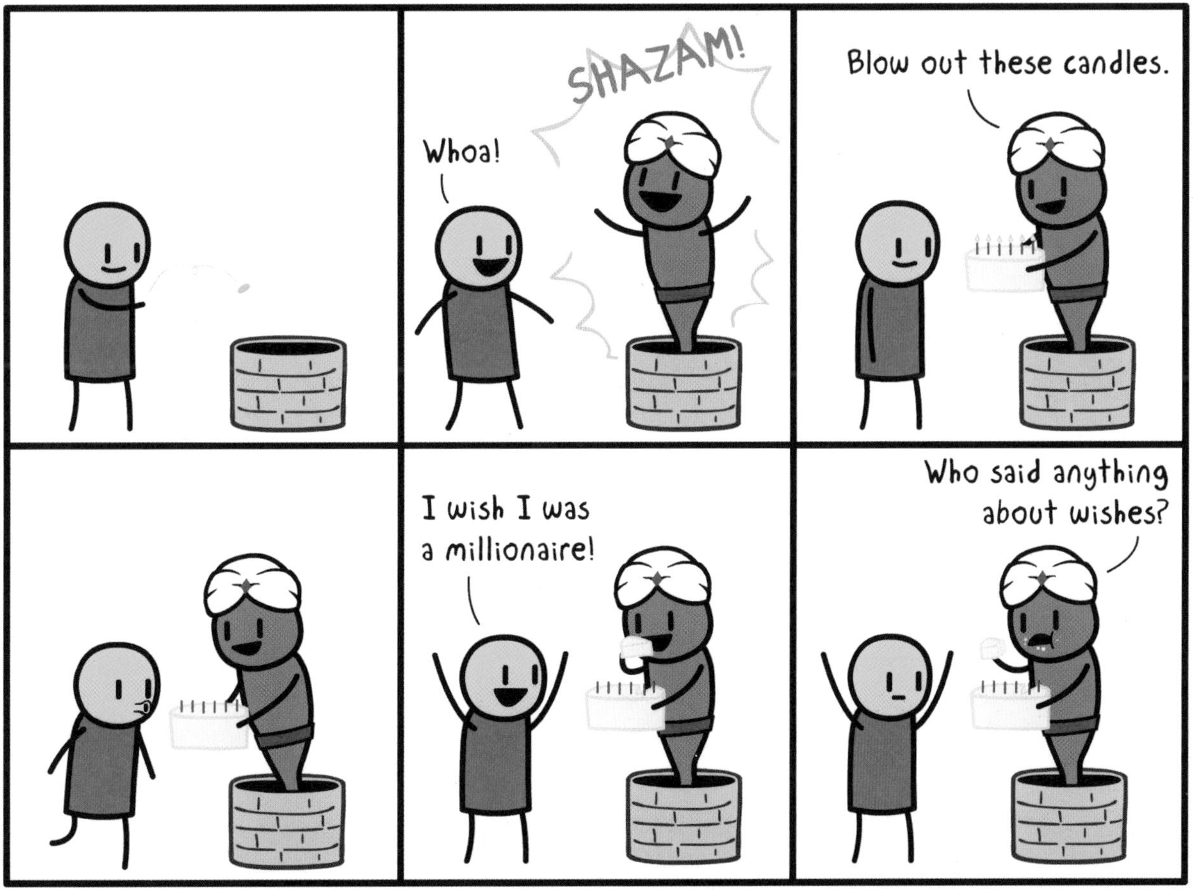
Whoa!
SHAZAM!
Blow out these candles.
I wish I was a millionaire!
Who said anything about wishes?

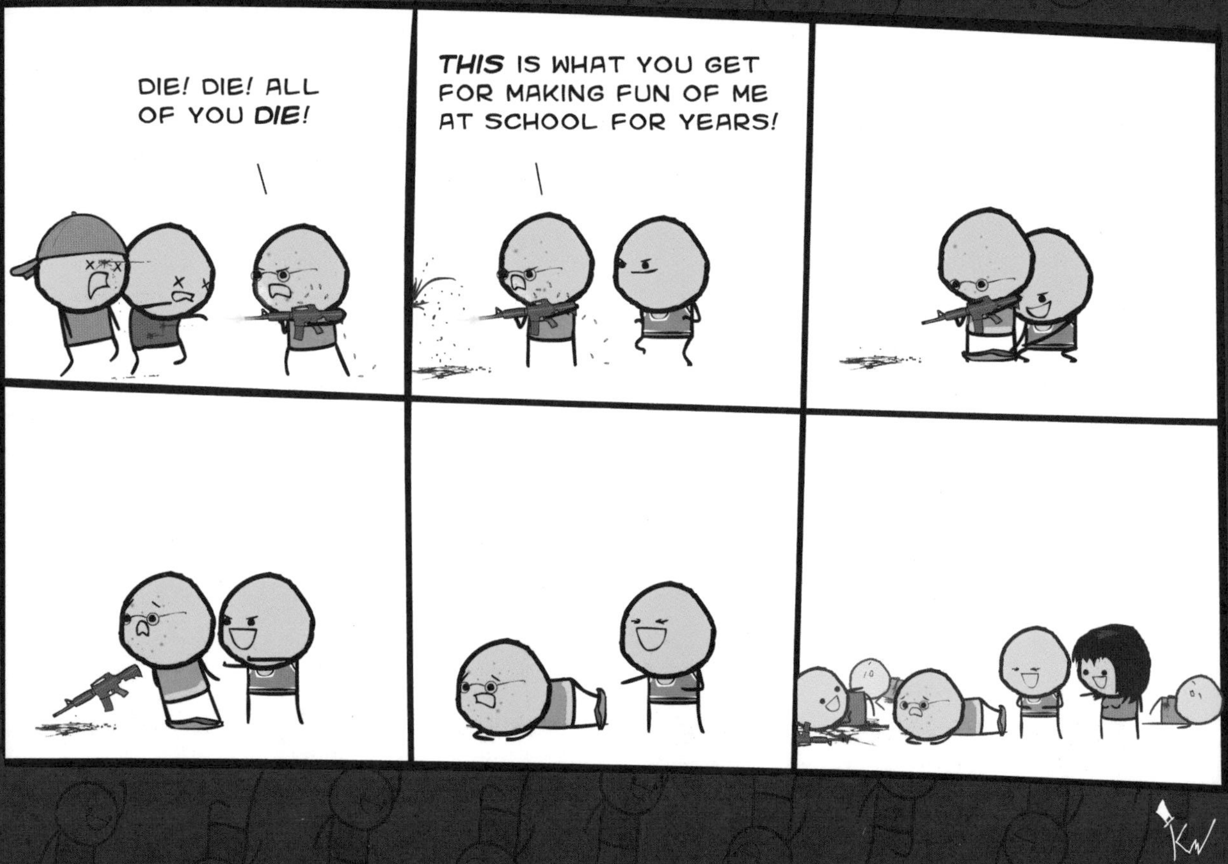
DIE! DIE! ALL OF YOU **DIE**!
THIS IS WHAT YOU GET FOR MAKING FUN OF ME AT SCHOOL FOR YEARS!
KW

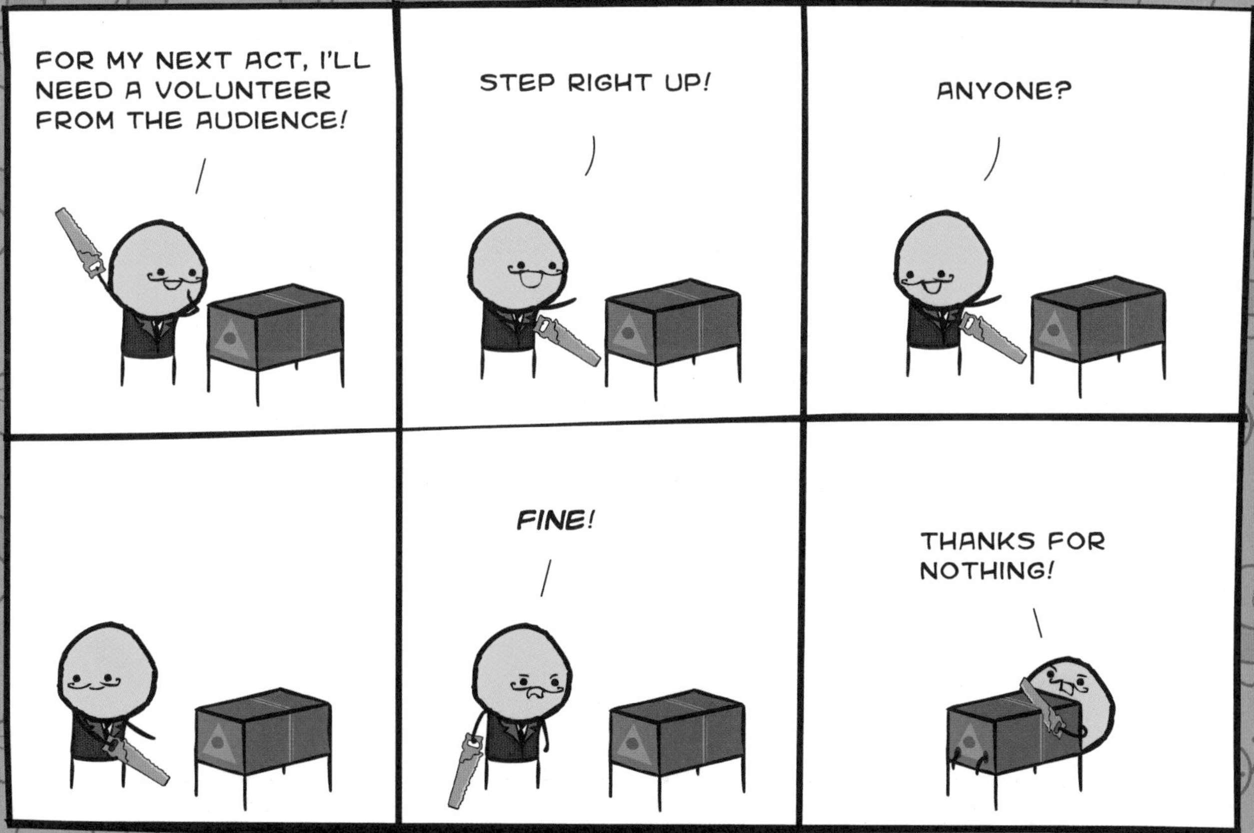
FOR MY NEXT ACT, I'LL NEED A VOLUNTEER FROM THE AUDIENCE!
STEP RIGHT UP!
ANYONE?
FINE!
THANKS FOR NOTHING!

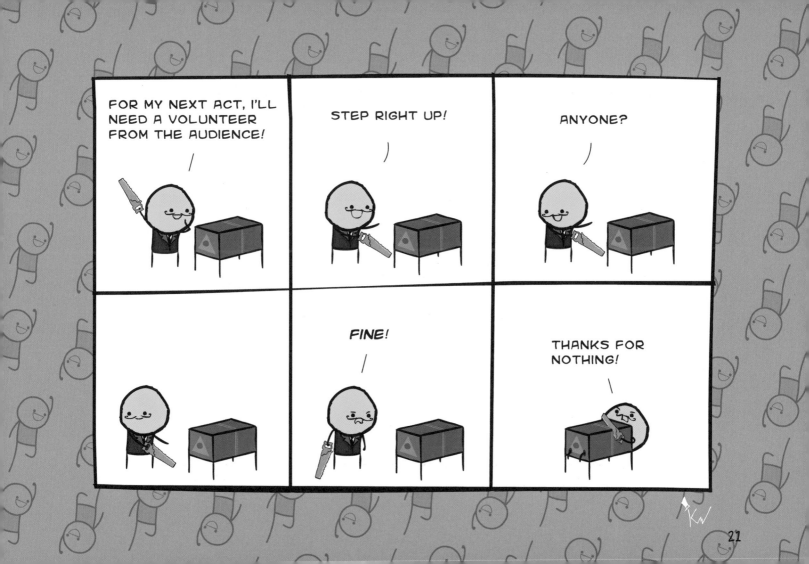

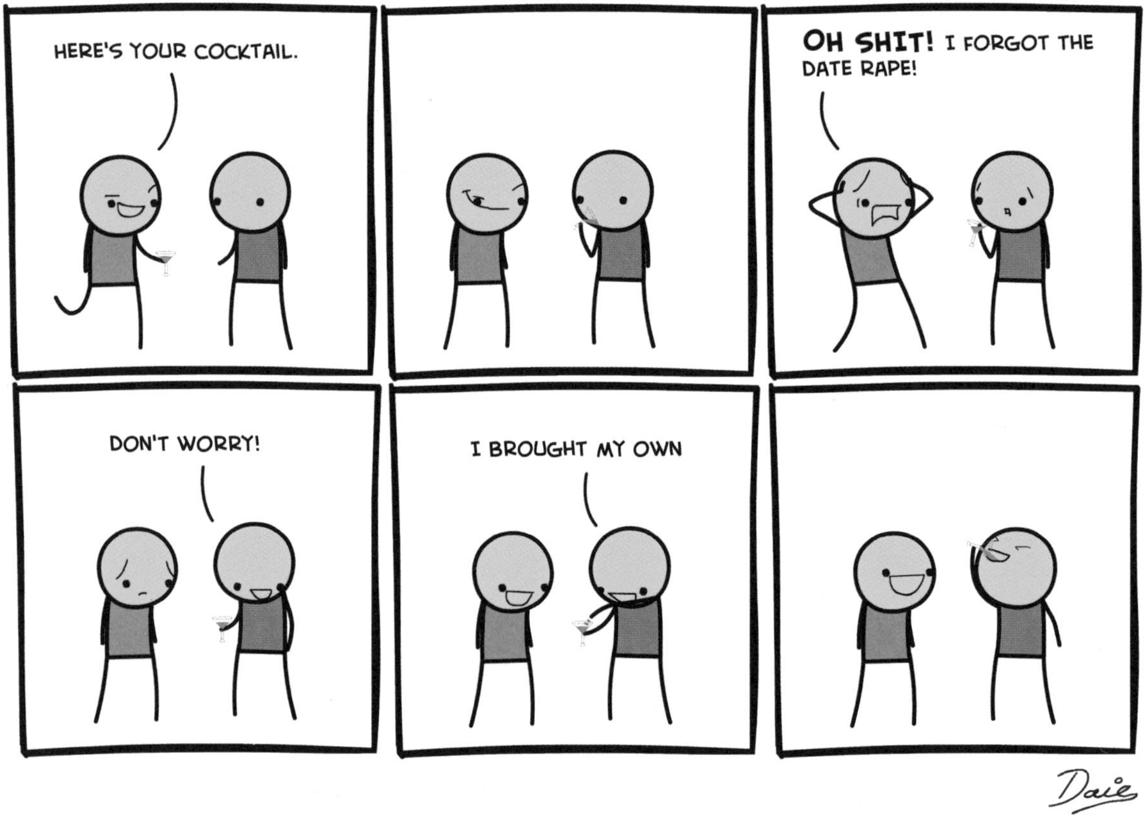
HERE'S YOUR COCKTAIL.
OH SHIT! I FORGOT THE DATE RAPE!
DON'T WORRY!
I BROUGHT MY OWN
Dave

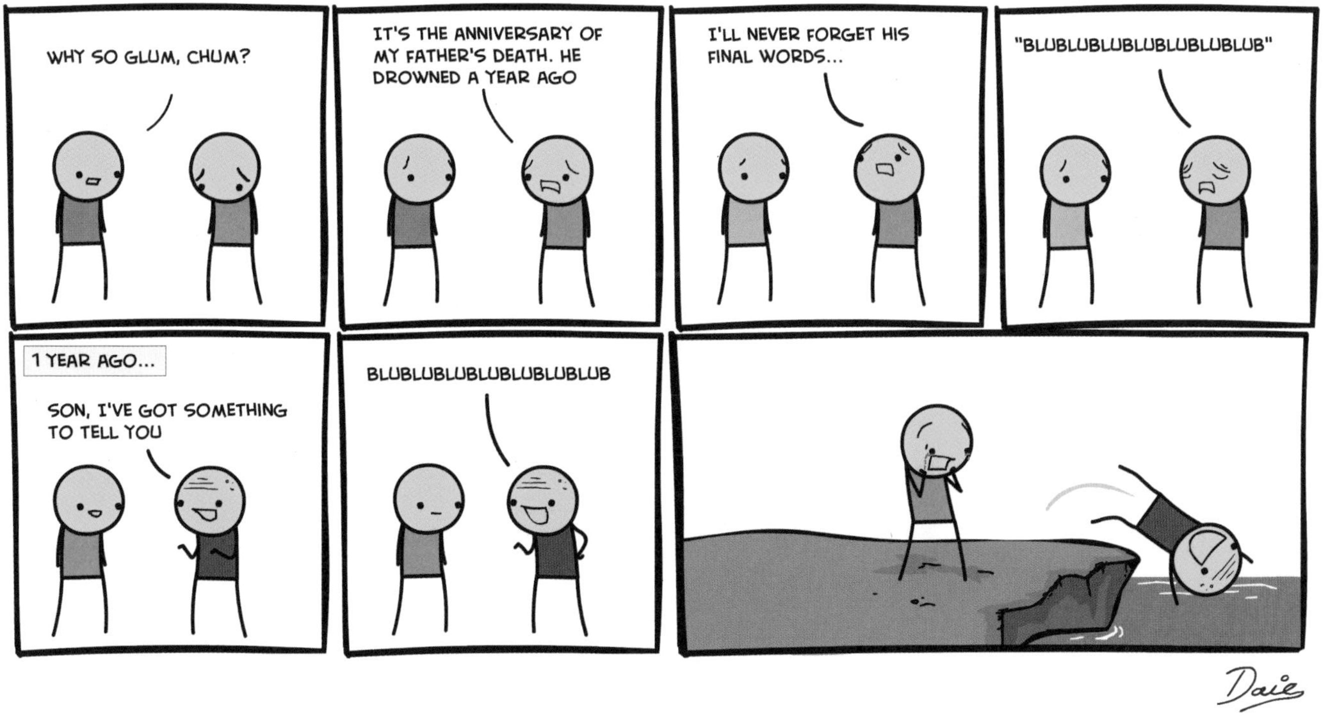
WHY SO GLUM, CHUM?
IT'S THE ANNIVERSARY OF MY FATHER'S DEATH. HE DROWNED A YEAR AGO
I'LL NEVER FORGET HIS FINAL WORDS...
"BLUBLUBLUBLUBLUBLUBLUB"
1 YEAR AGO...
SON, I'VE GOT SOMETHING TO TELL YOU
BLUBLUBLUBLUBLUBLUBLUB

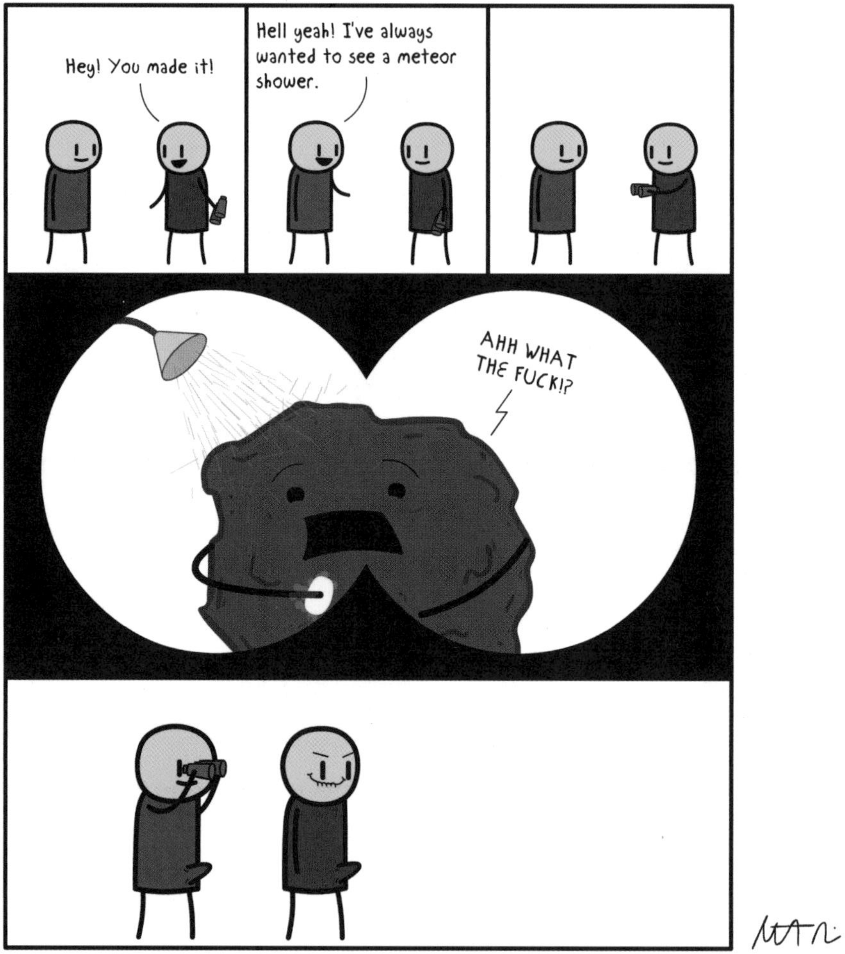
Hey! You made it!
Hell yeah! I've always wanted to see a meteor shower.
AHH WHAT THE FUCK!?

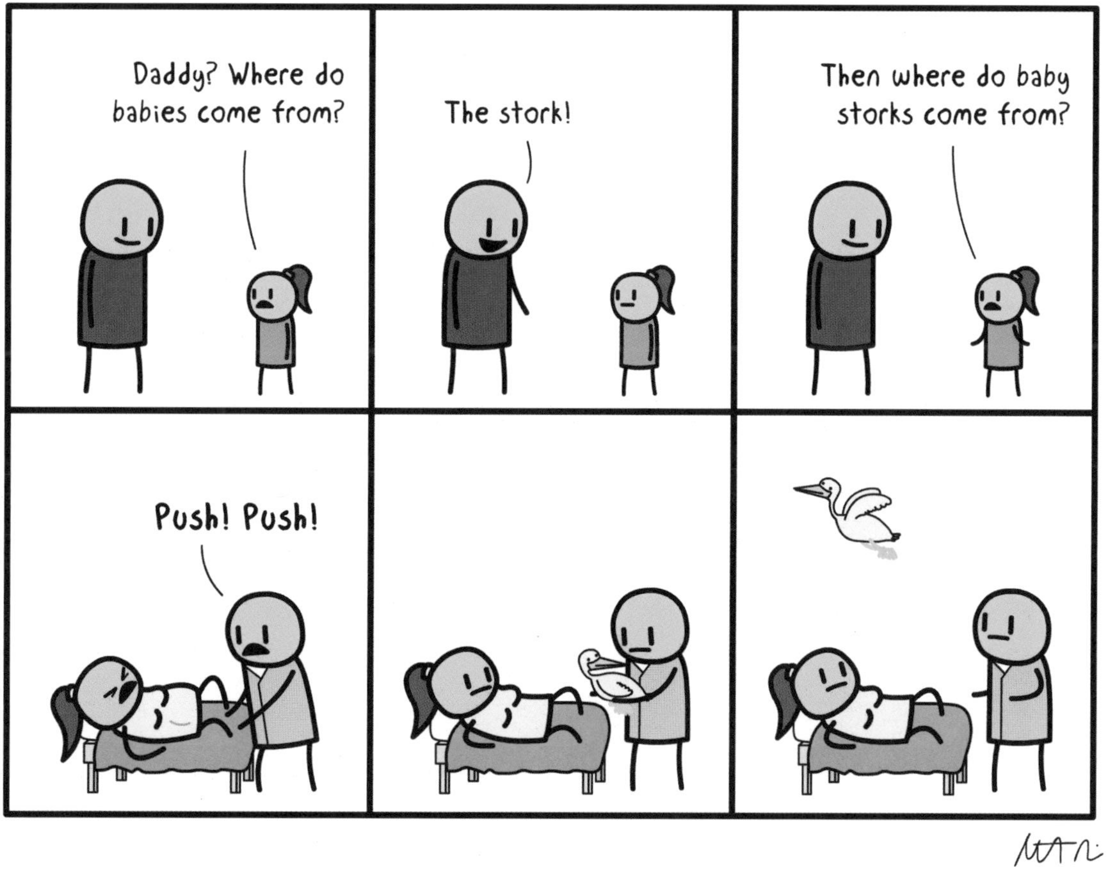
Daddy? Where do babies come from?
The stork!
Then where do baby storks come from?
Push! Push!

HEY BABY, WANT TO GO GET SUSHI TONIGHT?
NAH, I FEEL LIKE SHIT
AWWWWWWW, OKAY.
SAM'S HOUSE OF SHIT
Dave

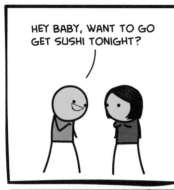

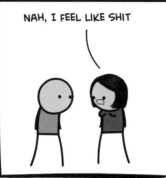

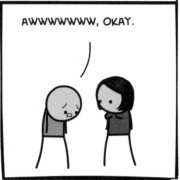

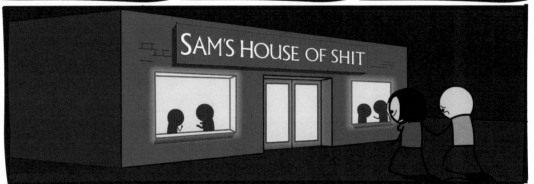

DAMNIT, I FORGOT TO TAKE MY MEDICINE THIS MORNING.
IS IT FOR YOUR FACE?
IT'S FOR MY LOW SELF-ESTEEM.
YOU'RE NOT TAKING ANYTHING FOR YOUR FACE?

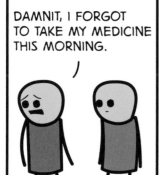

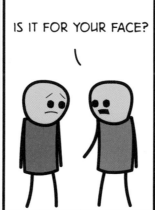

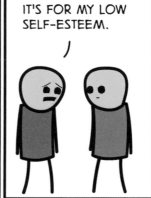

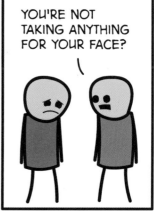

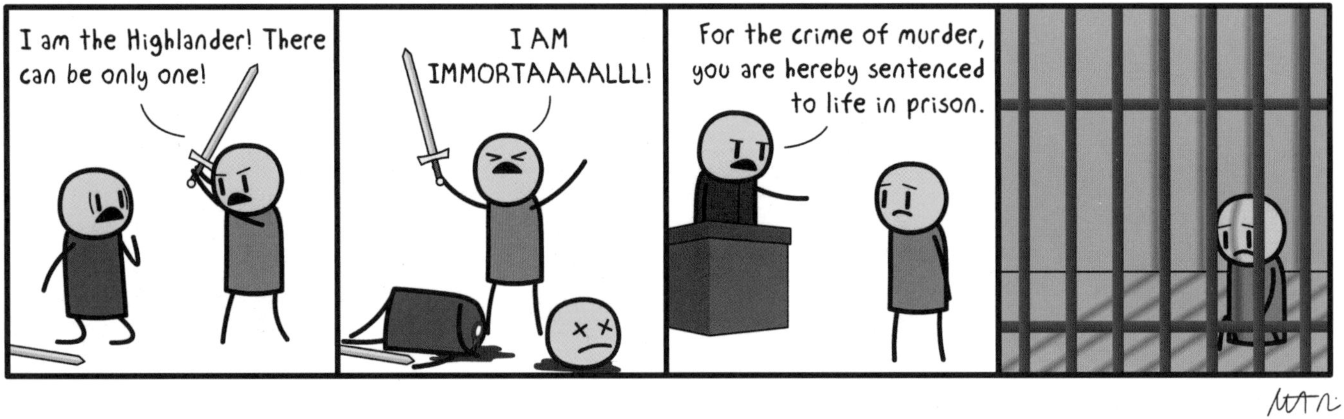
I am the Highlander! There can be only one!
I AM IMMORTAAAAALLL!
For the crime of murder, you are hereby sentenced to life in prison.

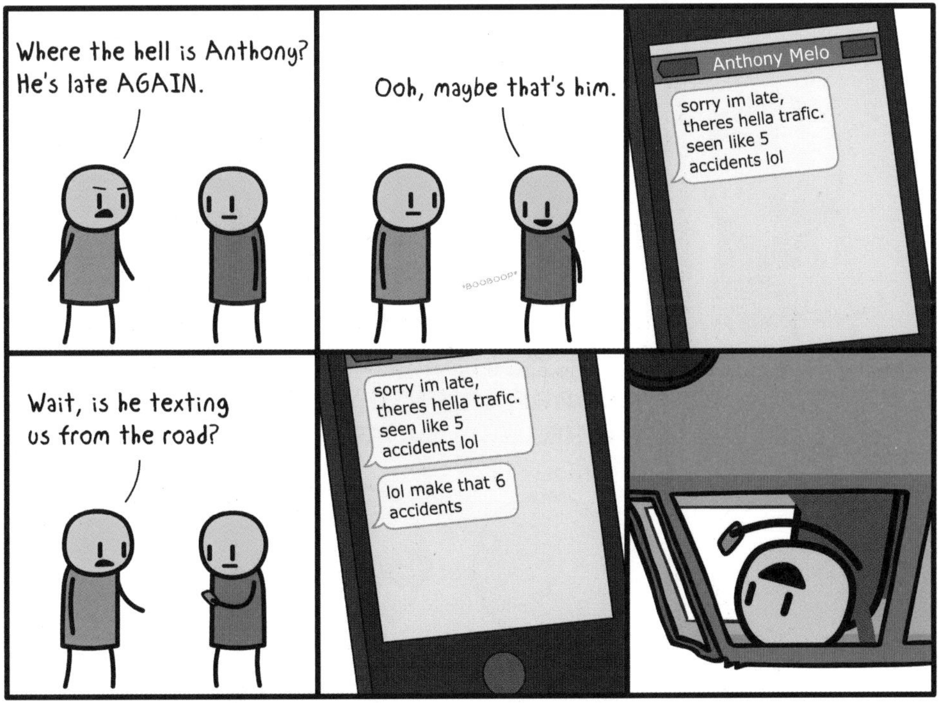
Where the hell is Anthony? He's late AGAIN.
Ooh, maybe that's him.
BOOBOOP
Anthony Melo
sorry im late, theres hella trafic. seen like 5 accidents lol
Wait, is he texting us from the road?
sorry im late, theres hella trafic. seen like 5 accidents lol
lol make that 6 accidents

DON'T BE A DICKHEAD. DON'T TEXT AND DRIVE.

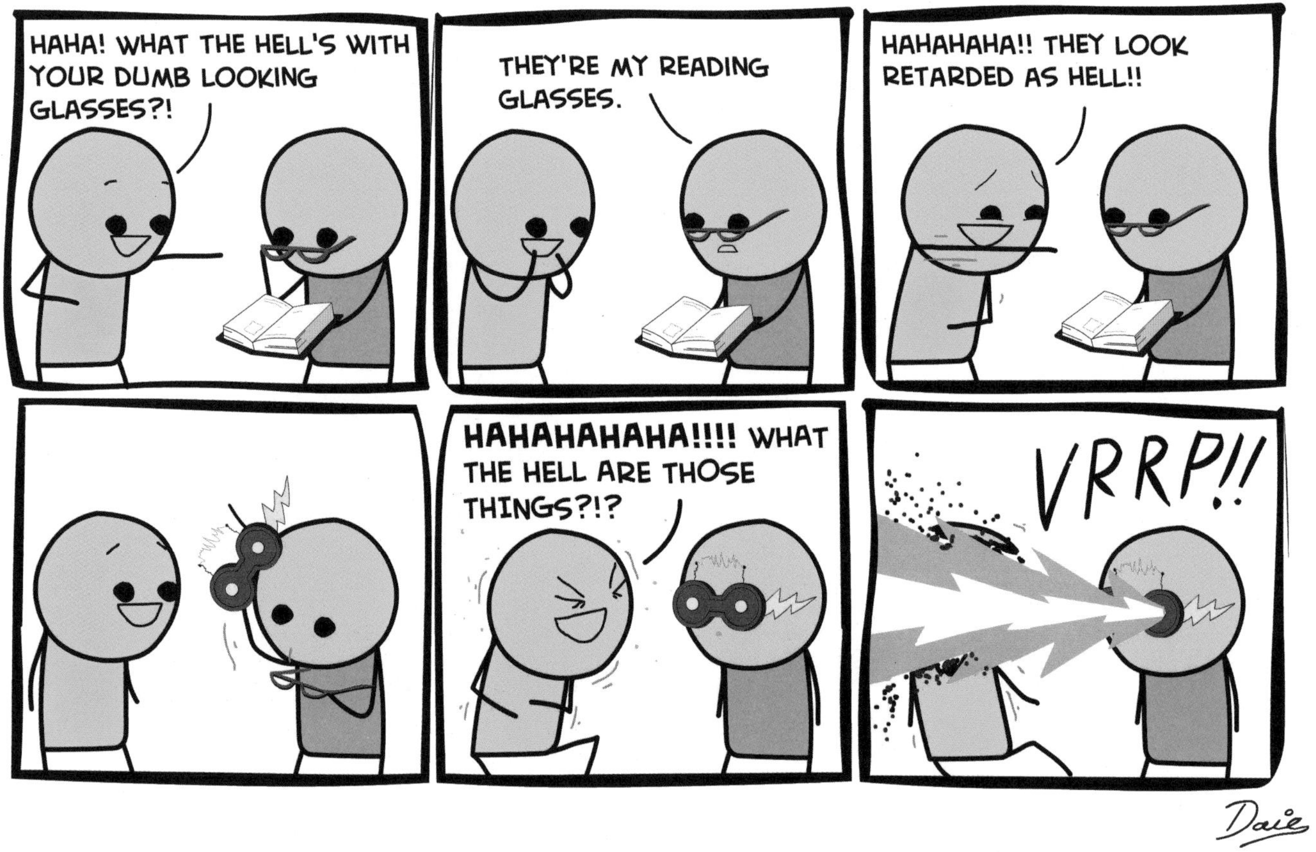
HAHA! WHAT THE HELL'S WITH YOUR DUMB LOOKING GLASSES?!
THEY'RE MY READING GLASSES.
HAHAHAHA!! THEY LOOK RETARDED AS HELL!!
HAHAHAHAHA!!!! WHAT THE HELL ARE THOSE THINGS?!?
VRRP!!
Dave

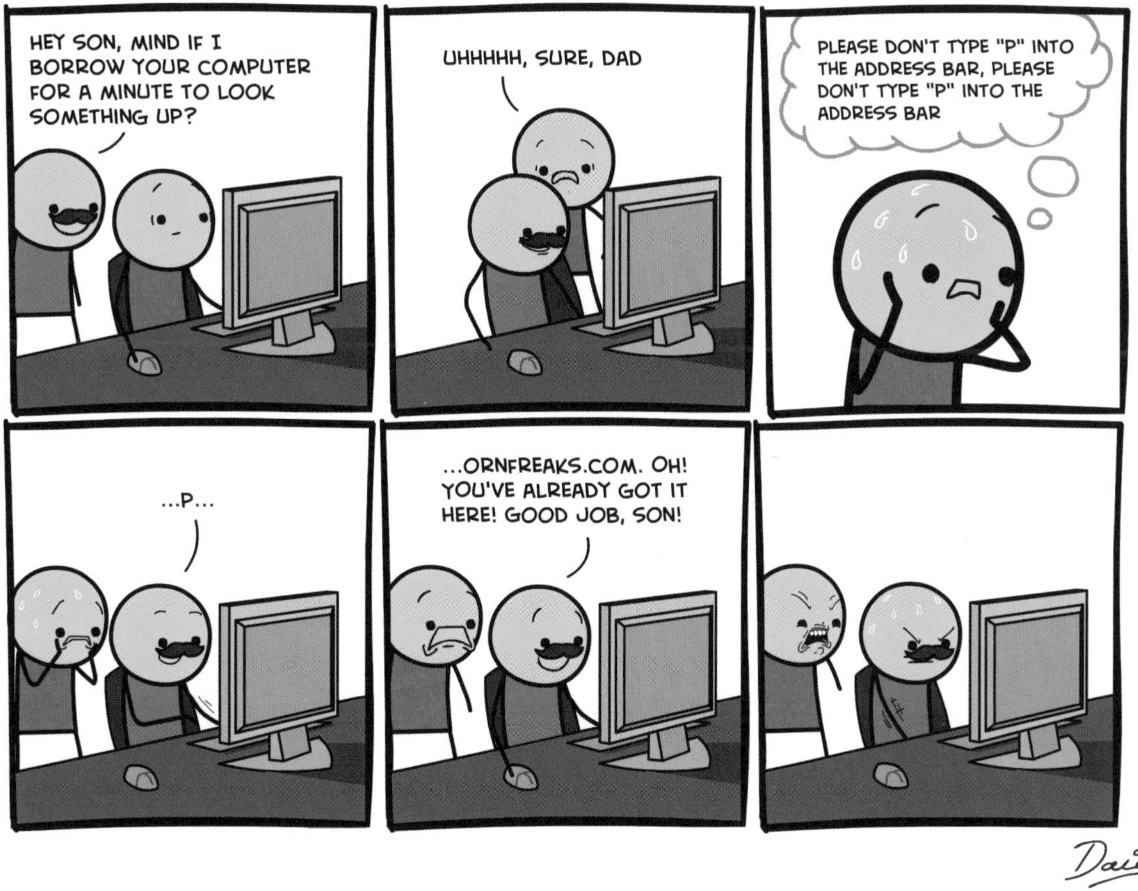
HEY SON, MIND IF I BORROW YOUR COMPUTER FOR A MINUTE TO LOOK SOMETHING UP?
UHHHHH, SURE, DAD
PLEASE DON'T TYPE "P" INTO THE ADDRESS BAR, PLEASE DON'T TYPE "P" INTO THE ADDRESS BAR
...P...
...ORNFREAKS.COM. OH! YOU'VE ALREADY GOT IT HERE! GOOD JOB, SON!
Dave

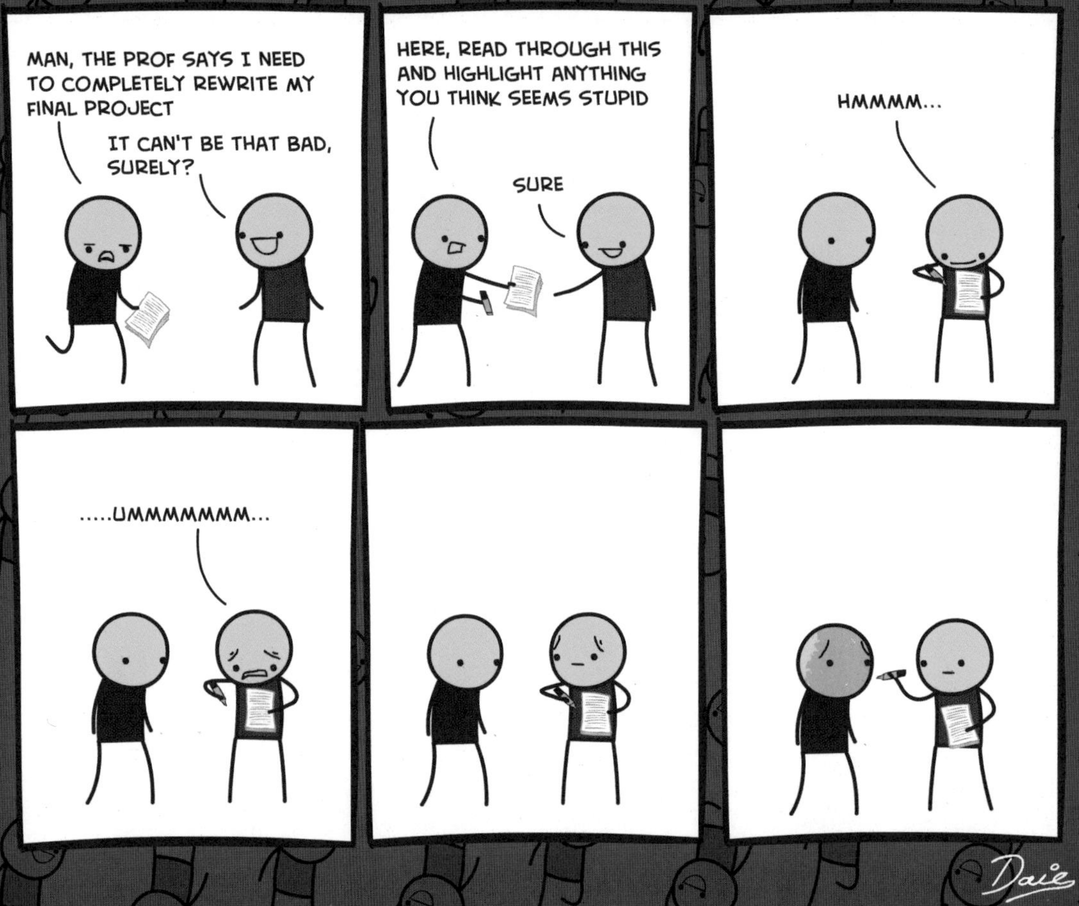
MAN, THE PROF SAYS I NEED TO COMPLETELY REWRITE MY FINAL PROJECT
IT CAN'T BE THAT BAD, SURELY?
HERE, READ THROUGH THIS AND HIGHLIGHT ANYTHING YOU THINK SEEMS STUPID
SURE
HMMMM...
.....UMMMMMMM...
Dave

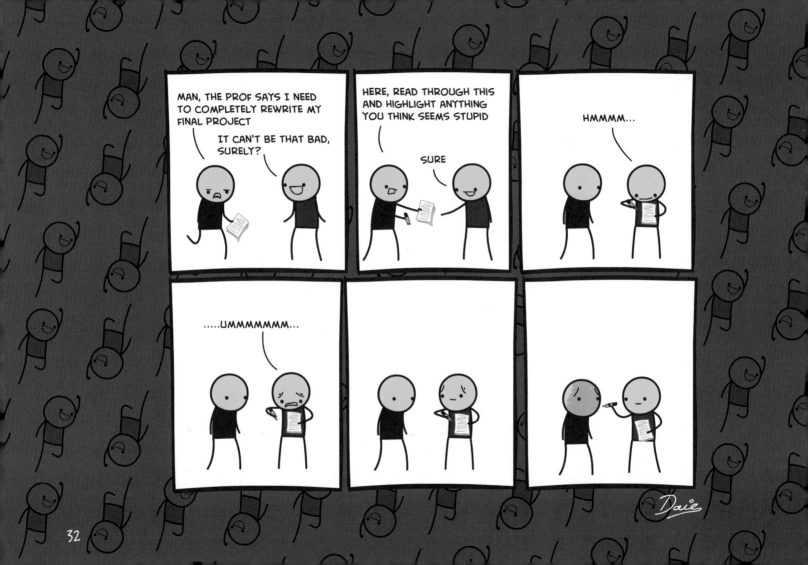

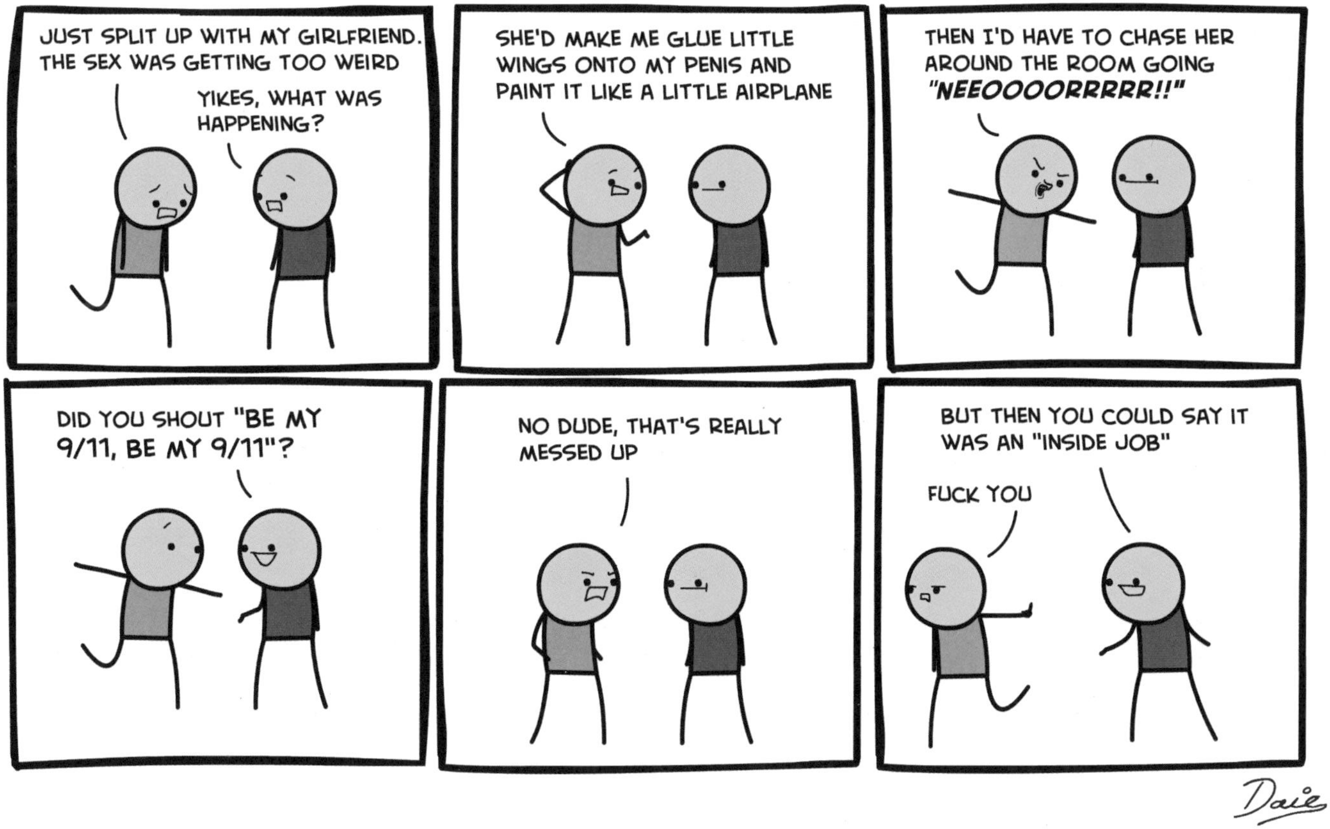
JUST SPLIT UP WITH MY GIRLFRIEND. THE SEX WAS GETTING TOO WEIRD
YIKES, WHAT WAS HAPPENING?
SHE'D MAKE ME GLUE LITTLE WINGS ONTO MY PENIS AND PAINT IT LIKE A LITTLE AIRPLANE
THEN I'D HAVE TO CHASE HER AROUND THE ROOM GOING "NEEOOOORRRRR!!"
DID YOU SHOUT "BE MY 9/11, BE MY 9/11"?
NO DUDE, THAT'S REALLY MESSED UP
BUT THEN YOU COULD SAY IT WAS AN "INSIDE JOB"
FUCK YOU
Dave

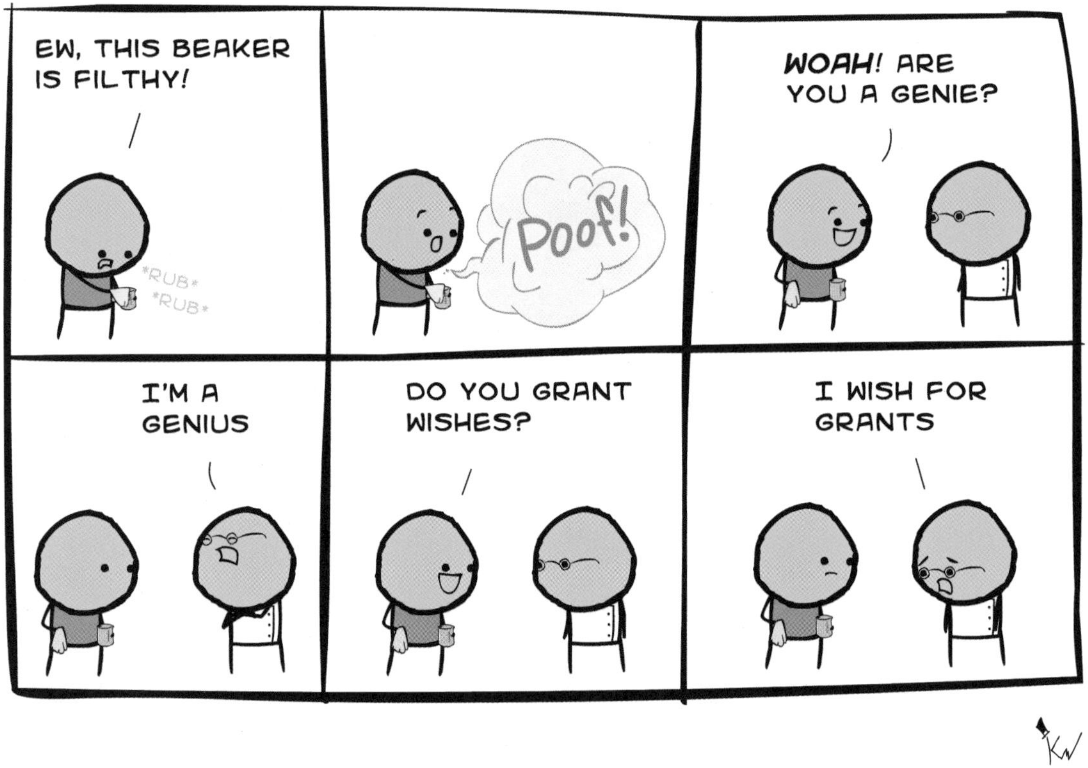
EW, THIS BEAKER IS FILTHY!
RUB *RUB*
Poof!
WOAH! ARE YOU A GENIE?
I'M A GENIUS
DO YOU GRANT WISHES?
I WISH FOR GRANTS

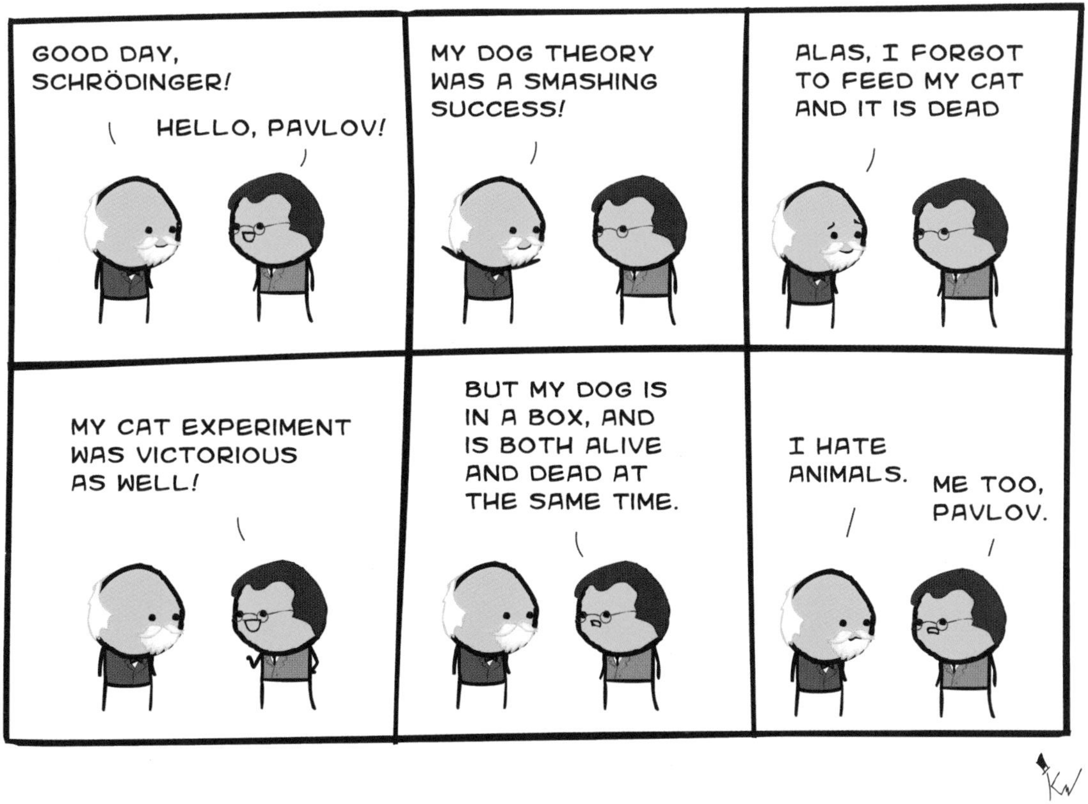
GOOD DAY, SCHRÖDINGER!
HELLO, PAVLOV!
MY DOG THEORY WAS A SMASHING SUCCESS!
ALAS, I FORGOT TO FEED MY CAT AND IT IS DEAD
MY CAT EXPERIMENT WAS VICTORIOUS AS WELL!
BUT MY DOG IS IN A BOX, AND IS BOTH ALIVE AND DEAD AT THE SAME TIME.
I HATE ANIMALS.
ME TOO, PAVLOV.

YOU SHOULD GO OUTSIDE MORE OFTEN. YOU SPEND TOO MUCH TIME ON THE INTERNET
ACTUALLY, MOTHER, I THINK YOU'LL FIND THAT THE INTERNET IS AN INFINITE, ENDLESSLY-GROWING SOURCE OF INFORMATION.
IT OFFERS ME A PORTAL TO AN ENDLESS ARRAY OF DISCUSSION, OPINIONS, NEWS AND FACTS THAT ALLOW ME TO IMPROVE MYSELF AS A HUMAN BEING, BOTH IN MY KNOWLEDGE OF THE WORLD WE LIVE IN AND MY INTERACTIONS WITH IT.
WELL... AS LONG AS YOU'RE BROADENING YOUR MIND... OKAY. CARRY ON.
HAAA, LOOK AT THAT FUCKIN' CAT

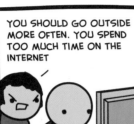

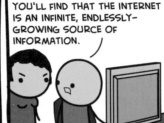

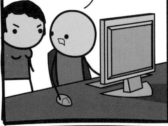

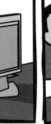

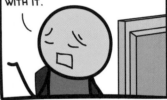

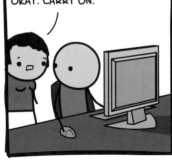

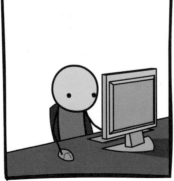

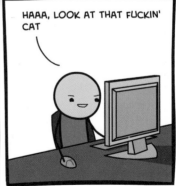

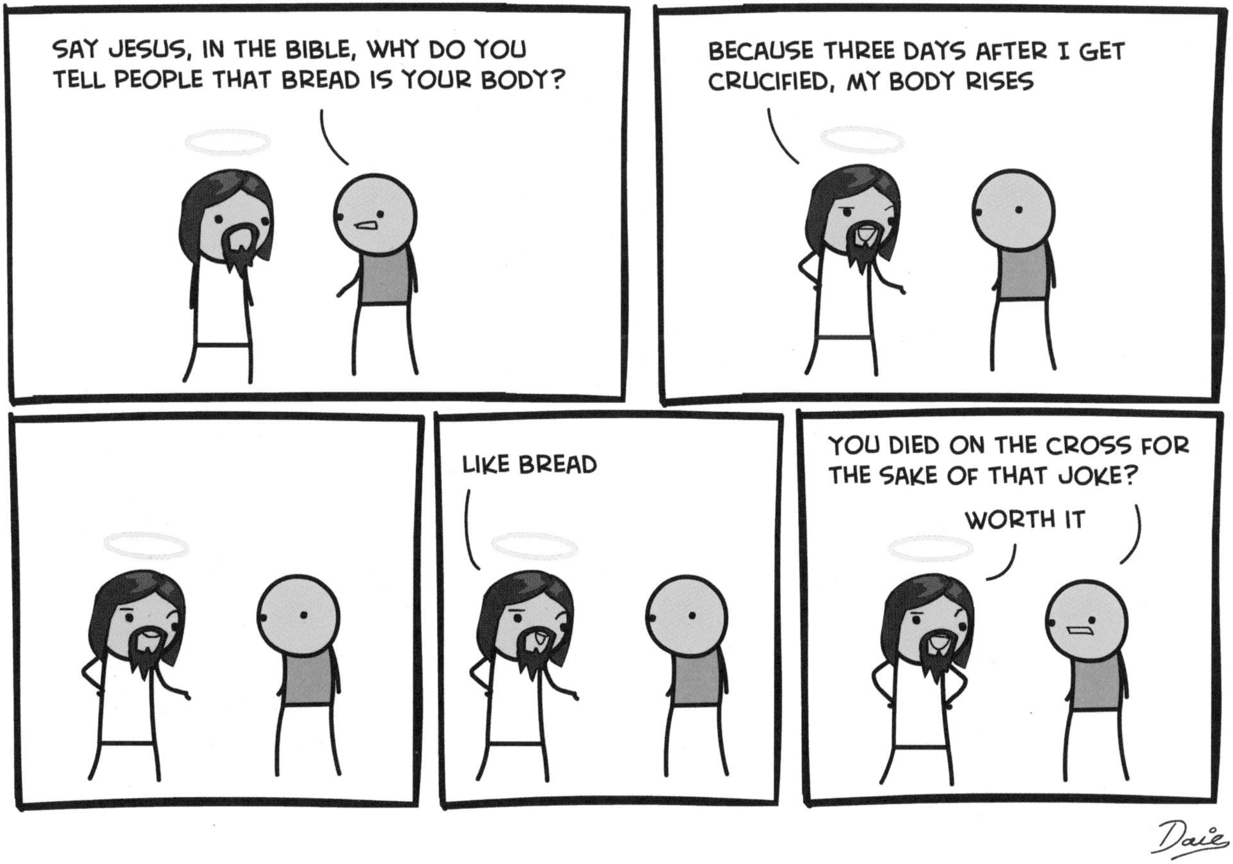

SAY JESUS, IN THE BIBLE, WHY DO YOU TELL PEOPLE THAT BREAD IS YOUR BODY?
BECAUSE THREE DAYS AFTER I GET CRUCIFIED, MY BODY RISES
LIKE BREAD
YOU DIED ON THE CROSS FOR THE SAKE OF THAT JOKE?
WORTH IT
Dave

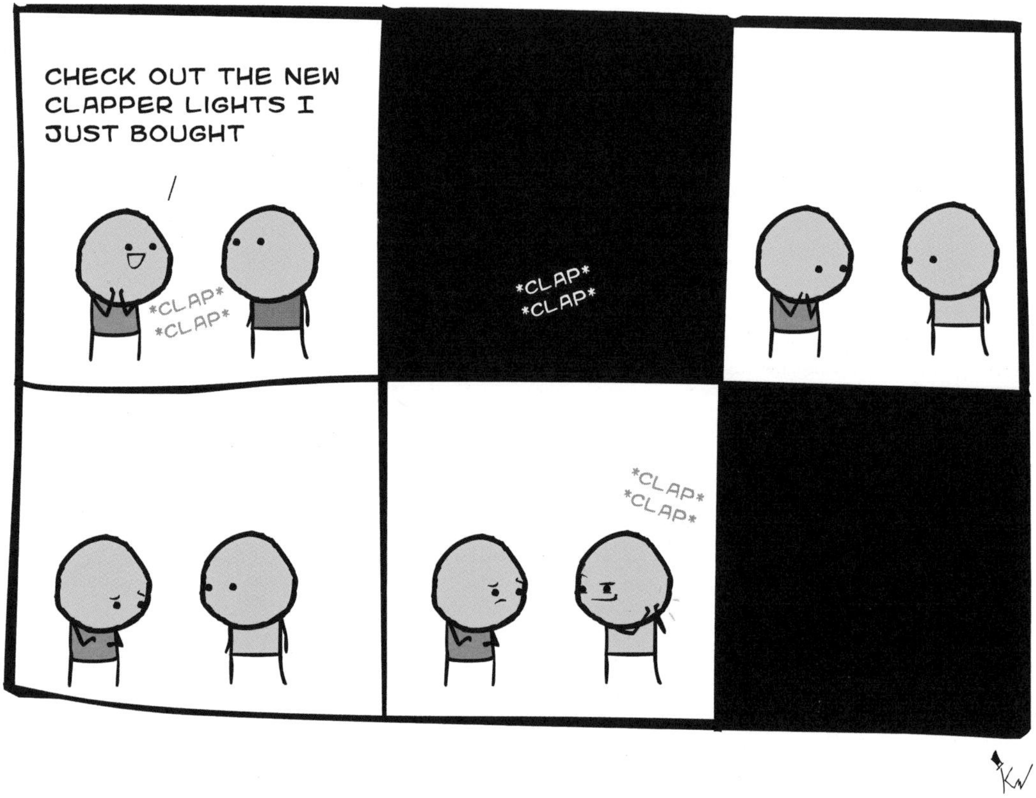
CHECK OUT THE NEW CLAPPER LIGHTS I JUST BOUGHT
CLAP *CLAP*
CLAP *CLAP*
CLAP *CLAP*

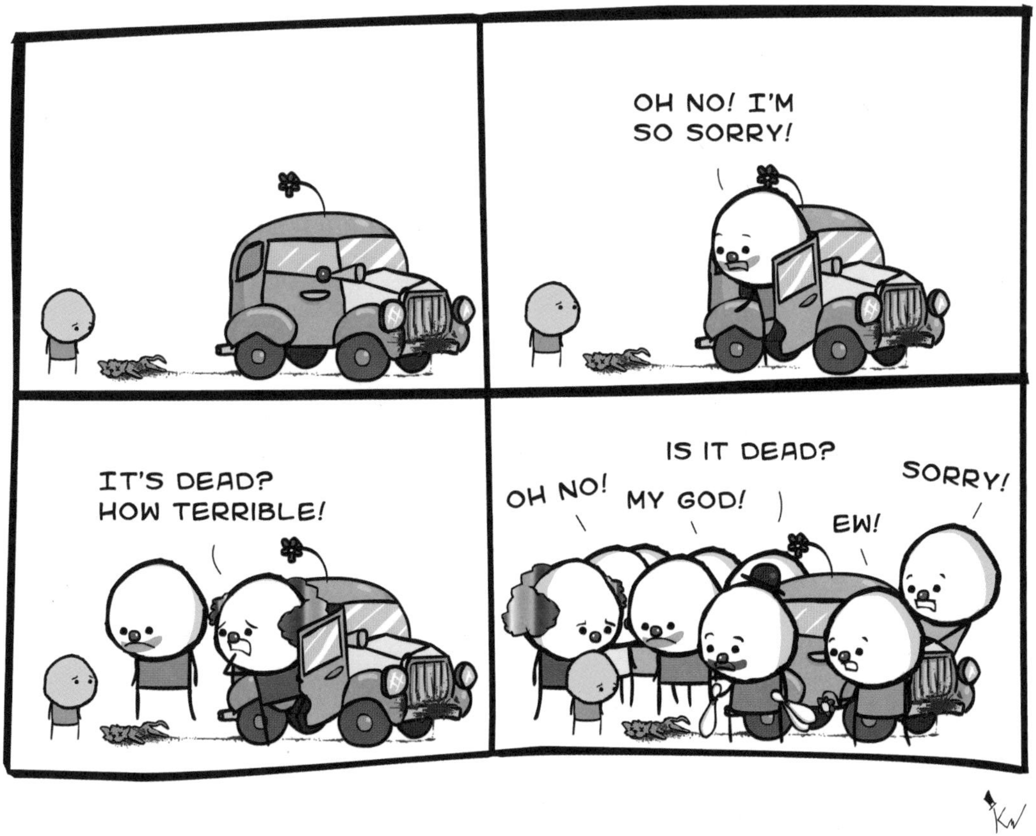
OH NO! I'M SO SORRY!
IT'S DEAD? HOW TERRIBLE!
IS IT DEAD?
OH NO!
MY GOD!
EW!
SORRY!
KW

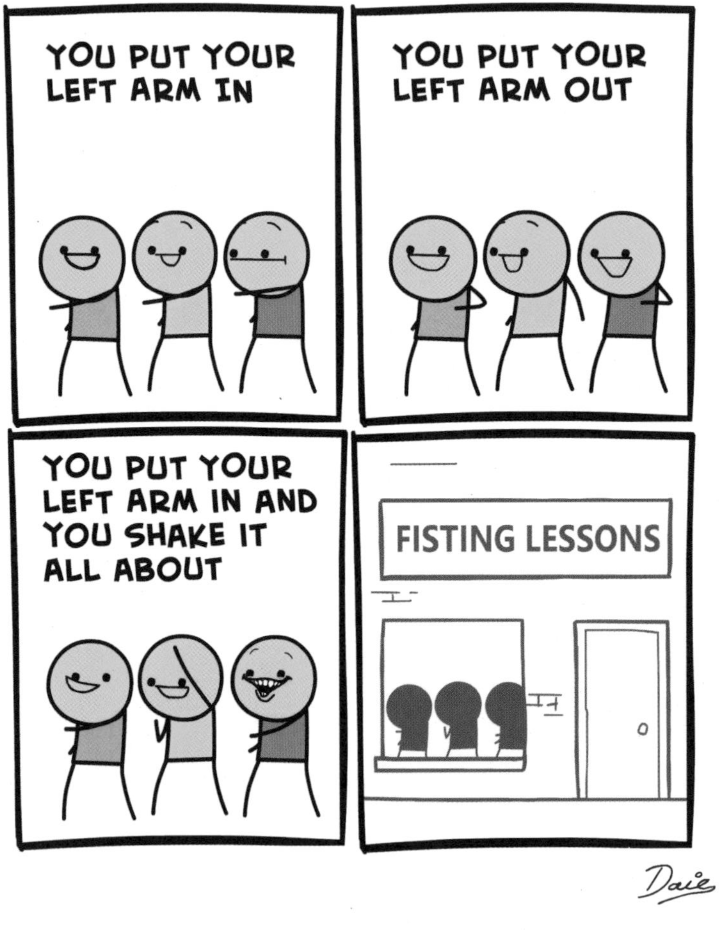
YOU PUT YOUR LEFT ARM IN
YOU PUT YOUR LEFT ARM OUT
YOU PUT YOUR LEFT ARM IN AND YOU SHAKE IT ALL ABOUT
FISTING LESSONS
Dave

ALL MY FRIENDS HAVE MOVED AWAY FROM HOME. I'M FED UP OF BEING LONELY AND SAD...
I KNOW! I'LL CLONE MYSELF!
THERE'S NOTHING TO DO
I'M SO BORED...
MAN I'M LONELY
I WANT TO CRY
I'M SO SAD
I MISS MY FRIENDS...
LIFE IS THE WORST
THIS SUCKS...
SIGHHH

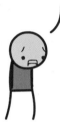

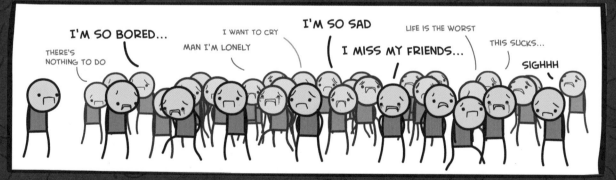

HOWDY! I'M JESUS CHRIST, AND I'M BACK FROM THE DEAD! DOO DE DOOO!

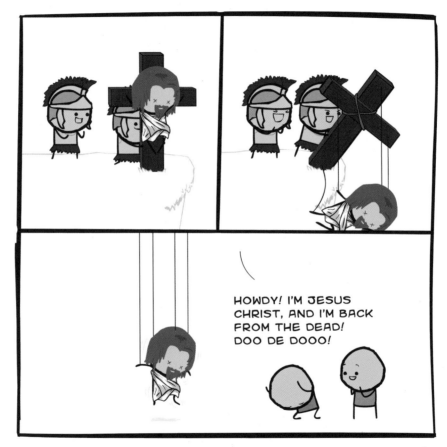

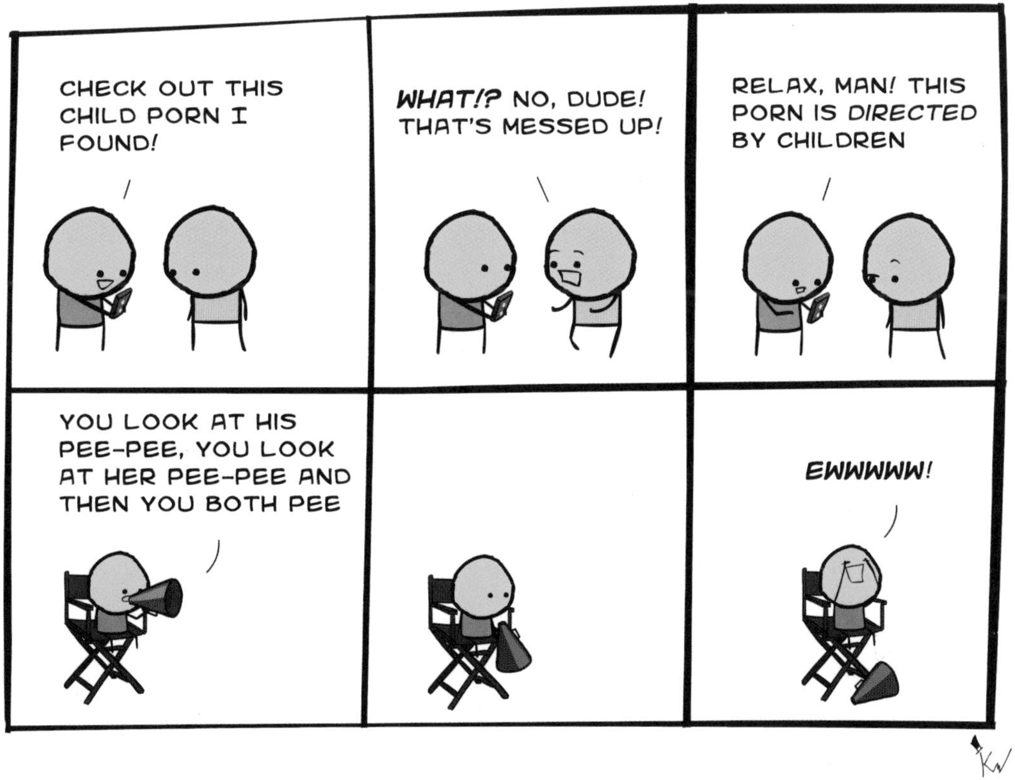
CHECK OUT THIS CHILD PORN I FOUND!
WHAT!? NO, DUDE! THAT'S MESSED UP!
RELAX, MAN! THIS PORN IS DIRECTED BY CHILDREN
YOU LOOK AT HIS PEE-PEE, YOU LOOK AT HER PEE-PEE AND THEN YOU BOTH PEE
EWWWWW!

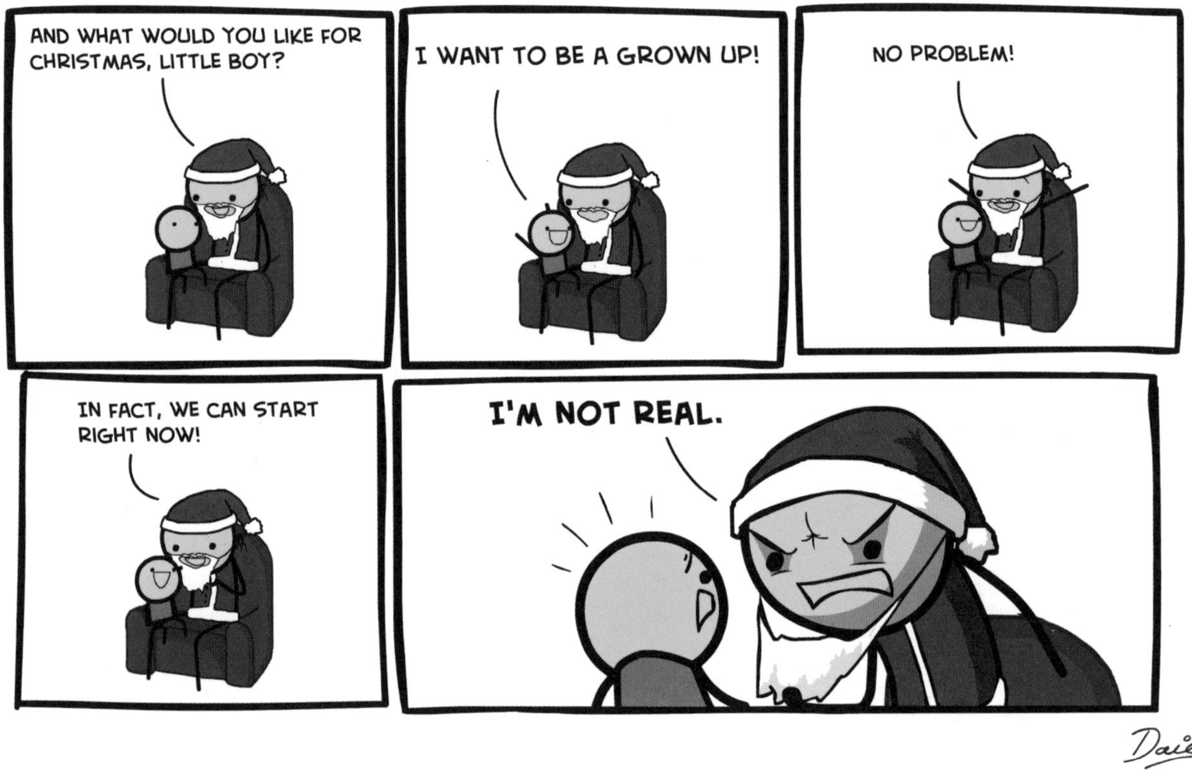
AND WHAT WOULD YOU LIKE FOR CHRISTMAS, LITTLE BOY?
I WANT TO BE A GROWN UP!
NO PROBLEM!
IN FACT, WE CAN START RIGHT NOW!
I'M NOT REAL.
Dave

YOU'LL BE A BIG MOVIE STAR, BABY! I SEE OSCARS AND TONYS IN YOUR FUTURE!
WHERE DO I SIGN!?
CONTRACT
OKAY OSCAR AND TONY, YOU'RE UP
SUPER BUM LOVE 7
Dave

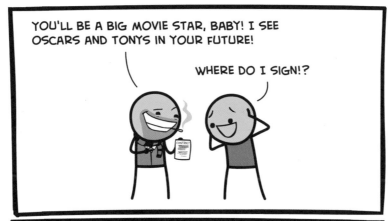

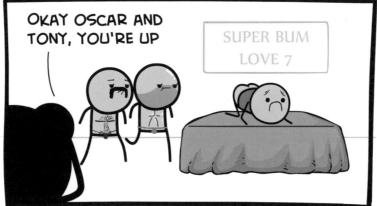

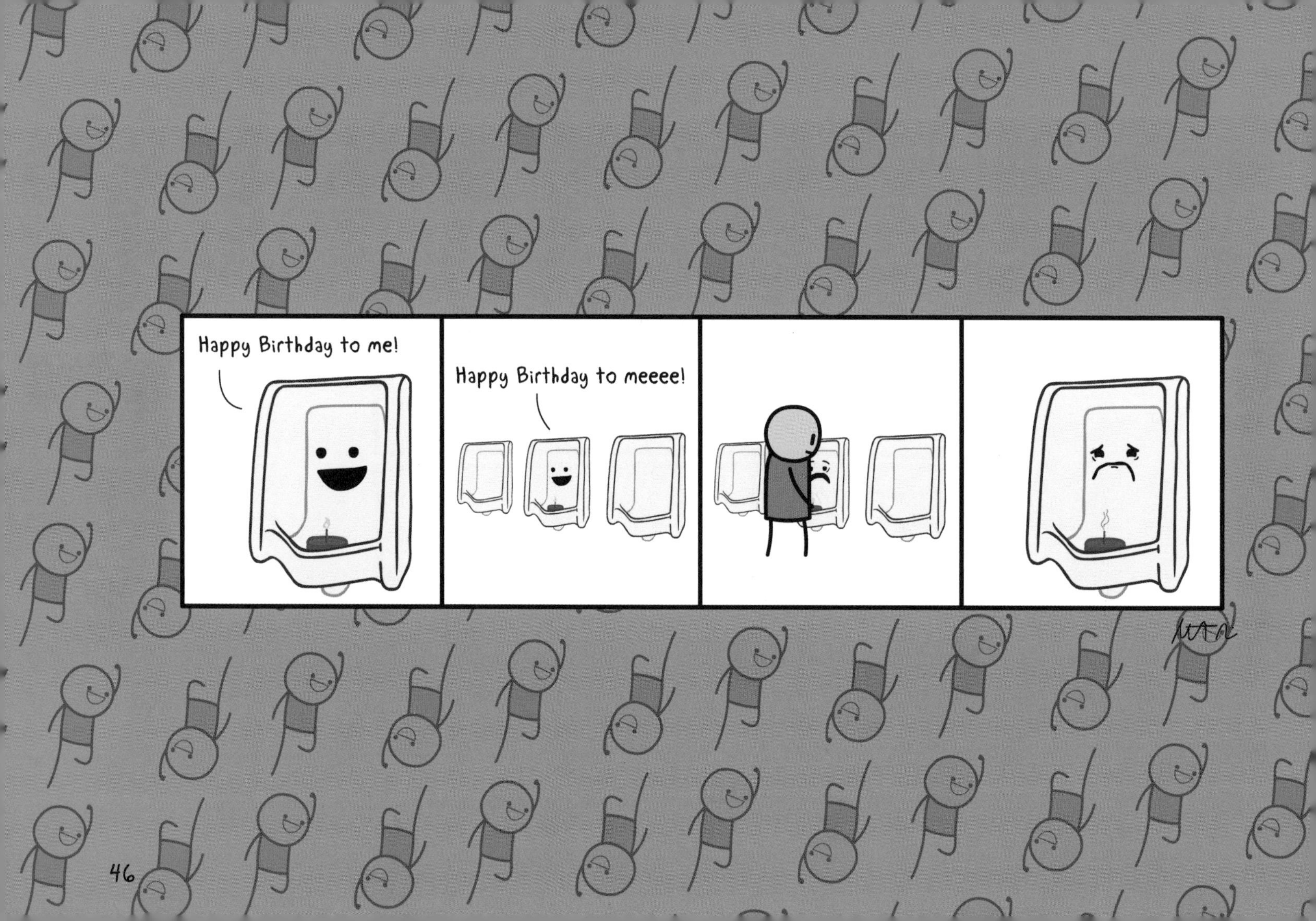
Happy Birthday to me!
Happy Birthday to meeee!

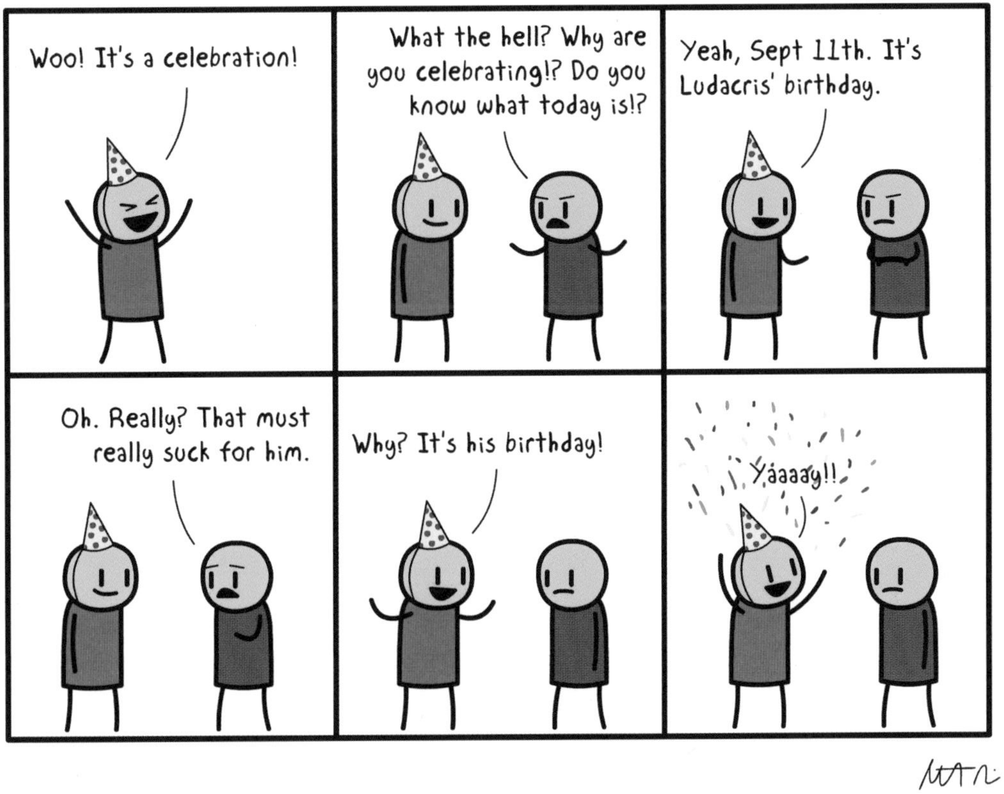
Woo! It's a celebration!
What the hell? Why are you celebrating!? Do you know what today is!?
Yeah, Sept 11th. It's Ludacris' birthday.
Oh. Really? That must really suck for him.
Why? It's his birthday!
Yaaaay!!

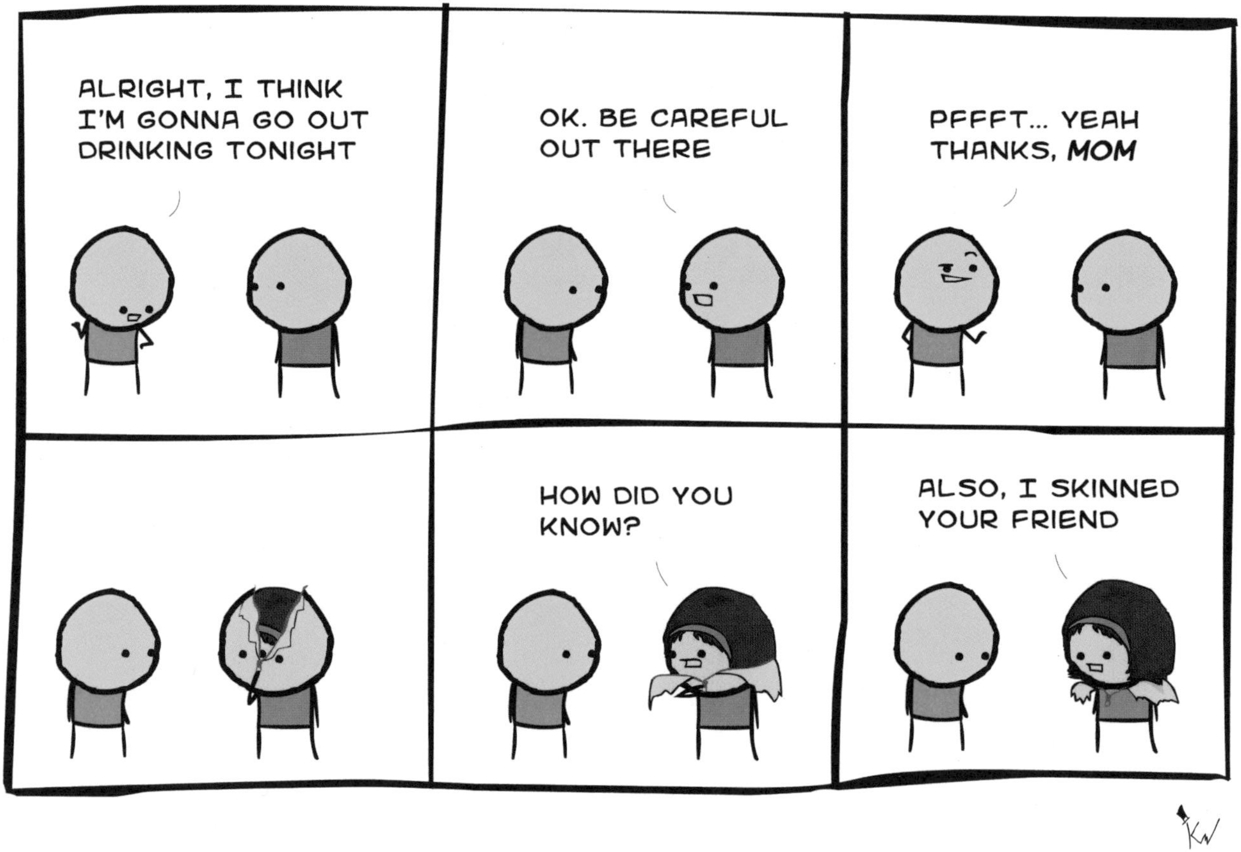
ALRIGHT, I THINK I'M GONNA GO OUT DRINKING TONIGHT
OK. BE CAREFUL OUT THERE
PFFFT... YEAH THANKS, MOM
HOW DID YOU KNOW?
ALSO, I SKINNED YOUR FRIEND

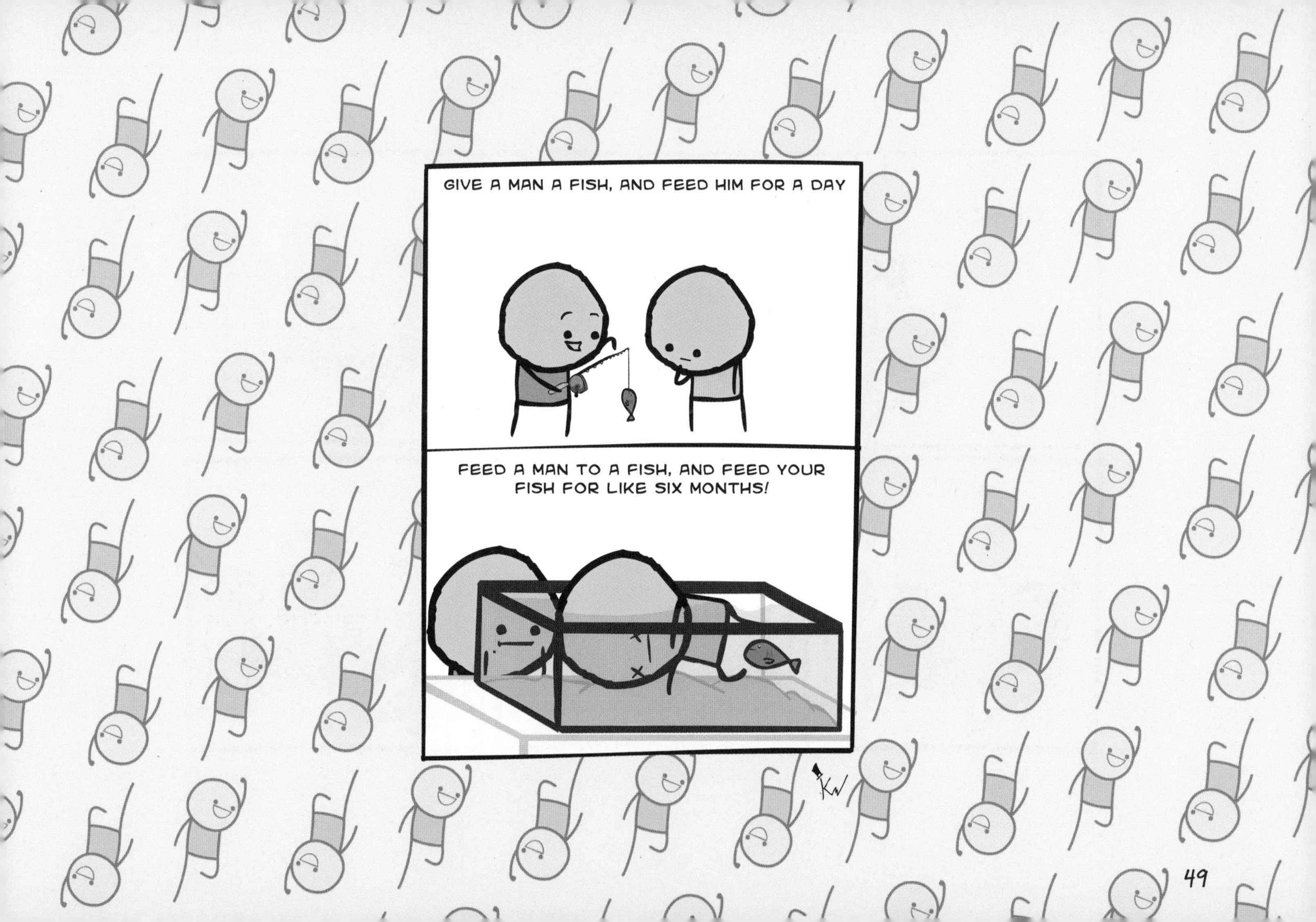
GIVE A MAN A FISH, AND FEED HIM FOR A DAY
FEED A MAN TO A FISH, AND FEED YOUR FISH FOR LIKE SIX MONTHS!

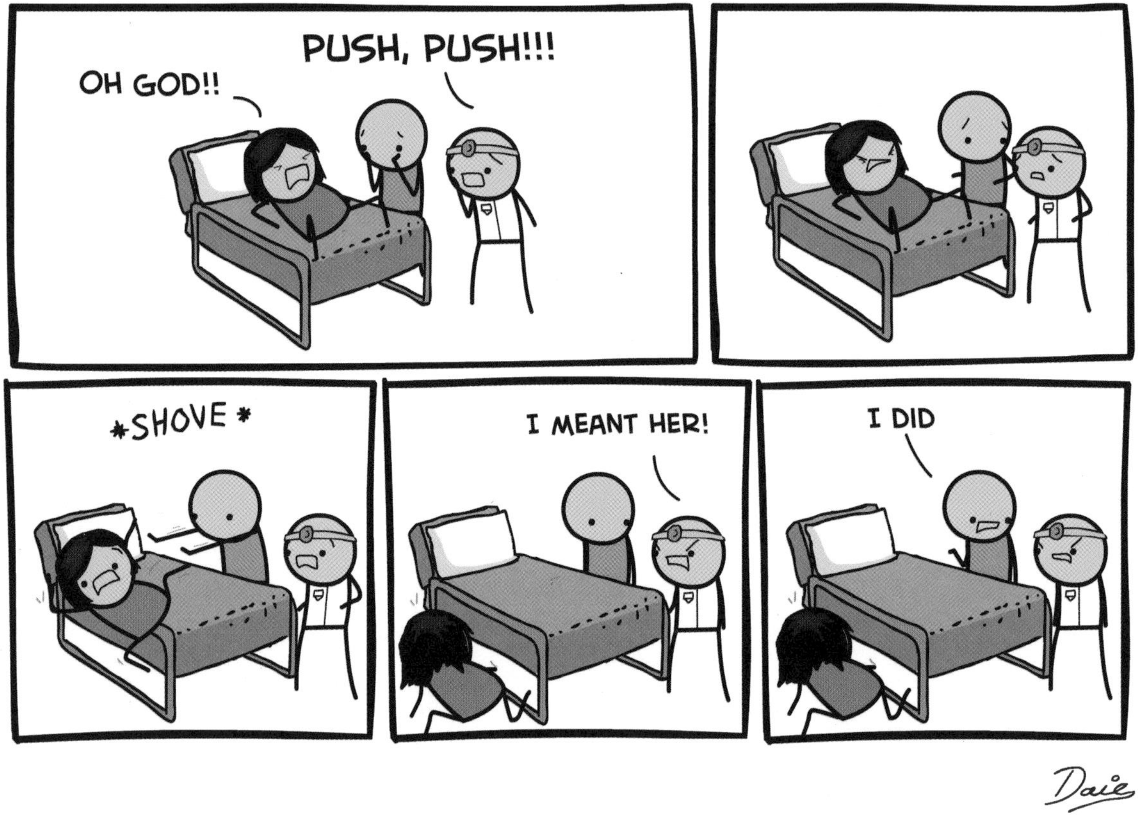
OH GOD!!
PUSH, PUSH!!!
SHOVE
I MEANT HER!
I DID

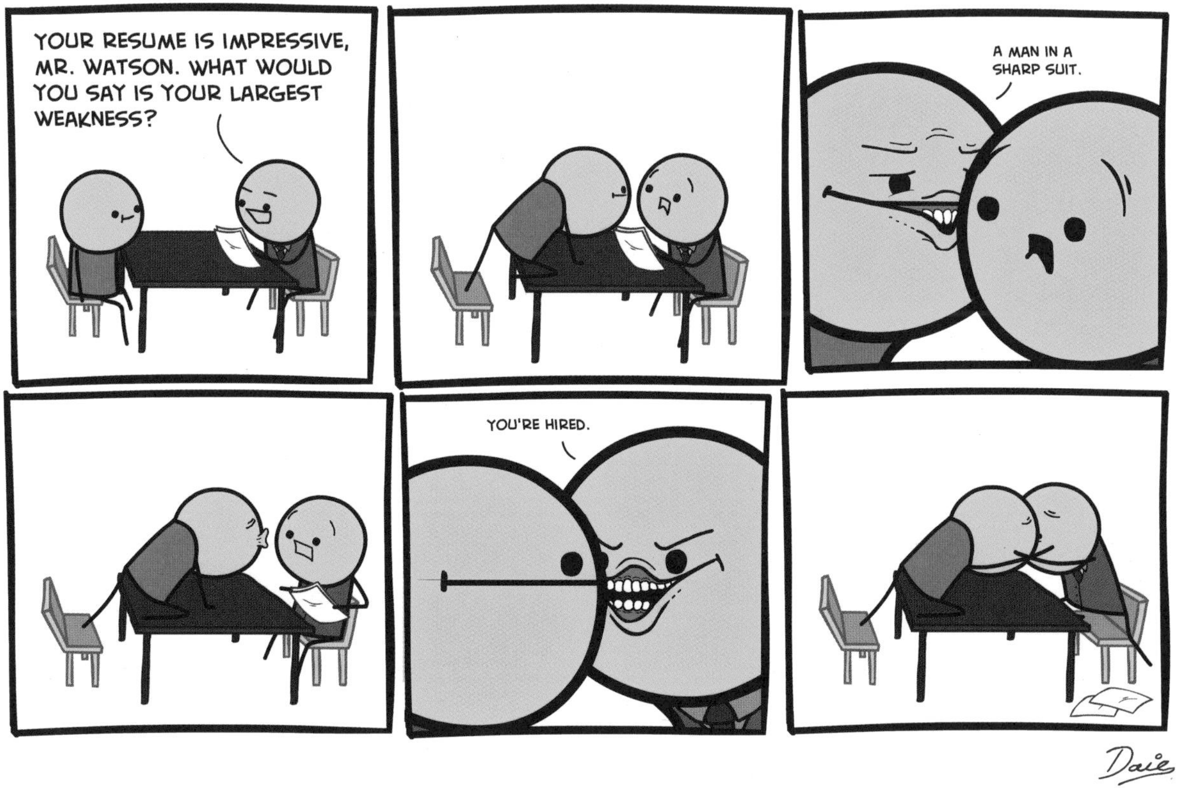
YOUR RESUME IS IMPRESSIVE, MR. WATSON. WHAT WOULD YOU SAY IS YOUR LARGEST WEAKNESS?
A MAN IN A SHARP SUIT.
YOU'RE HIRED.
Dave

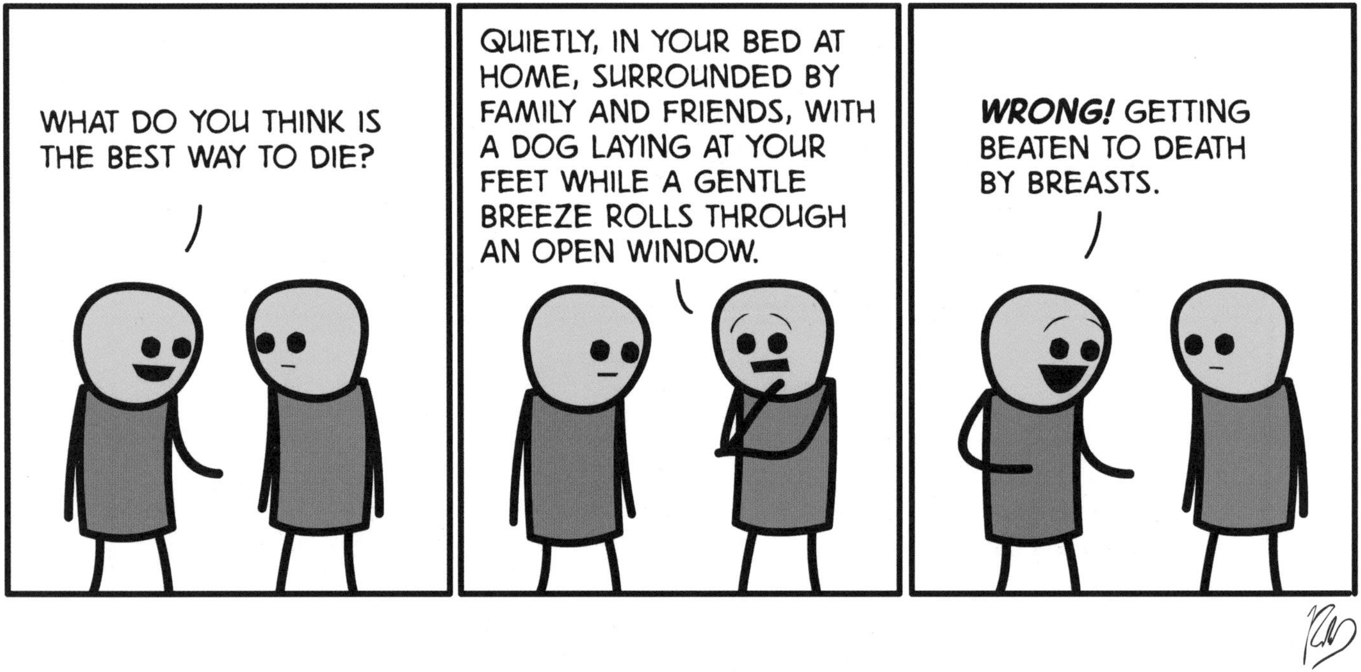
WHAT DO YOU THINK IS THE BEST WAY TO DIE?
QUIETLY, IN YOUR BED AT HOME, SURROUNDED BY FAMILY AND FRIENDS, WITH A DOG LAYING AT YOUR FEET WHILE A GENTLE BREEZE ROLLS THROUGH AN OPEN WINDOW.
WRONG! GETTING BEATEN TO DEATH BY BREASTS.

THAT CANDY BAR HAS YOUR NAME ON IT!
I WISH YOU HADN'T NAMED ME BUTTERFINGER, DAD.
I WISH YOU HADN'T BEEN BORN.

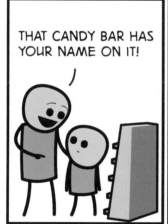

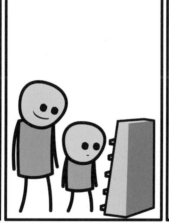

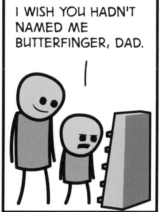

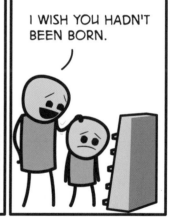

HMPH! NO MATTER HOW MUCH I PLAY MY FLUTE, I JUST CAN'T SEEM TO CHARM THE SNAKE!
HEY THERE, HAVING TROUBLE SNAKE CHARMING? HERE, LET ME TRY
WELL HELLO THERE, YOU SLITHERY SLITHERY SNAKE. HOW YOU DOIN' TONIGHT?
OH GOD, WHAT DID I DO LAST NIGHT!?
YAWN
Dave

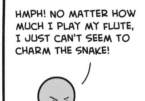

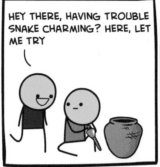

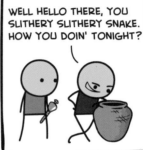

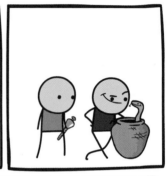

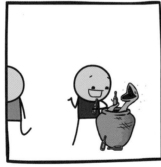

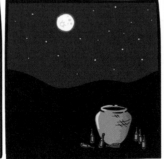

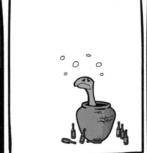

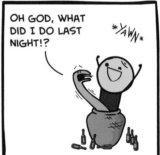

WHAT IS THE SQUARE ROOT OF 128?
√128 =
WHO GIVES A SHIT?
√128 =
HUH... YOU'RE RIGHT
√128 =
Dave

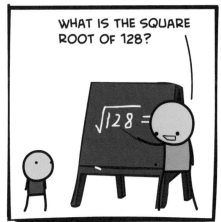

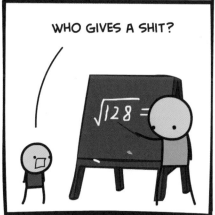

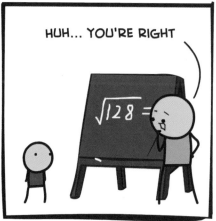

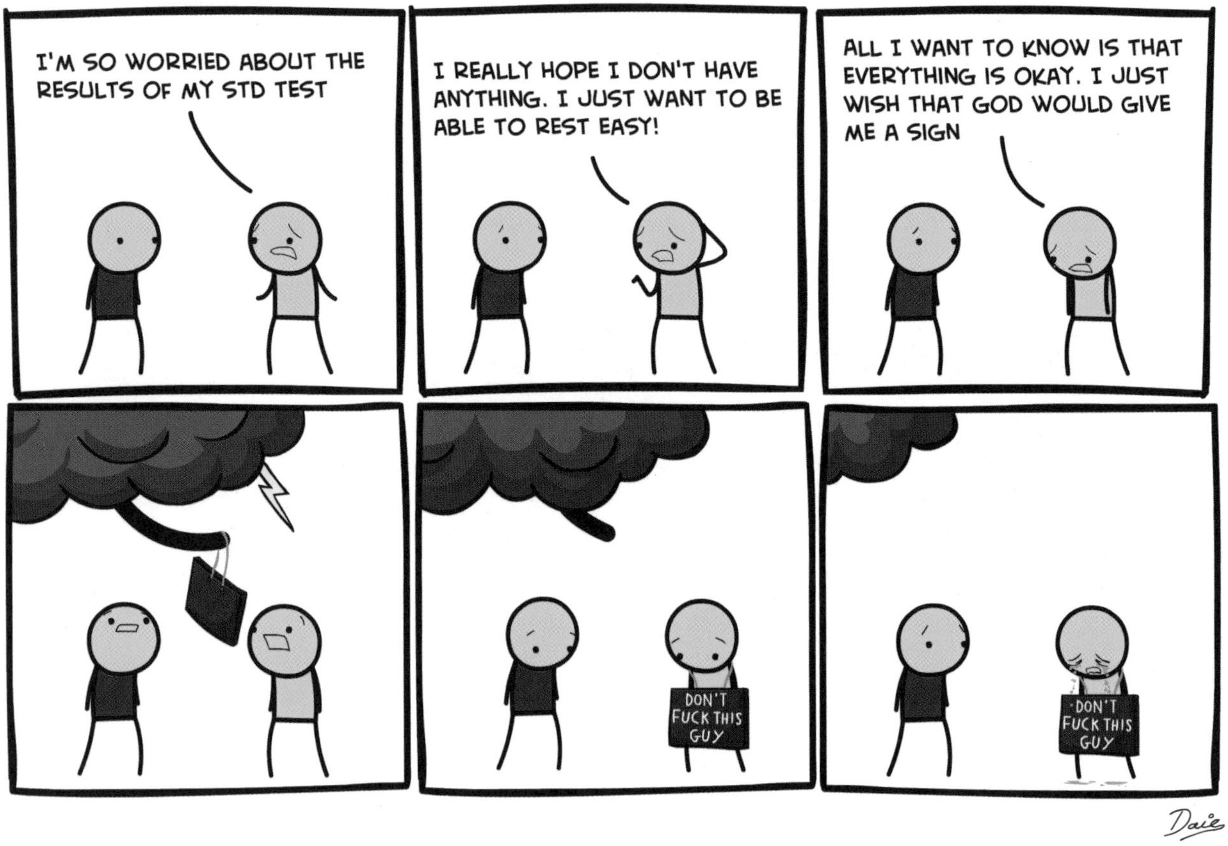
I'M SO WORRIED ABOUT THE RESULTS OF MY STD TEST
I REALLY HOPE I DON'T HAVE ANYTHING. I JUST WANT TO BE ABLE TO REST EASY!
ALL I WANT TO KNOW IS THAT EVERYTHING IS OKAY. I JUST WISH THAT GOD WOULD GIVE ME A SIGN
DON'T FUCK THIS GUY
DON'T FUCK THIS GUY
Dave

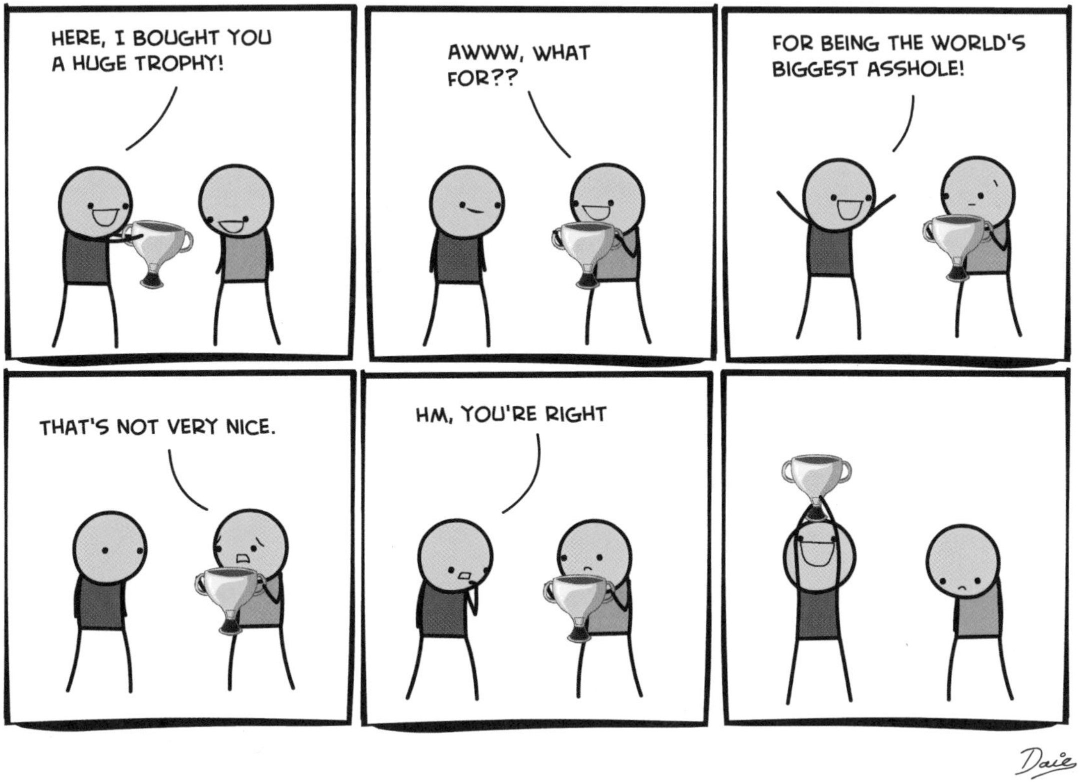
HERE, I BOUGHT YOU A HUGE TROPHY!
AWWW, WHAT FOR??
FOR BEING THE WORLD'S BIGGEST ASSHOLE!
THAT'S NOT VERY NICE.
HM, YOU'RE RIGHT
Dave

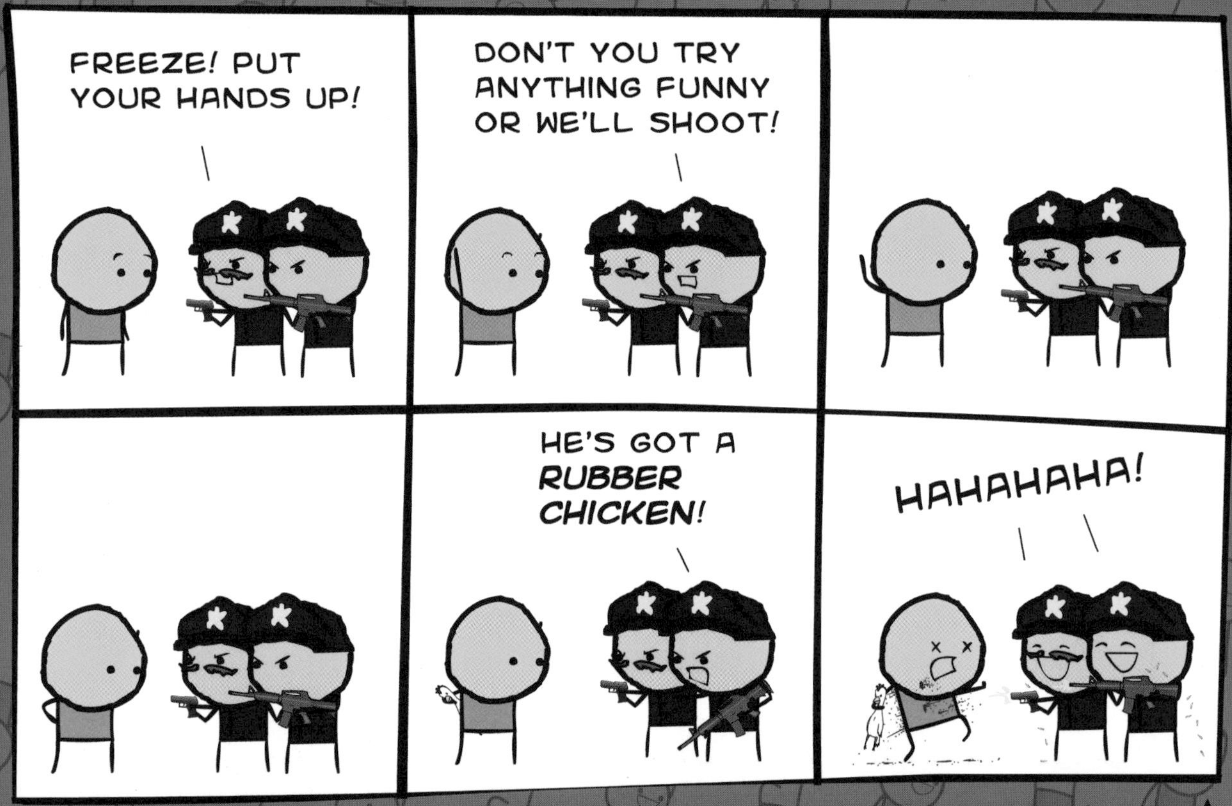
FREEZE! PUT YOUR HANDS UP!
DON'T YOU TRY ANYTHING FUNNY OR WE'LL SHOOT!
HE'S GOT A RUBBER CHICKEN!
HAHAHAHA!

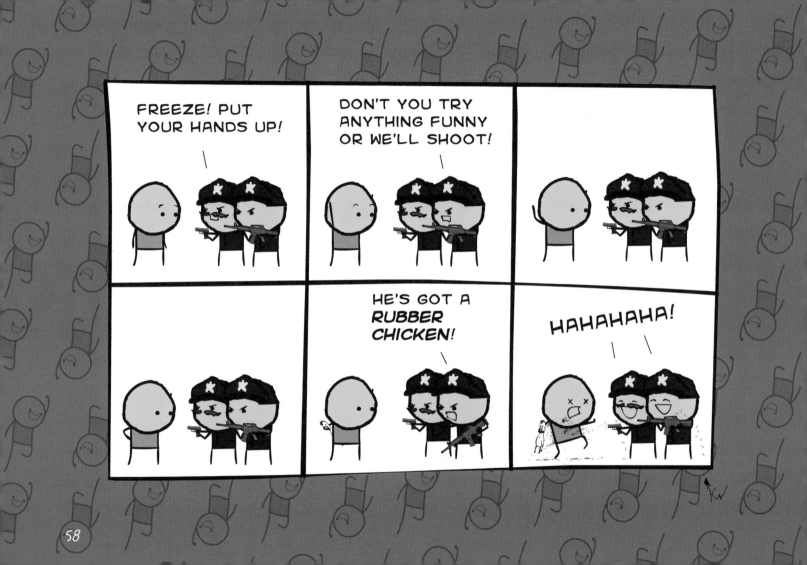

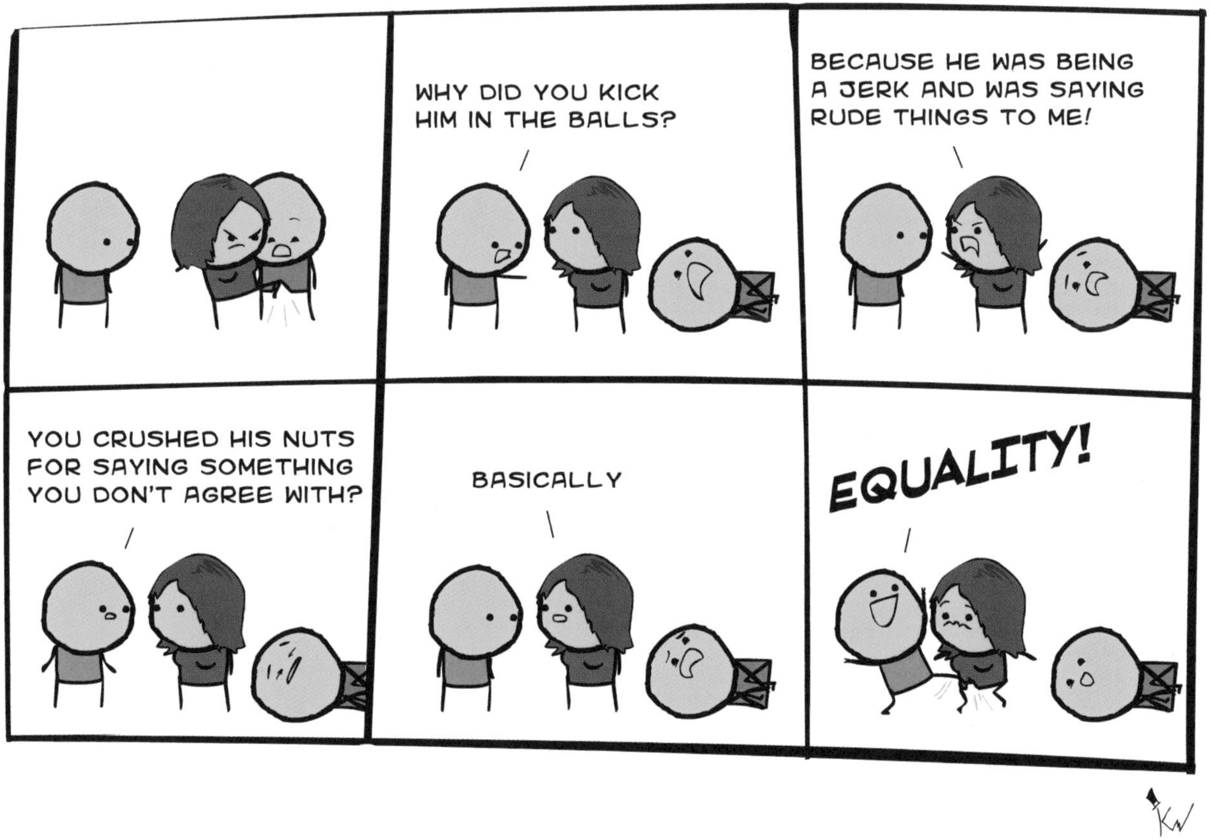
WHY DID YOU KICK HIM IN THE BALLS?
BECAUSE HE WAS BEING A JERK AND WAS SAYING RUDE THINGS TO ME!
YOU CRUSHED HIS NUTS FOR SAYING SOMETHING YOU DON'T AGREE WITH?
BASICALLY
EQUALITY!

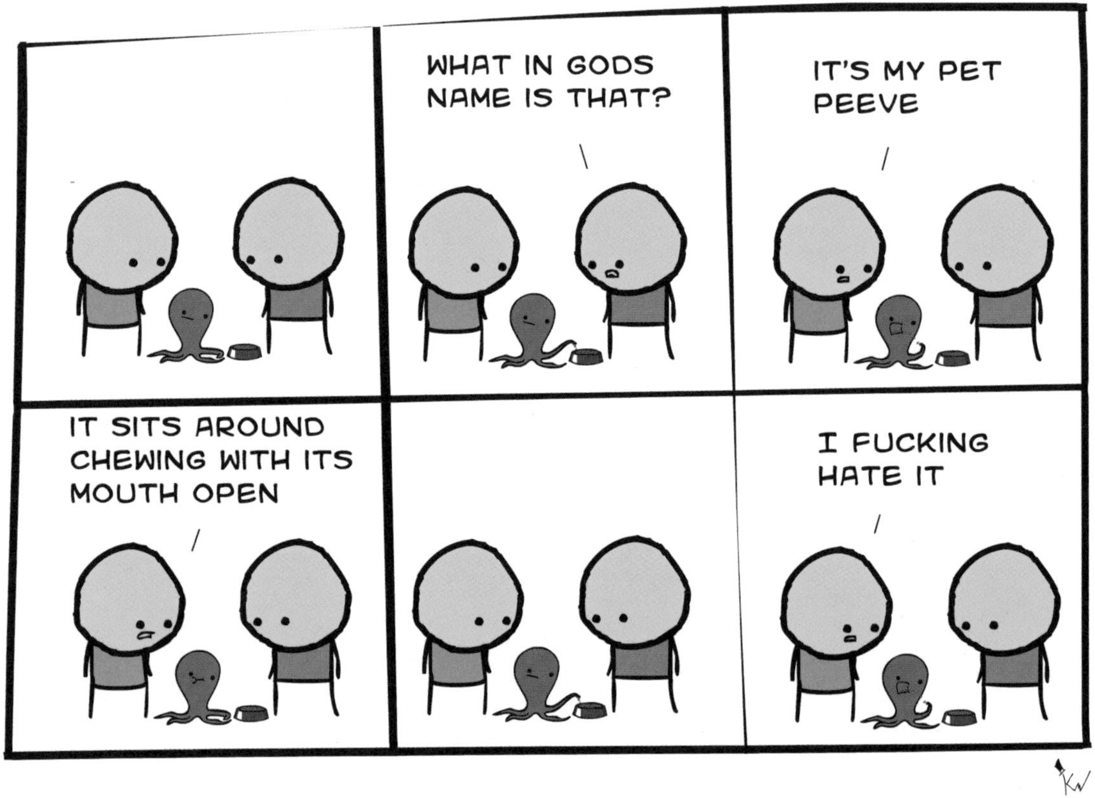
WHAT IN GODS NAME IS THAT?
IT'S MY PET PEEVE
IT SITS AROUND CHEWING WITH ITS MOUTH OPEN
I FUCKING HATE IT

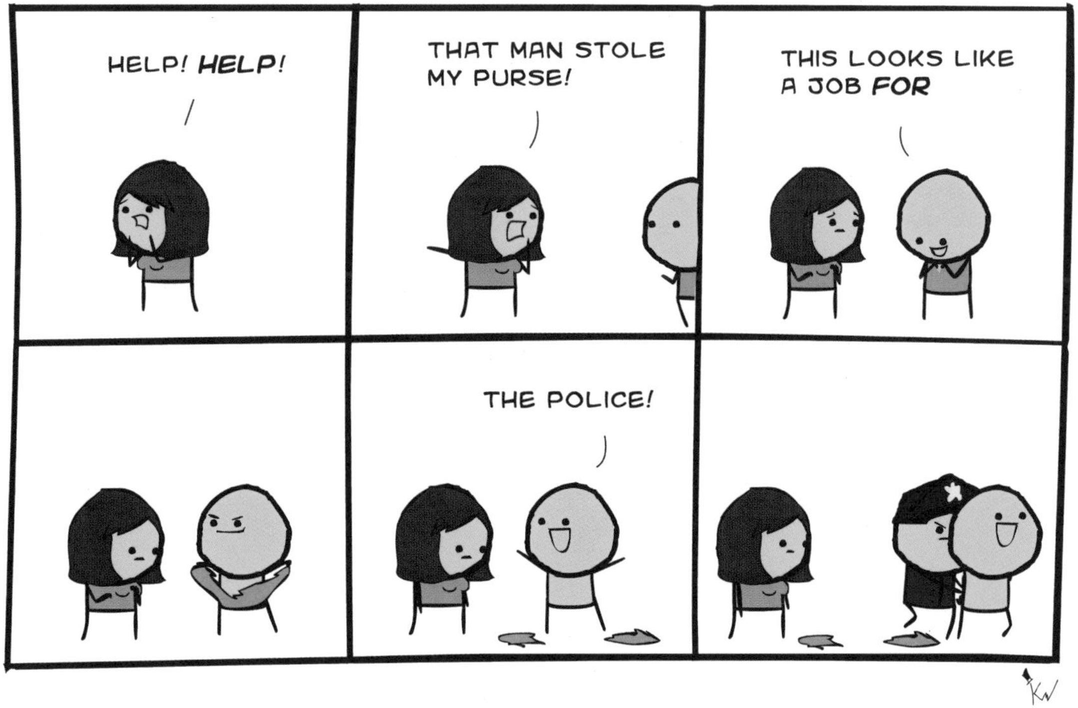
HELP! **HELP!**
THAT MAN STOLE MY PURSE!
THIS LOOKS LIKE A JOB **FOR**
THE POLICE!

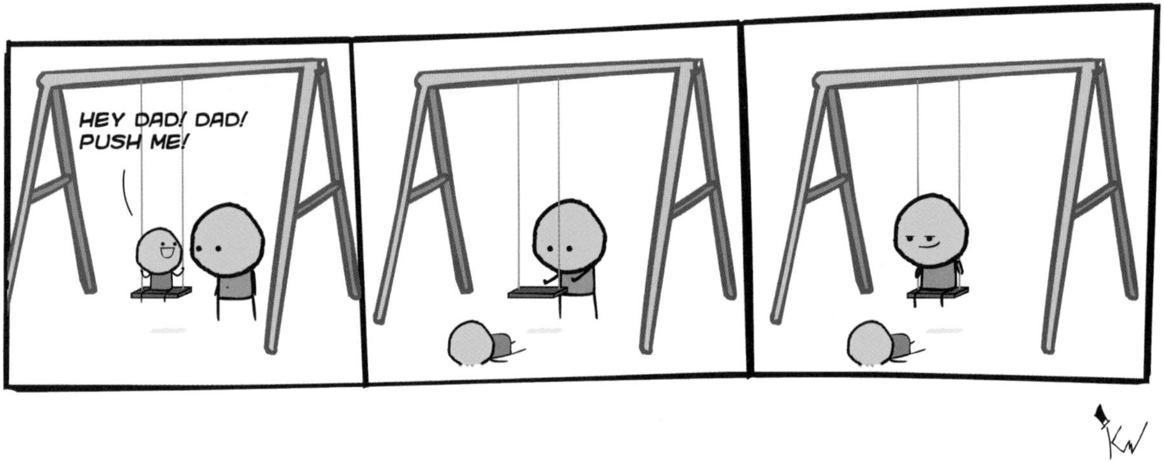
HEY DAD! DAD!
PUSH ME!
KW

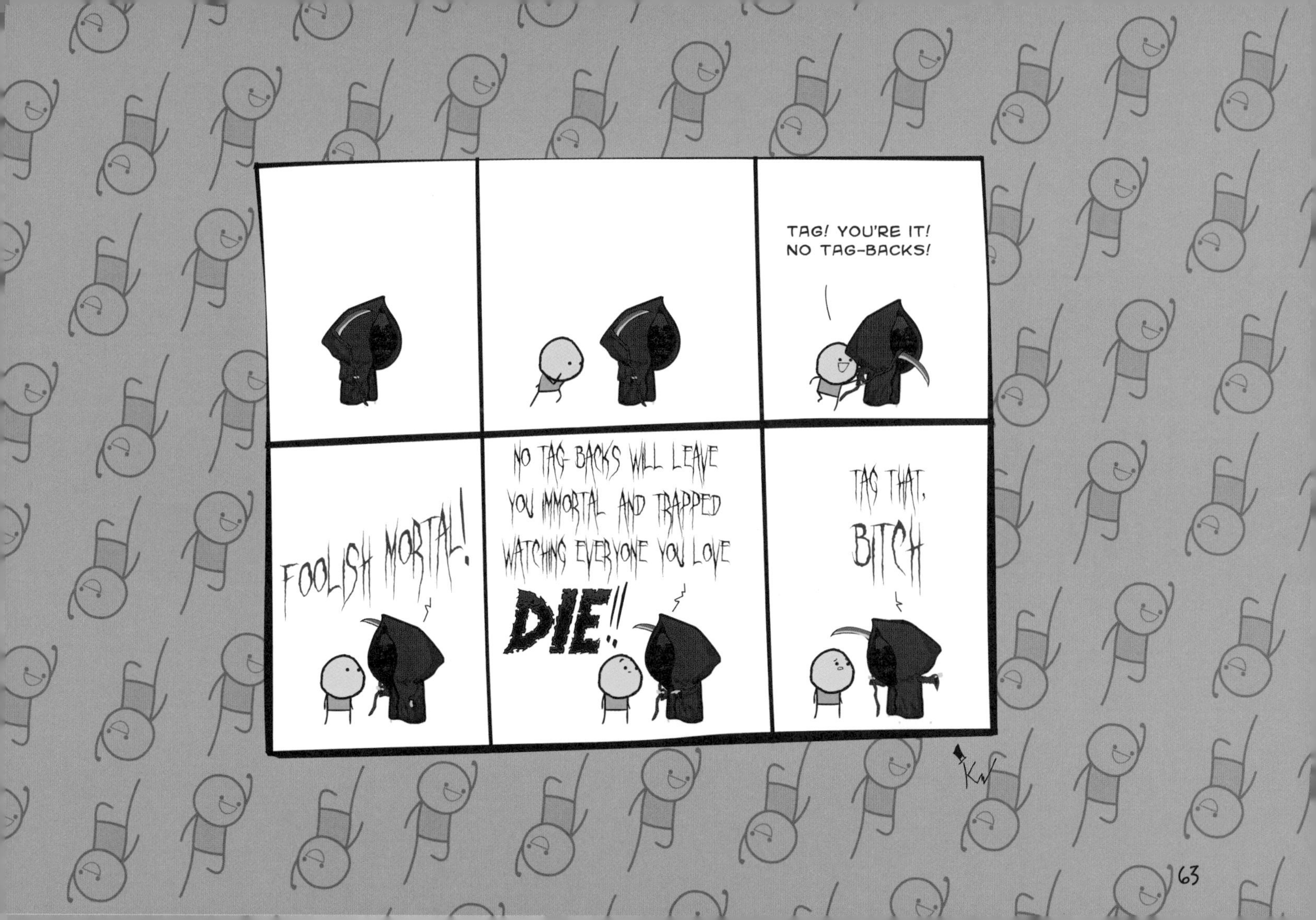
TAG! YOU'RE IT!
NO TAG-BACKS!
FOOLISH MORTAL!
NO TAG-BACKS WILL LEAVE
YOU IMMORTAL AND TRAPPED
WATCHING EVERYONE YOU LOVE
DIE!!
TAG THAT,
BITCH

I CAN'T BELIEVE YOU CHEATED ON ME, CHARLES! HOW COULD YOU!?
I CAN'T HELP IT! I HAVE THAT THING TIGER WOODS HAS.
SEX ADDICTION?
A HUGE BLACK DICK.

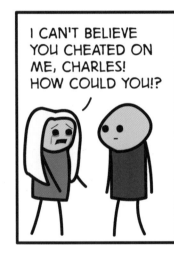

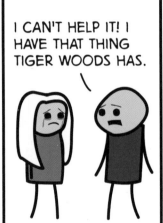

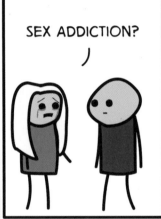

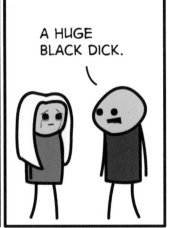

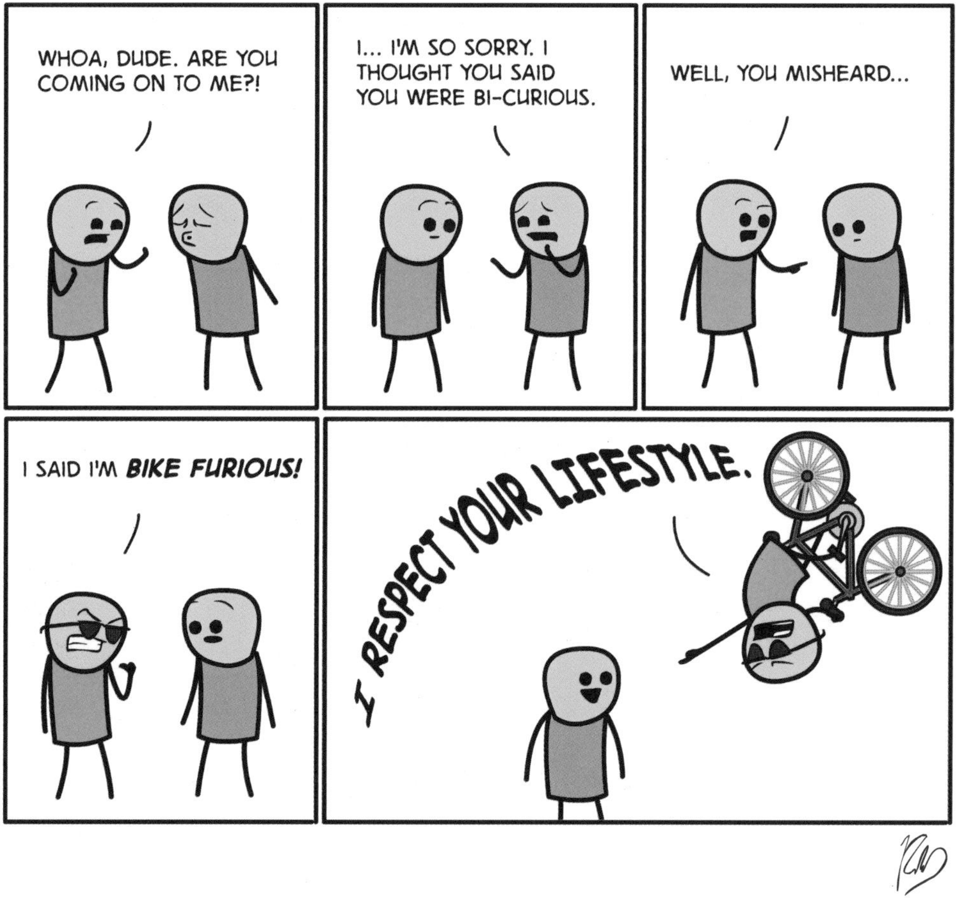
WHOA, DUDE. ARE YOU COMING ON TO ME?!
I... I'M SO SORRY. I THOUGHT YOU SAID YOU WERE BI-CURIOUS.
WELL, YOU MISHEARD...
I SAID I'M BIKE FURIOUS!
I RESPECT YOUR LIFESTYLE.

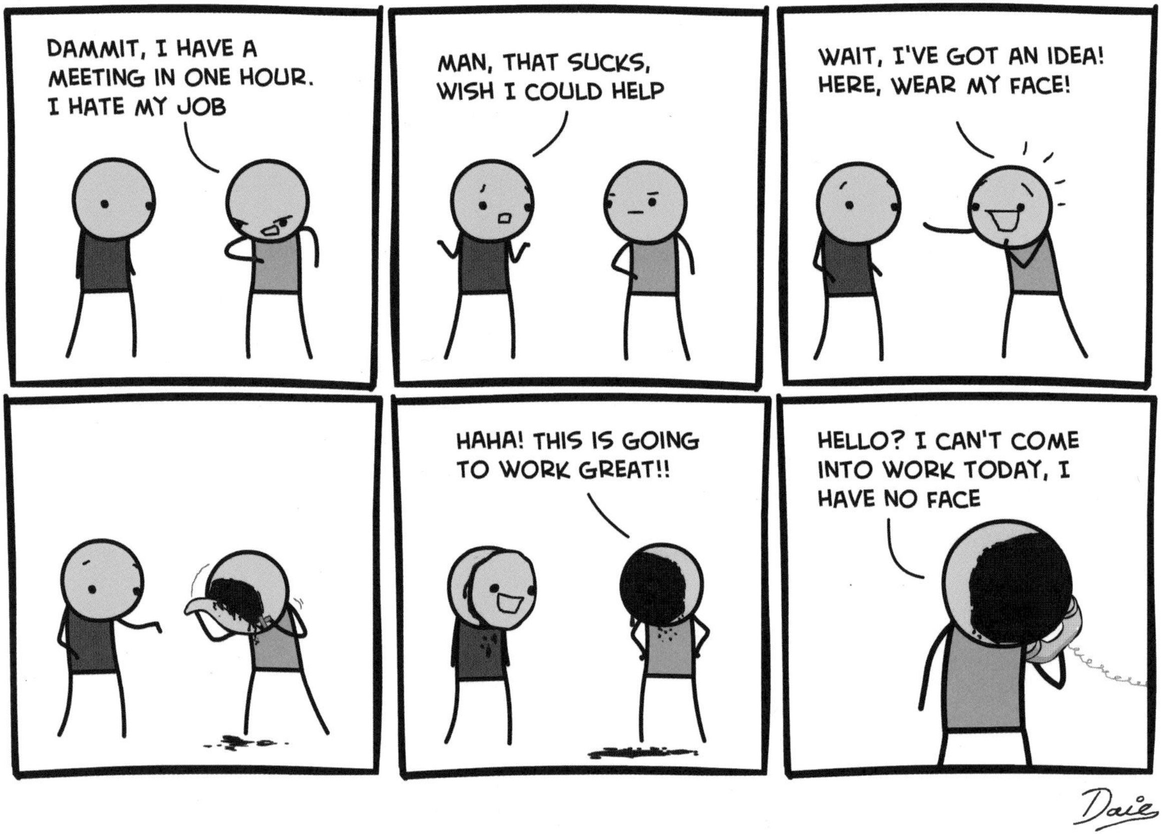
DAMMIT, I HAVE A MEETING IN ONE HOUR. I HATE MY JOB
MAN, THAT SUCKS, WISH I COULD HELP
WAIT, I'VE GOT AN IDEA! HERE, WEAR MY FACE!
HAHA! THIS IS GOING TO WORK GREAT!!
HELLO? I CAN'T COME INTO WORK TODAY, I HAVE NO FACE
Dave

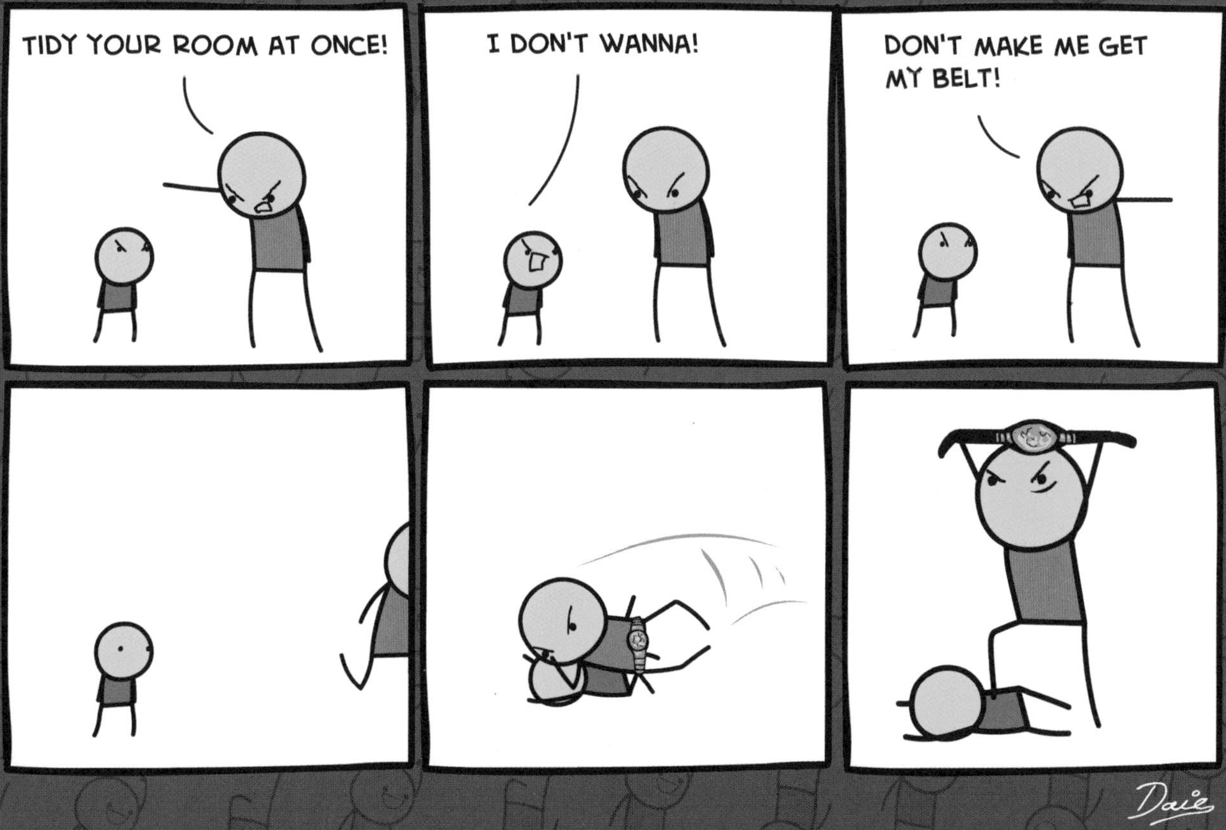
TIDY YOUR ROOM AT ONCE!
I DON'T WANNA!
DON'T MAKE ME GET MY BELT!
Dave

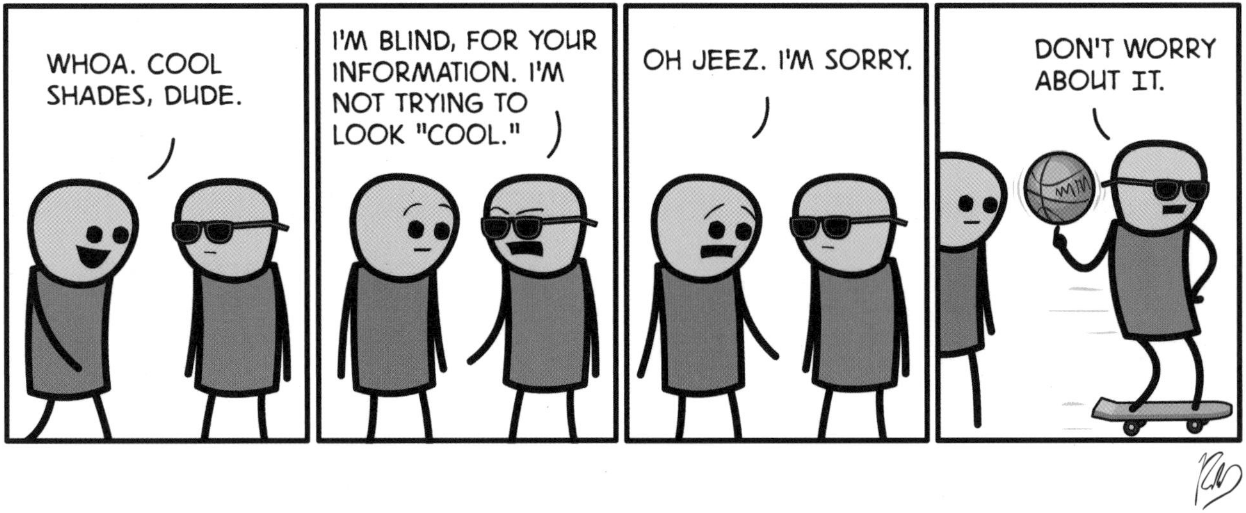
WHOA. COOL SHADES, DUDE.
I'M BLIND, FOR YOUR INFORMATION. I'M NOT TRYING TO LOOK "COOL."
OH JEEZ. I'M SORRY.
DON'T WORRY ABOUT IT.

HMM... BLURRY VISION? TUMMY ACHE?
HEART RACING?
THESE ARE SYMPTOMS OF A LITTLE CONDITION CALLED BEING IN LOVE.
AND THE SHITTING BLOOD, TOO?
SOMETIMES!

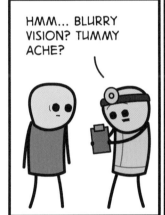

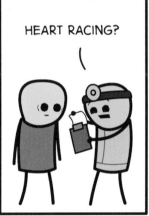

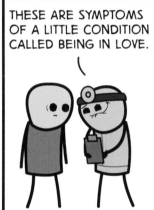

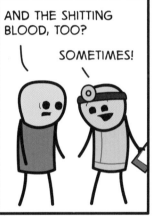

OK, MR. JOHNSON, ALL WE NEED IS A SEMEN SAMPLE AND THEN WE'RE DONE.
A SEMEN SAMPLE?
DON'T WORRY, MR. JOHNSON. I KNOW IT CAN BE A LITTLE AWKWARD AT FIRST
AND YEAH, IT'S IN A COLD AND STERILE ENVIRONMENT INSIDE THE MOST DEPRESSING BUILDING IMAGINABLE
NOT TO MENTION YOU MIGHT HEAR A BABY CRYING, OR HEAR SOMEONE DIE IN A NEARBY ROOM, BUT AT LEAST IT-
I'M DONE.

HOW DO THE RESULTS LOOK, DR. SEUSS?
I LOOKED AT YOUR LUNGS, I LOOKED AT YOUR HEART...
YOU HAVE SO MANY THINGS WRONG, I DON'T KNOW WHERE TO START!
YOUR LIVER IS BLUE, AND YOUR TONGUE IS BLUE TOO, I'D WRITE UP MY WILL, IF I WERE YOU
I'M SORRY, SO SORRY YOUNG DAUGHTER AND WIFE, NOTHING COULD BE DONE TO SAVE THE MAN'S LIFE
KW

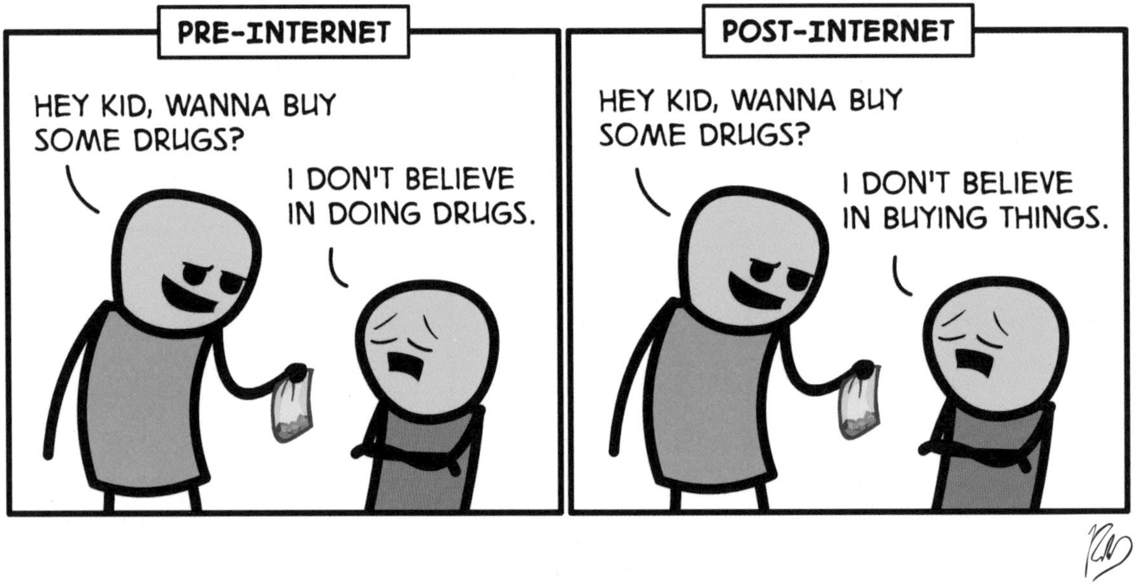
PRE-INTERNET
HEY KID, WANNA BUY SOME DRUGS?
I DON'T BELIEVE IN DOING DRUGS.
POST-INTERNET
HEY KID, WANNA BUY SOME DRUGS?
I DON'T BELIEVE IN BUYING THINGS.

EMOTIONAL ROLLERCOASTER
HONEY, WE'VE BEEN TOGETHER FOR A LONG TIME NOW, AND...
...I WANT TO TRY ANAL...
...WITH OTHER GUYS.

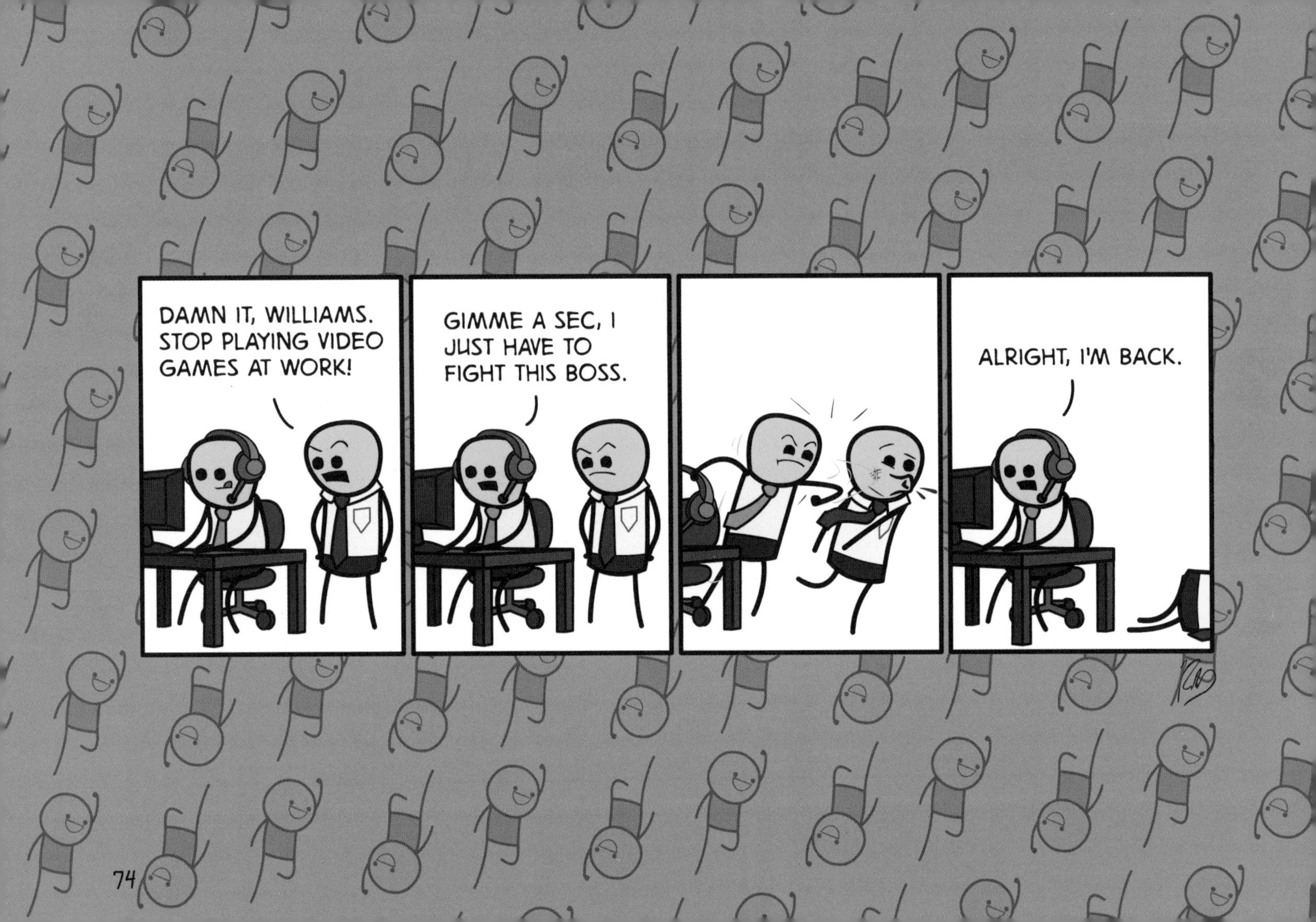
DAMN IT, WILLIAMS. STOP PLAYING VIDEO GAMES AT WORK!
GIMME A SEC, I JUST HAVE TO FIGHT THIS BOSS.
ALRIGHT, I'M BACK.

MY NAME'S GEORGE, AND I'M AN ALCOHOLIC.
UH... THIS IS A BOOK CLUB.
AND I NEED A GODDAMN DRINK.

DUDE, I'VE GOT THIS WEIRD GREEN MOLD ON MY BALLS!
YOU SHOULD PROBABLY GET IT LOOKED AT.
GOOD IDEA.

ALAS, POOR YORICK!
OH HEY, YOU FOUND MY SKULL. THANKS, BUDDY.
NO PROBS, YORICK.

WELL ACCORDING TO MY CLIPBOARD, YOU'VE GOT A FRACTURED SKULL.
UH, I THINK THAT'S A MISTAKE. I CAME HERE BECAUSE MY STOMACH HURTS!
I'M THE DOCTOR!!

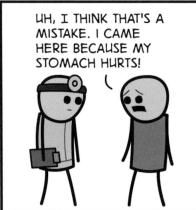

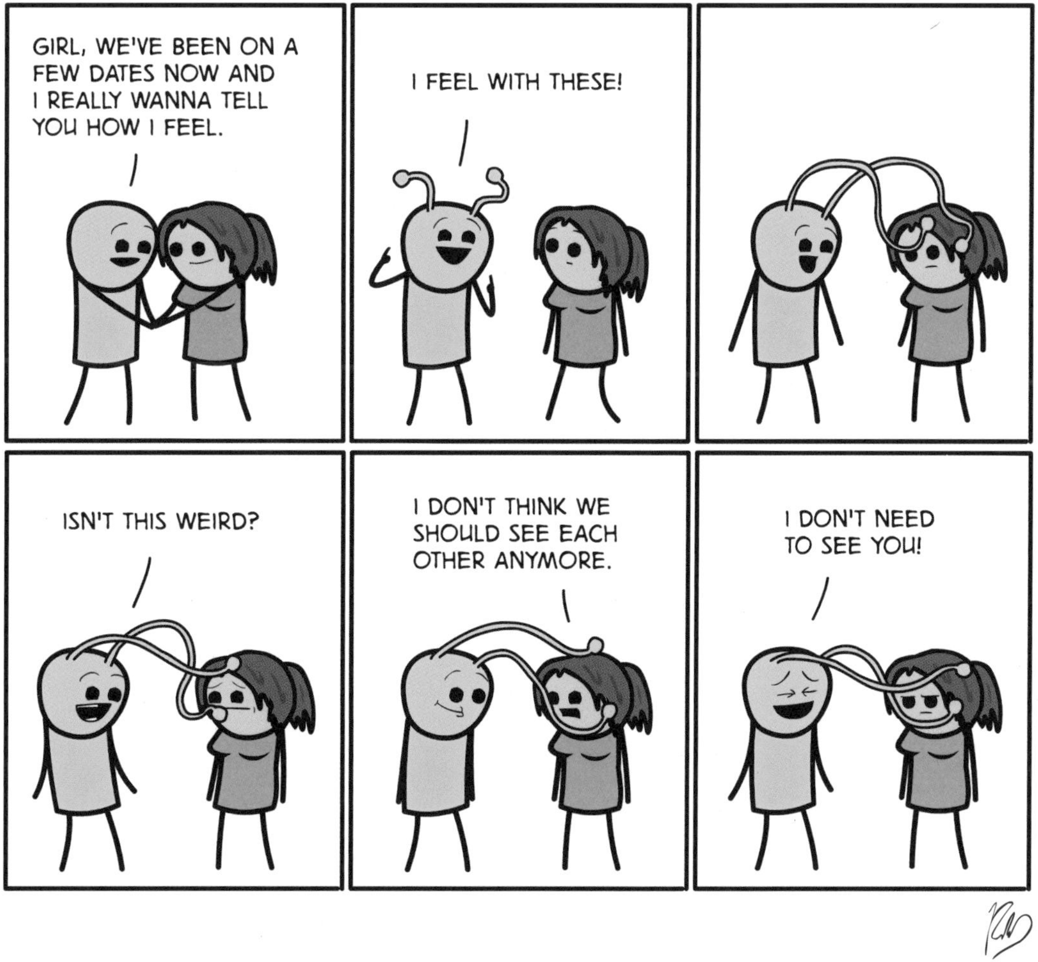
GIRL, WE'VE BEEN ON A FEW DATES NOW AND I REALLY WANNA TELL YOU HOW I FEEL.
I FEEL WITH THESE!
ISN'T THIS WEIRD?
I DON'T THINK WE SHOULD SEE EACH OTHER ANYMORE.
I DON'T NEED TO SEE YOU!

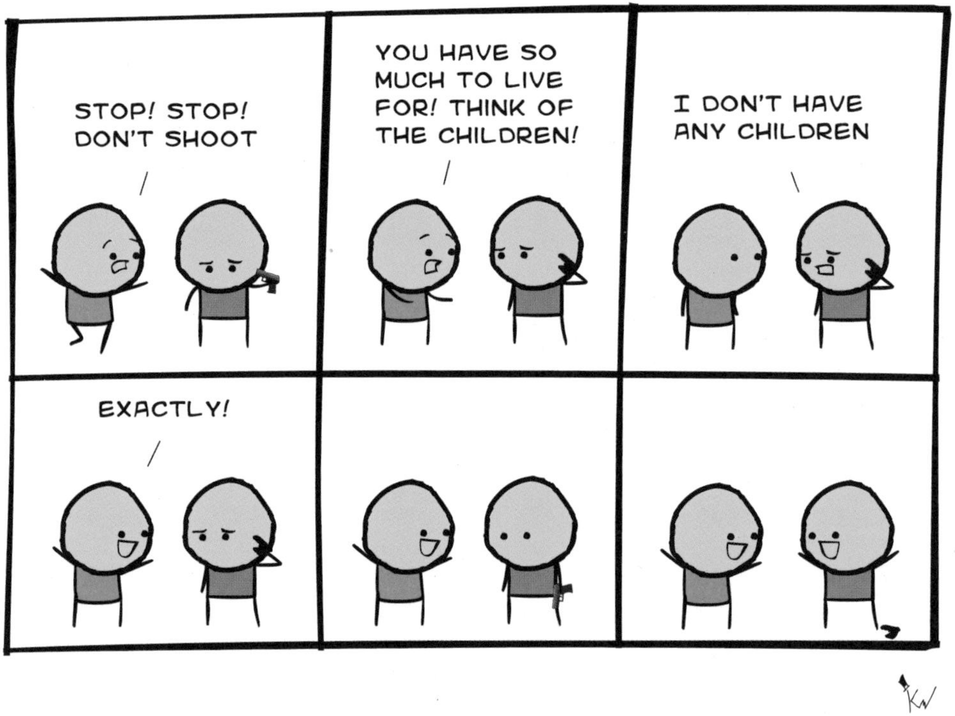
STOP! STOP!
DON'T SHOOT
YOU HAVE SO
MUCH TO LIVE
FOR! THINK OF
THE CHILDREN!
I DON'T HAVE
ANY CHILDREN
EXACTLY!

I HAVE THE WORST HABIT OF TALKING IN MY SLEEP
OH YEAH, I'VE HAD THAT BEFORE. IT MIGHT BE CAUSED BY STRESS OR CERTAIN MEDICATIONS
YOU CAN FIX THAT BY NOT EATING A LARGE MEAL BEFORE YOU GO TO SLEEP
IT ALSO HELPS TO FOLLOW A NATURAL SLEEP ROUTINE
YAWN
OH, HEY THERE. GOOD MORNING

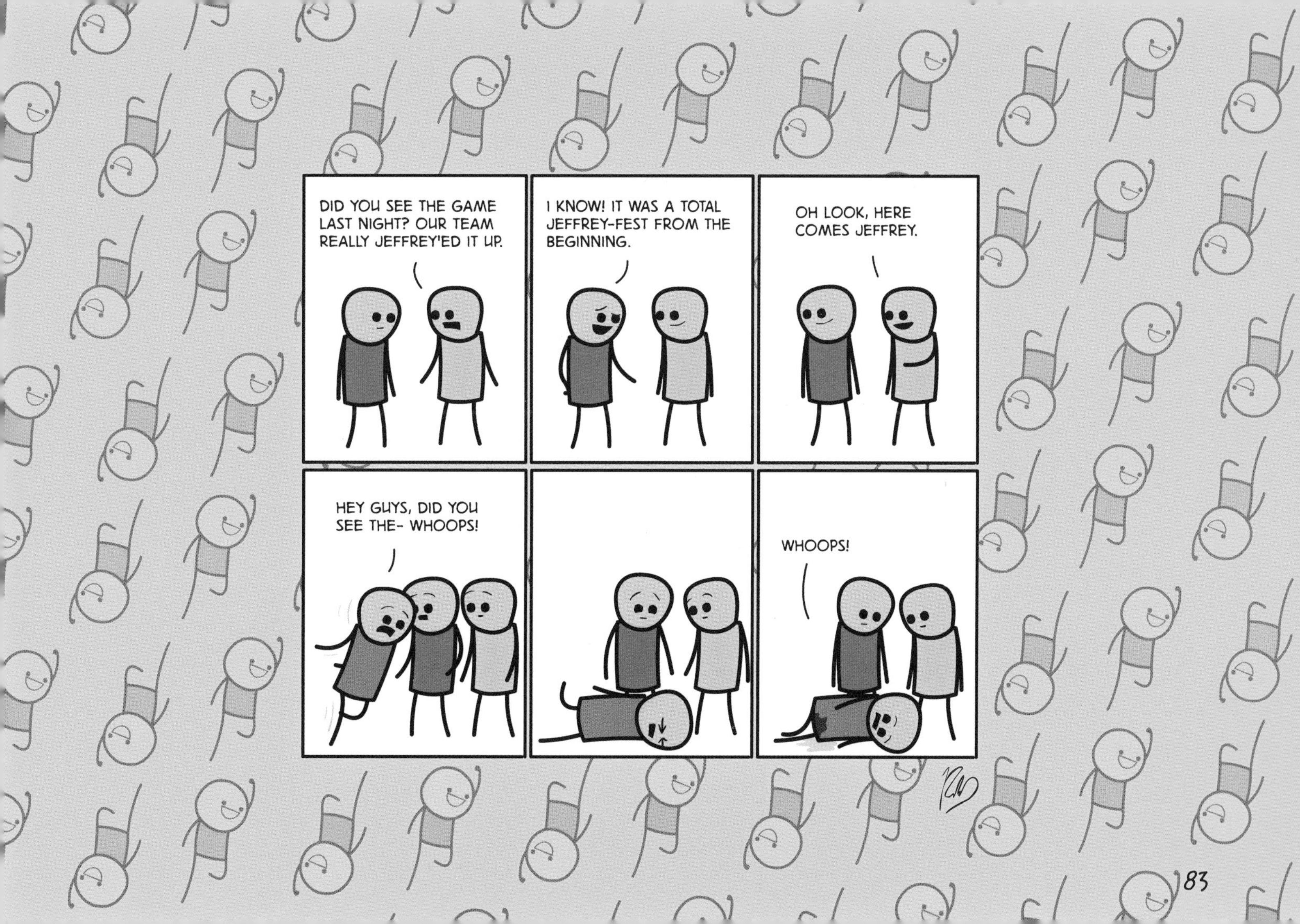
DID YOU SEE THE GAME LAST NIGHT? OUR TEAM REALLY JEFFREY'ED IT UP.
I KNOW! IT WAS A TOTAL JEFFREY-FEST FROM THE BEGINNING.
OH LOOK, HERE COMES JEFFREY.
HEY GUYS, DID YOU SEE THE- WHOOPS!
WHOOPS!

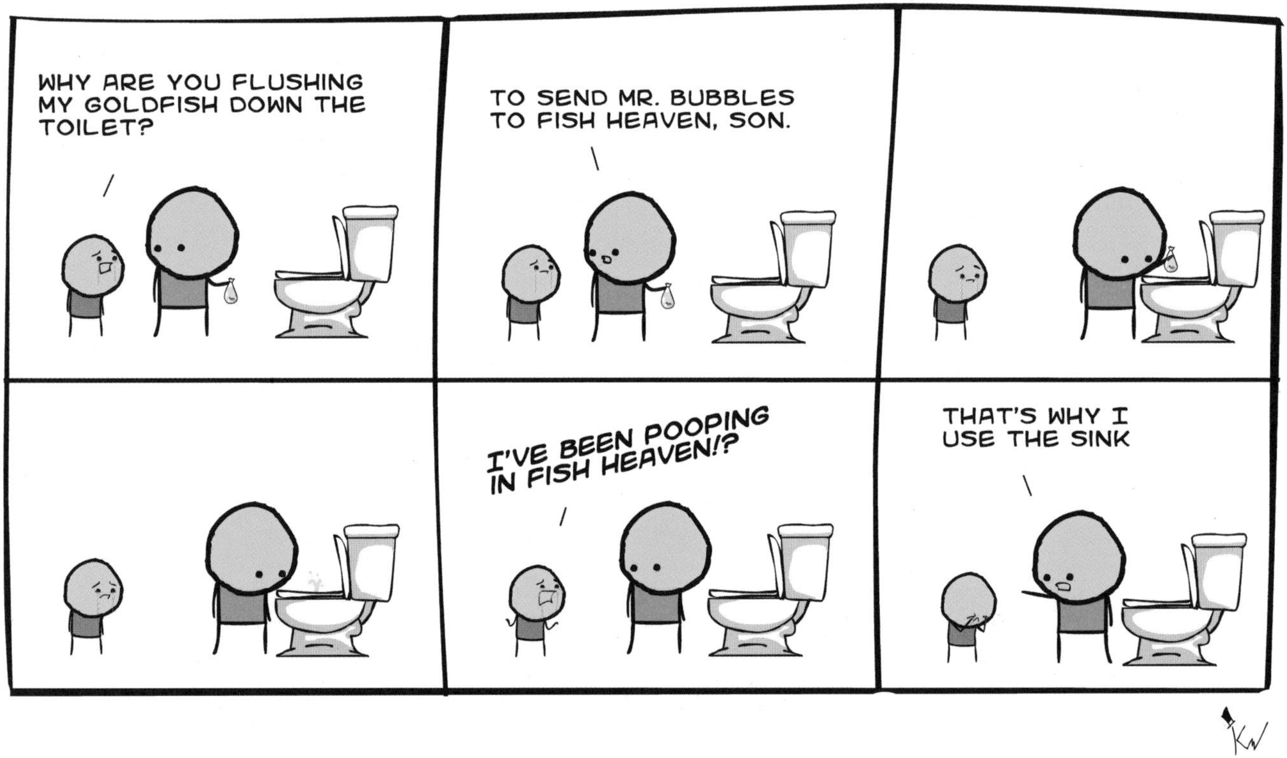
WHY ARE YOU FLUSHING MY GOLDFISH DOWN THE TOILET?
TO SEND MR. BUBBLES TO FISH HEAVEN, SON.
I'VE BEEN POOPING IN FISH HEAVEN!?
THAT'S WHY I USE THE SINK

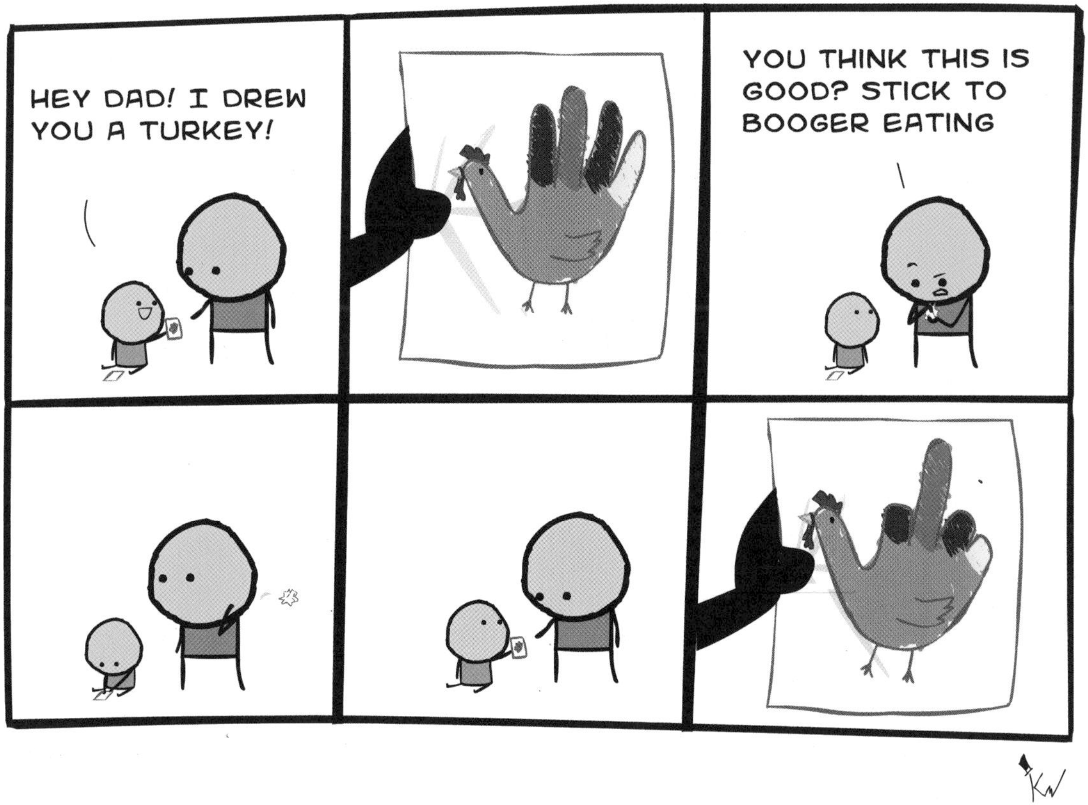
HEY DAD! I DREW YOU A TURKEY!
YOU THINK THIS IS GOOD? STICK TO BOOGER EATING

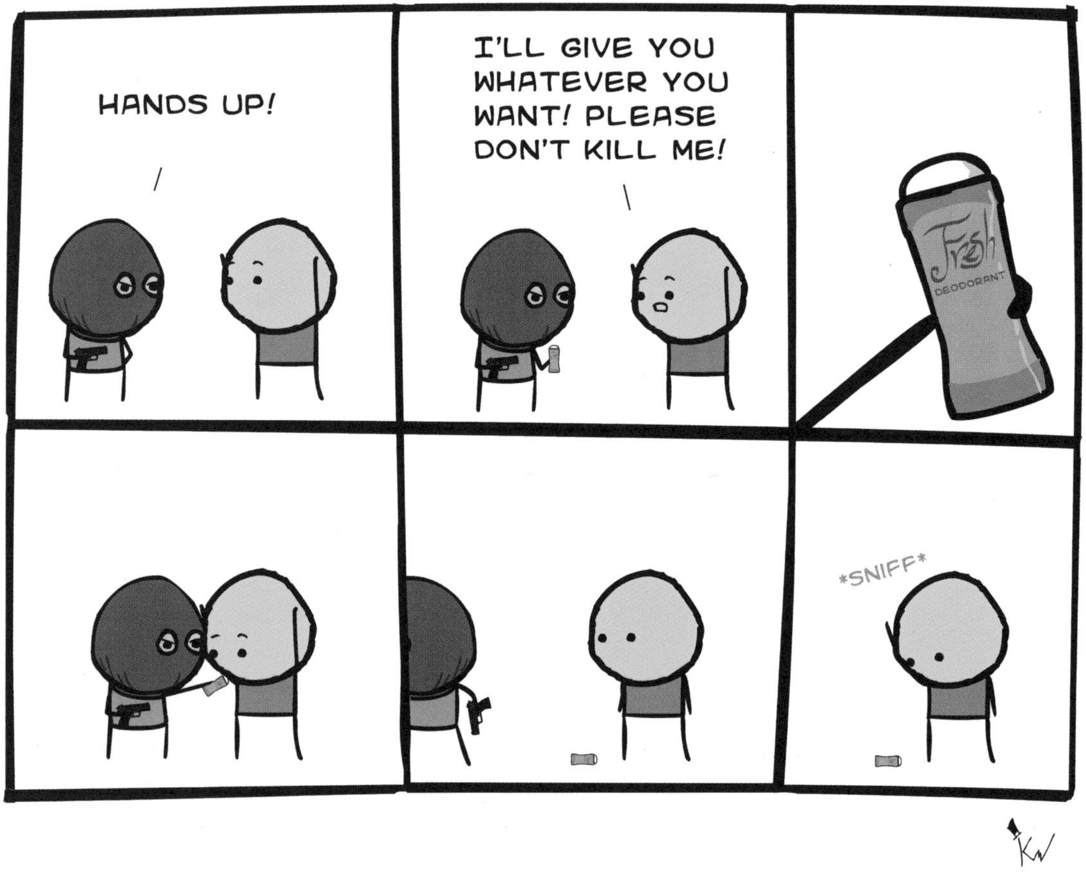
HANDS UP!
I'LL GIVE YOU WHATEVER YOU WANT! PLEASE DON'T KILL ME!
Fresh
DEODORANT
SNIFF

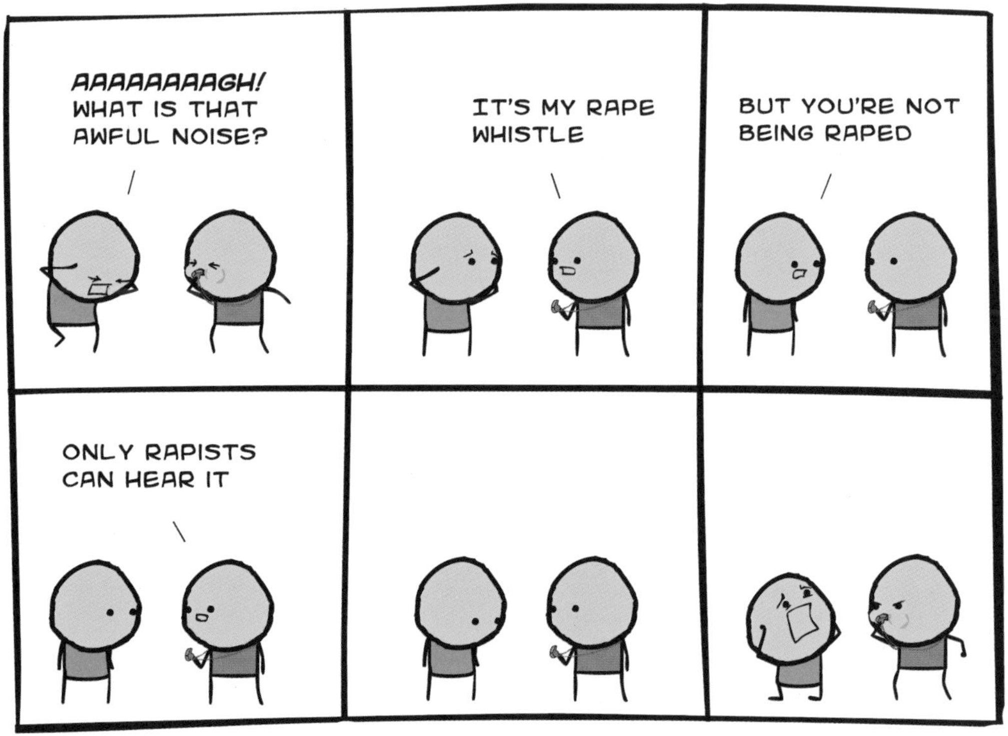
AAAAAAAAAGH! WHAT IS THAT AWFUL NOISE?
IT'S MY RAPE WHISTLE
BUT YOU'RE NOT BEING RAPED
ONLY RAPISTS CAN HEAR IT

I'M SORRY, MACGYVER. IT LOOKS LIKE YOU HAVE ERECTILE DYSFUNCTION.

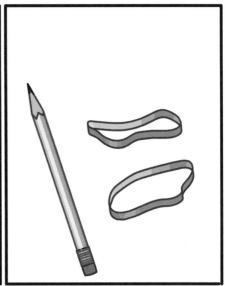

I MADE SOME MIX CD'S! WHAT KIND OF MUSIC DO YOU LIKE?
I'LL LISTEN TO *ANYTHING!*
WHAT ABOUT YOUR PARENTS HAVING SEX?
MEH, THEIR OLDER STUFF WAS BETTER.

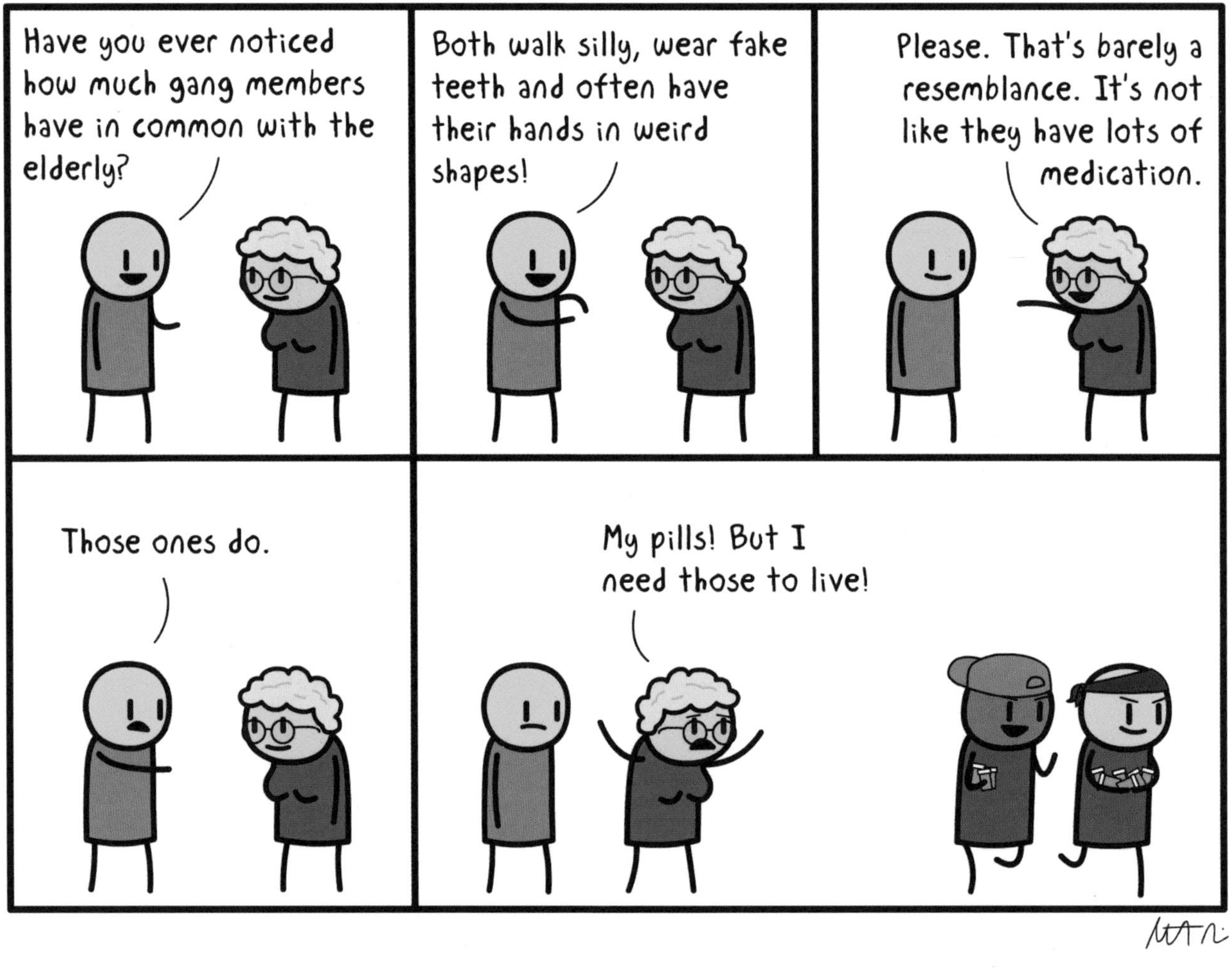
Have you ever noticed how much gang members have in common with the elderly?
Both walk silly, wear fake teeth and often have their hands in weird shapes!
Please. That's barely a resemblance. It's not like they have lots of medication.
Those ones do.
My pills! But I need those to live!

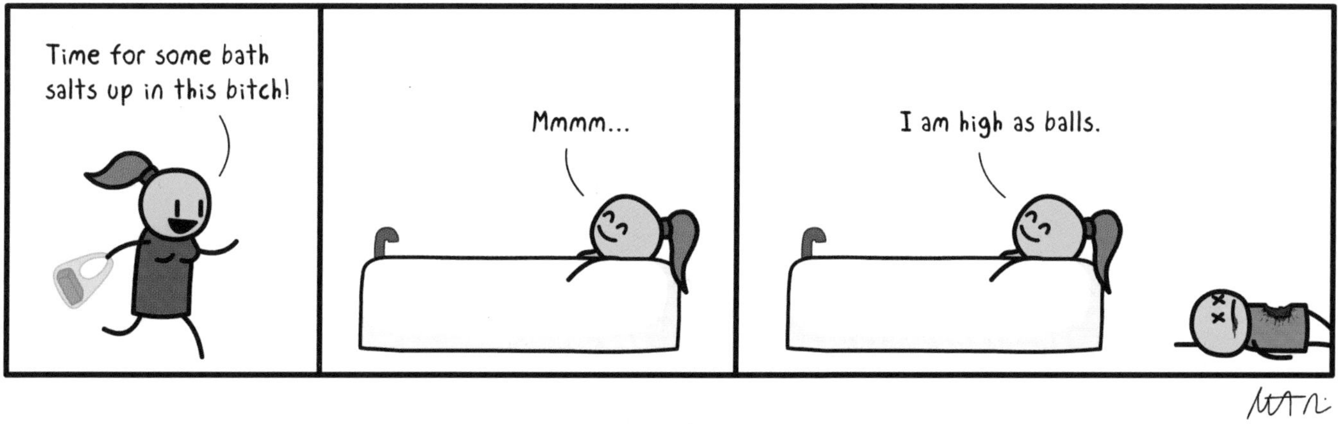
Time for some bath salts up in this bitch!
Mmmm...
I am high as balls.

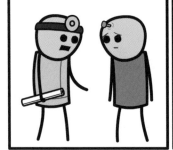

WELL, I WASN'T ABLE
TO GET THE NAIL OUT
OF YOUR HEAD...

BUT I WAS ABLE TO
PHOTOSHOP IT OUT
OF YOUR HEAD!

HOW'S THAT
SUPPOSED
TO HELP?

BEHOLD, IT IS I... MINDFUCK!
WHAT'S YOUR POWER?
I CAN PSYCHICALLY HAVE SEX WITH ANY WOMAN SIMPLY BY MAKING EYE CONTACT WITH HER.
HOLY COW! YOU CAN MAKE GIRLS ORGASM WITH A SINGLE GLANCE?
NOT THEM... JUST ME. OTHERWISE MY POWERS MIGHT BE REVEALED!
SO YOUR SUPERPOWER IS EJACULATING EVERY TIME YOU SEE A WOMAN?
I THINK YOU'RE OVERSIMPLIFYING IT.
MF

DOCTOR, HELP! I TOOK VIAGRA AND MY ERECTION IS LONGER THAN FOUR INCHES.
YOU MEAN HOURS?
NO, IT'S MINE.

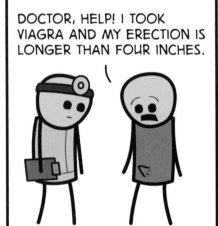

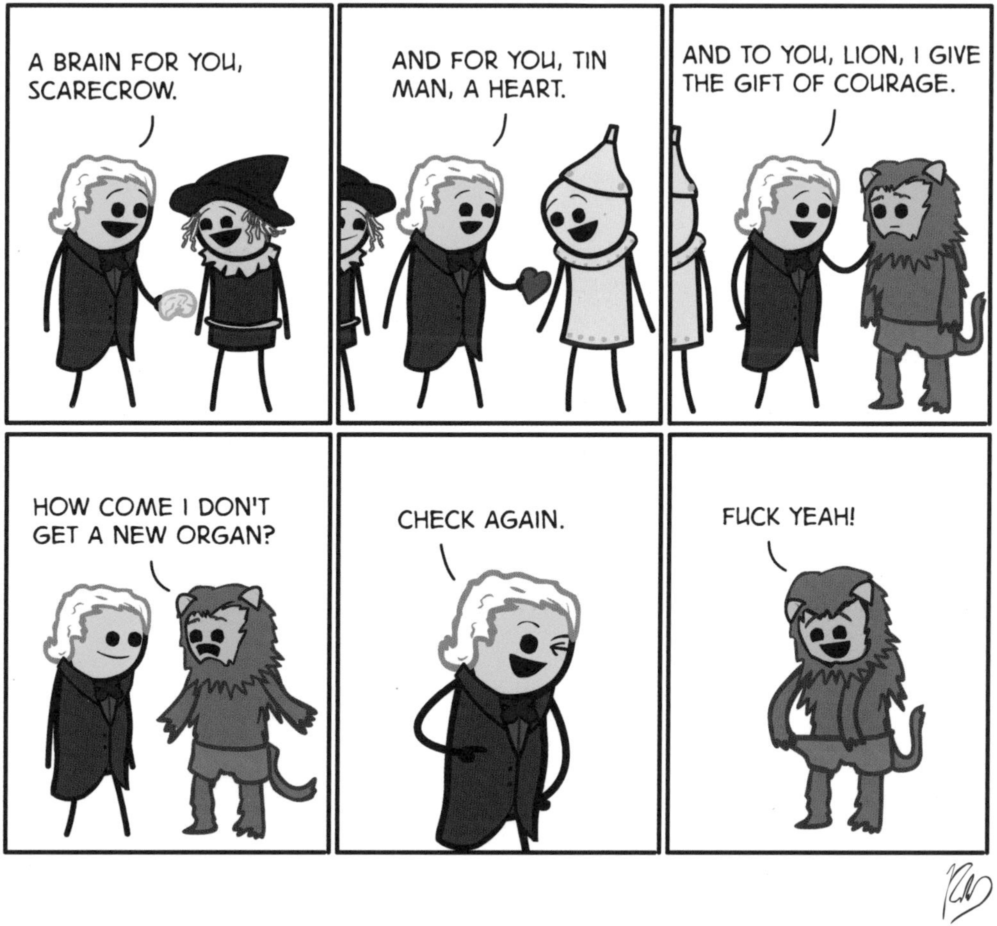
A BRAIN FOR YOU, SCARECROW.
AND FOR YOU, TIN MAN, A HEART.
AND TO YOU, LION, I GIVE THE GIFT OF COURAGE.
HOW COME I DON'T GET A NEW ORGAN?
CHECK AGAIN.
FUCK YEAH!

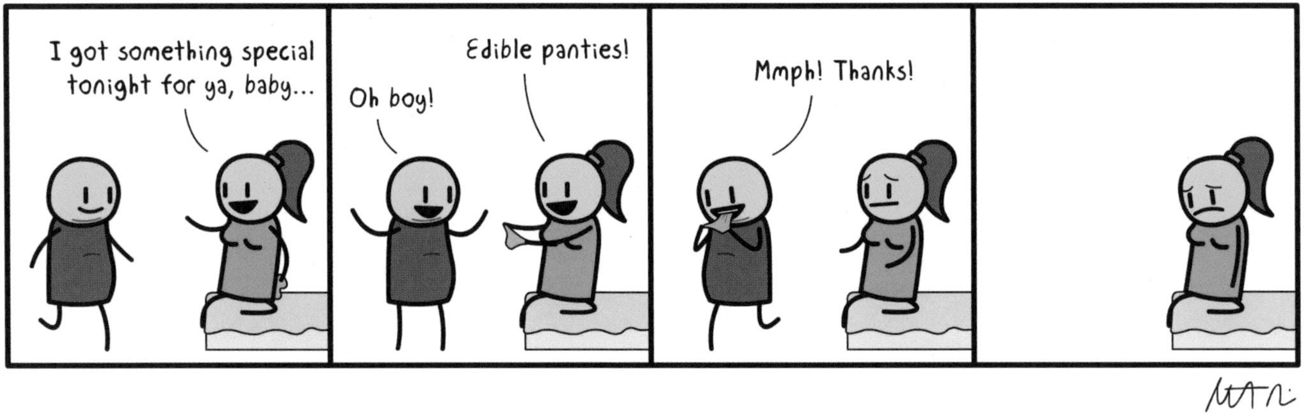
I got something special tonight for ya, baby...
Oh boy!
Edible panties!
Mmph! Thanks!

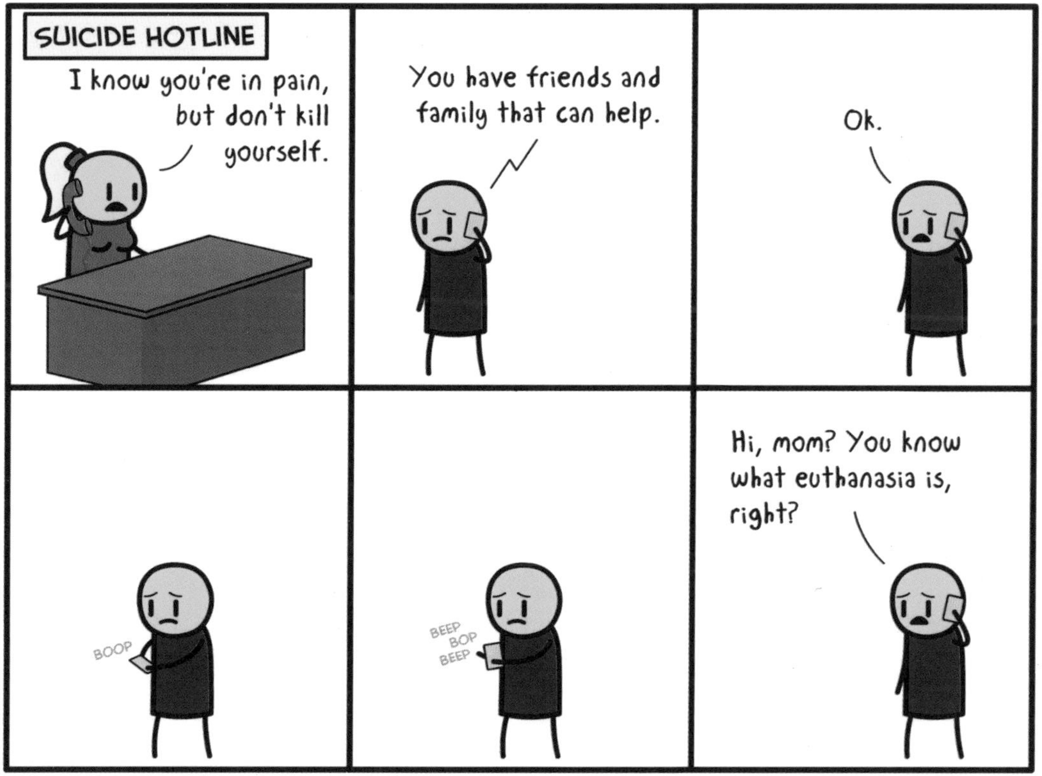
SUICIDE HOTLINE
I know you're in pain, but don't kill yourself.
You have friends and family that can help.
Ok.
BOOP
BEEP BOP BEEP
Hi, mom? You know what euthanasia is, right?

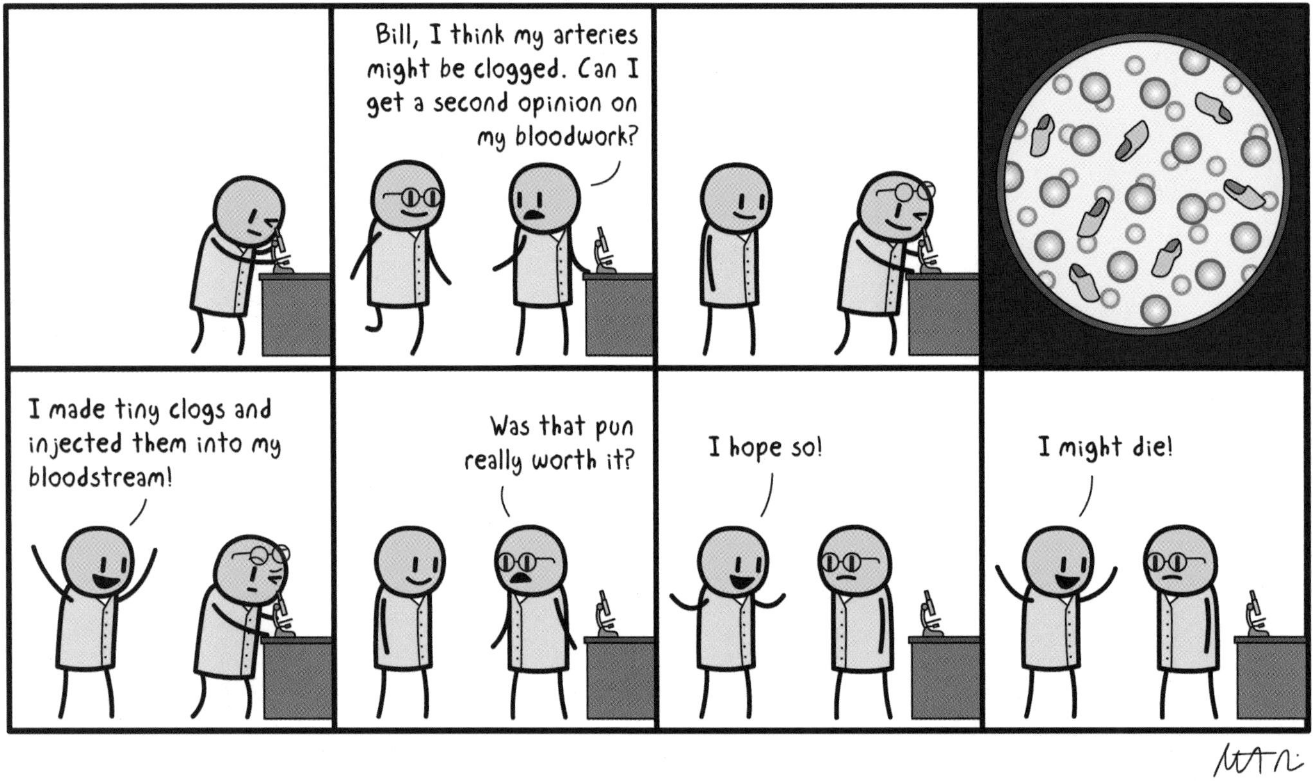
Bill, I think my arteries might be clogged. Can I get a second opinion on my bloodwork?
I made tiny clogs and injected them into my bloodstream!
Was that pun really worth it?
I hope so!
I might die!

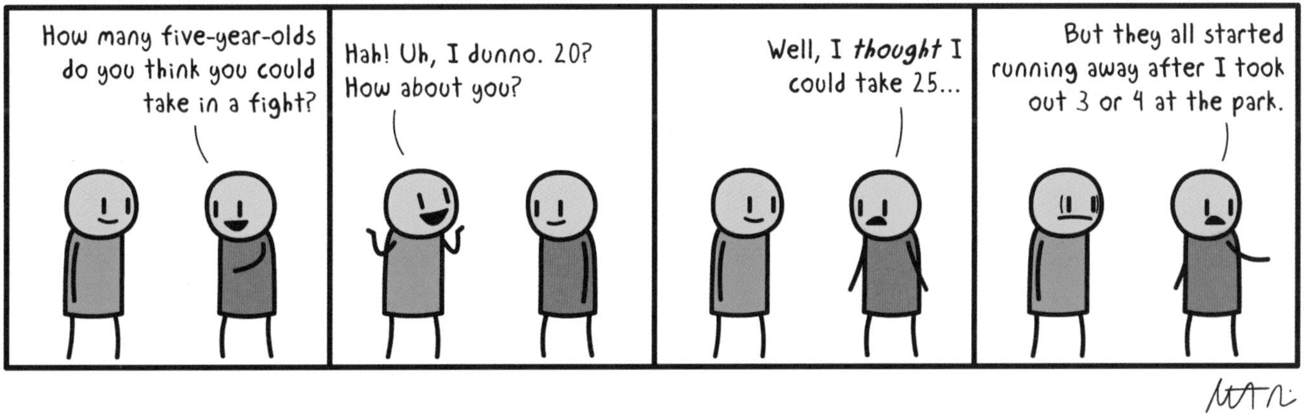
How many five-year-olds do you think you could take in a fight?
Hah! Uh, I dunno. 20? How about you?
Well, I *thought* I could take 25...
But they all started running away after I took out 3 or 4 at the park.

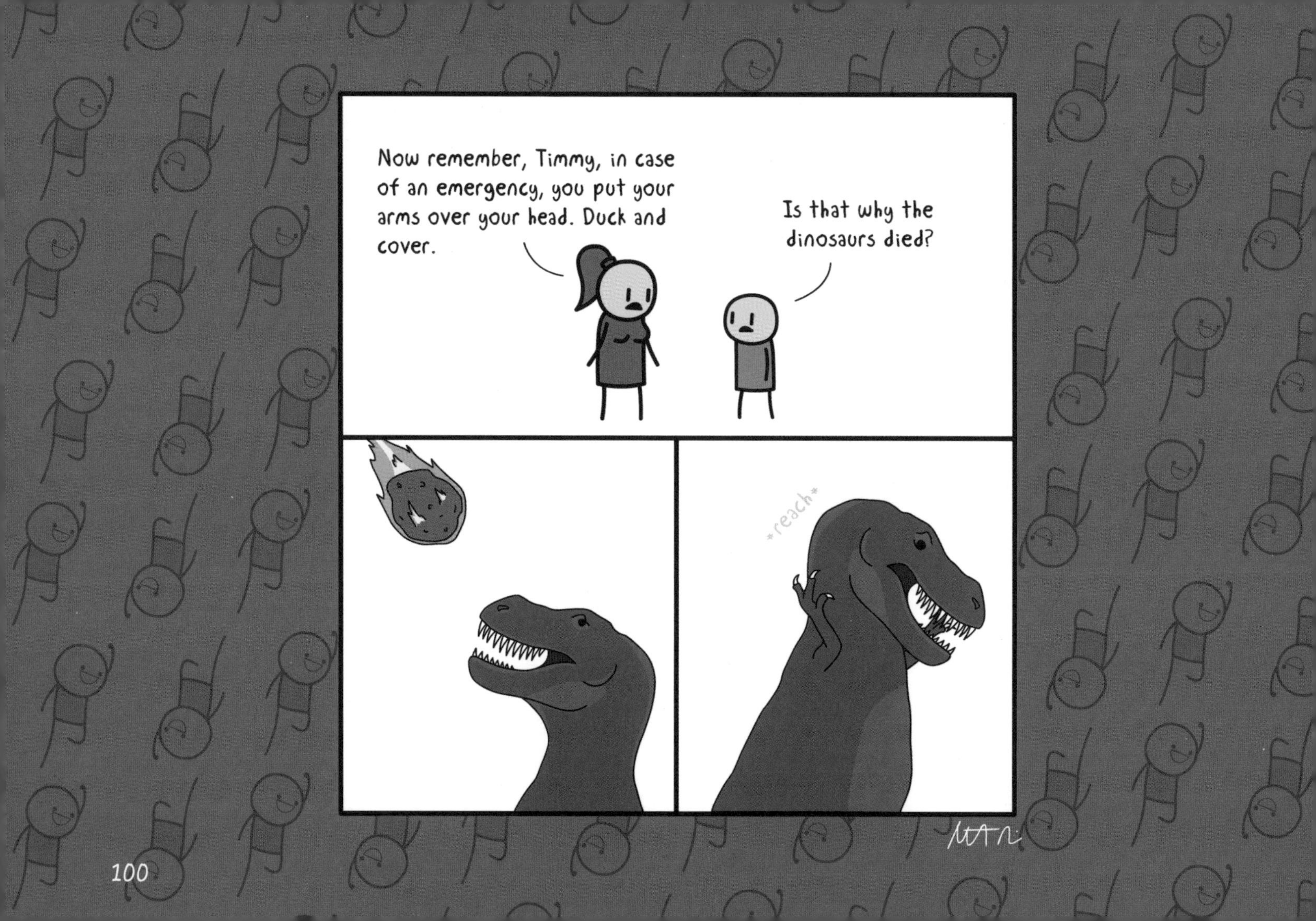
Now remember, Timmy, in case of an emergency, you put your arms over your head. Duck and cover.
Is that why the dinosaurs died?
reach

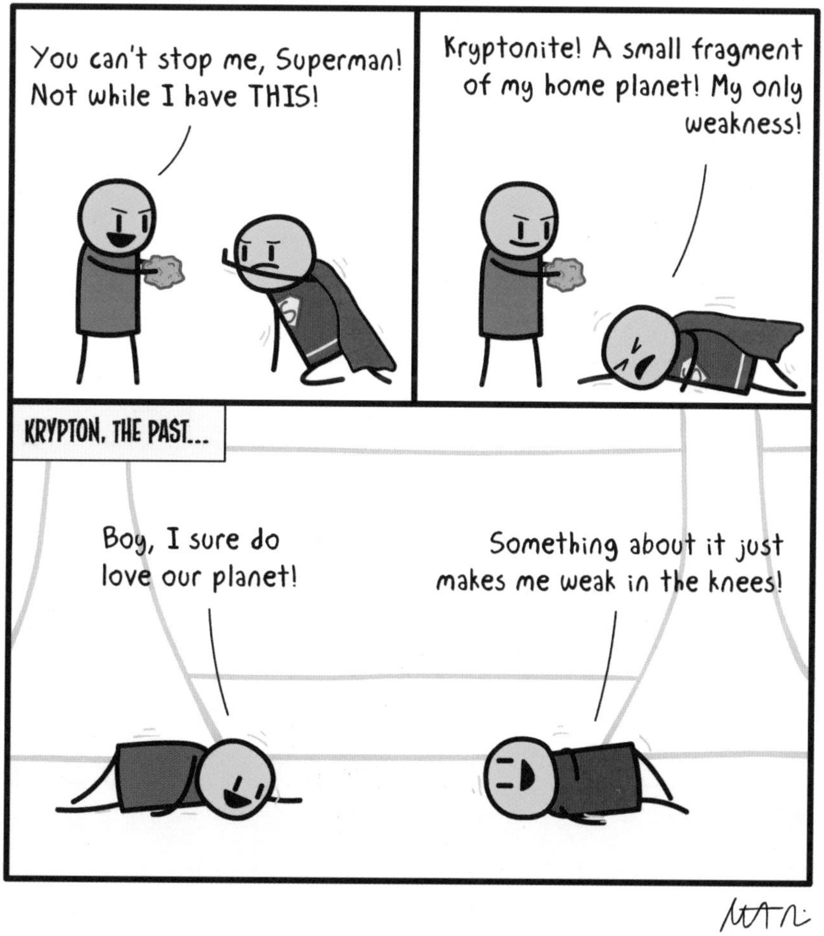
You can't stop me, Superman! Not while I have THIS!
Kryptonite! A small fragment of my home planet! My only weakness!
KRYPTON, THE PAST...
Boy, I sure do love our planet!
Something about it just makes me weak in the knees!

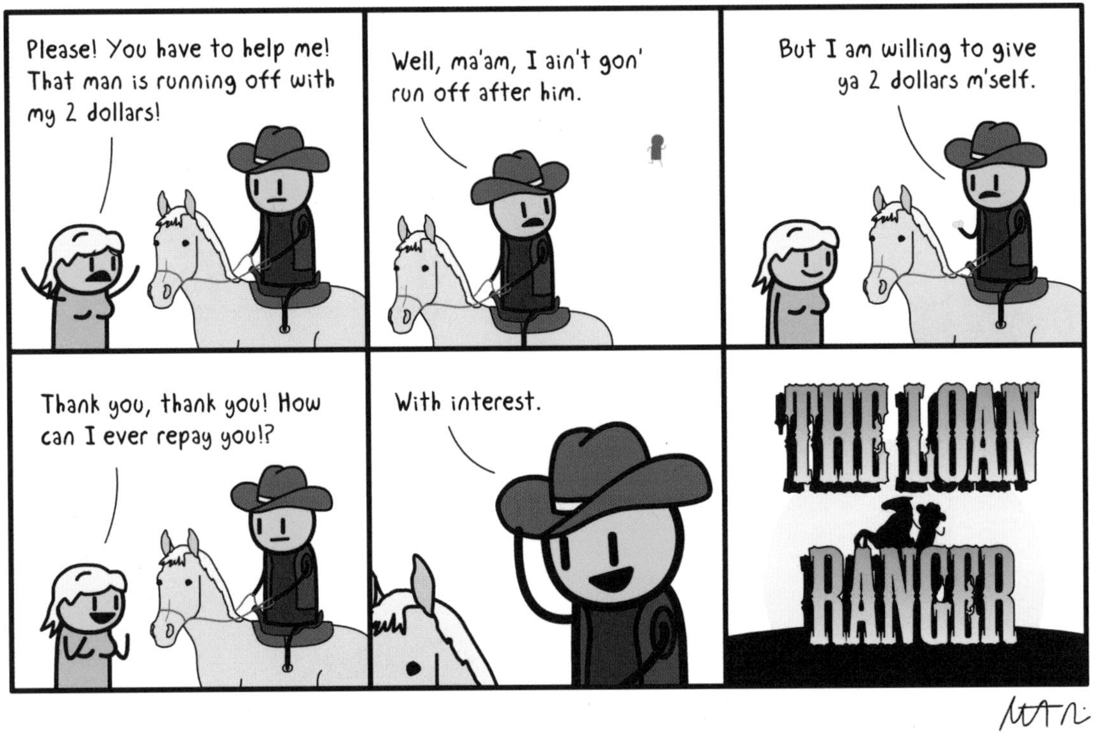

Please! You have to help me! That man is running off with my 2 dollars!
Well, ma'am, I ain't gon' run off after him.
But I am willing to give ya 2 dollars m'self.
Thank you, thank you! How can I ever repay you!?
With interest.
THE LOAN RANGER

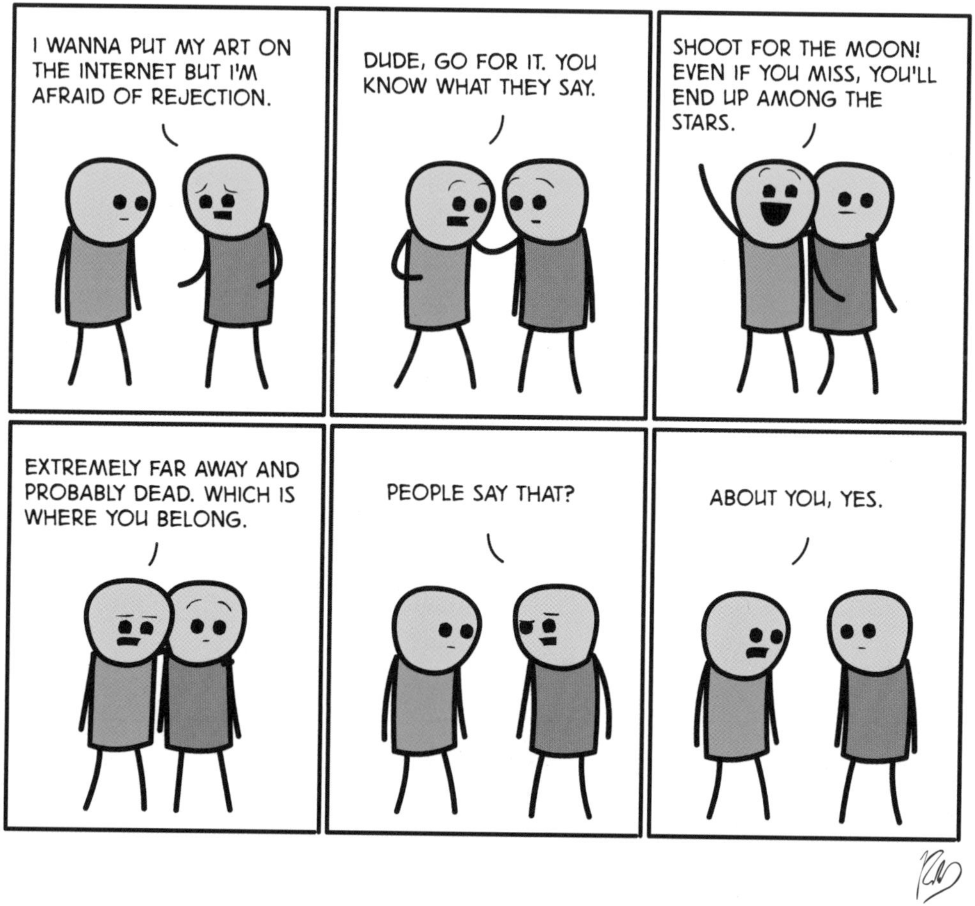
I WANNA PUT MY ART ON THE INTERNET BUT I'M AFRAID OF REJECTION.
DUDE, GO FOR IT. YOU KNOW WHAT THEY SAY.
SHOOT FOR THE MOON! EVEN IF YOU MISS, YOU'LL END UP AMONG THE STARS.
EXTREMELY FAR AWAY AND PROBABLY DEAD. WHICH IS WHERE YOU BELONG.
PEOPLE SAY THAT?
ABOUT YOU, YES.

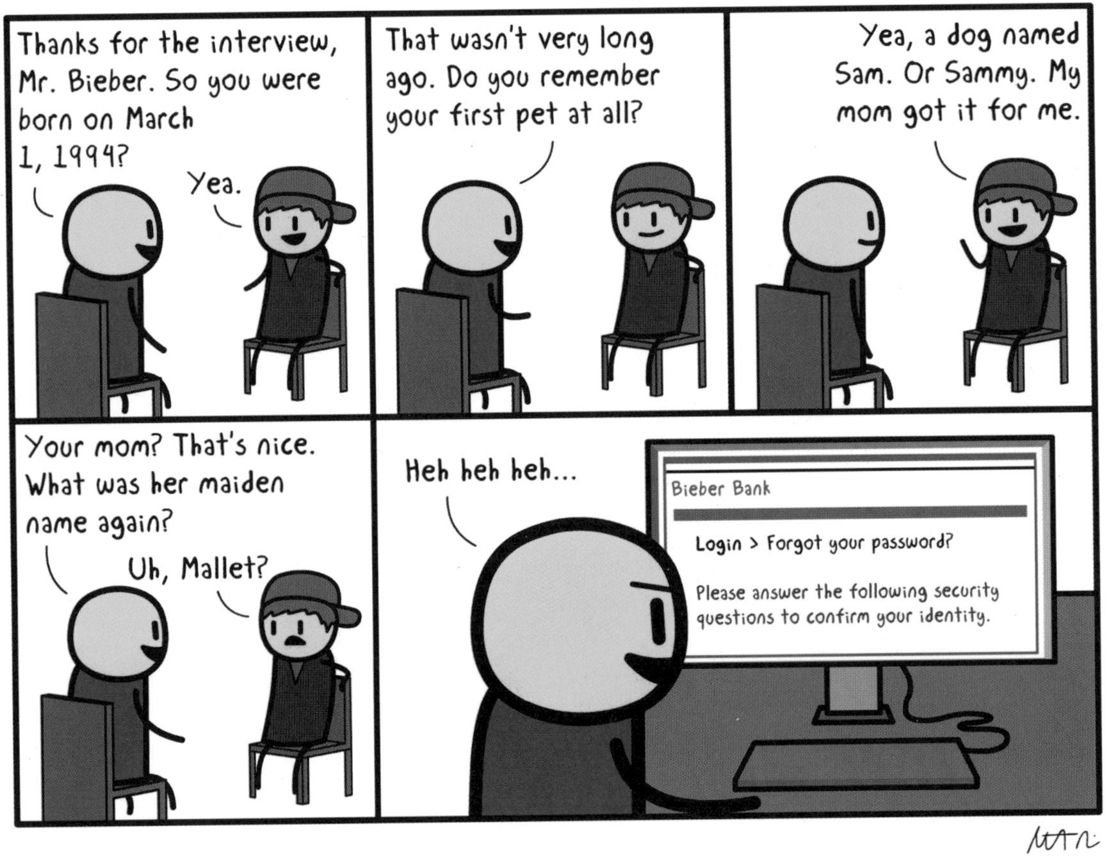

Thanks for the interview, Mr. Bieber. So you were born on March 1, 1994?
Yea.
That wasn't very long ago. Do you remember your first pet at all?
Yea, a dog named Sam. Or Sammy. My mom got it for me.
Your mom? That's nice. What was her maiden name again?
Uh, Mallet?
Heh heh heh...
Bieber Bank
Login > Forgot your password?
Please answer the following security questions to confirm your identity.

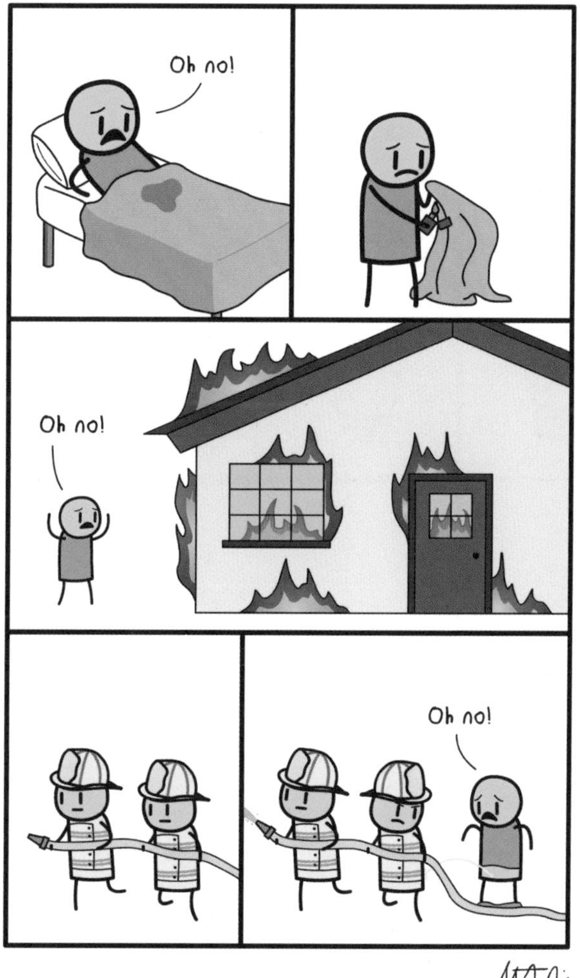
Oh no!
Oh no!
Oh no!

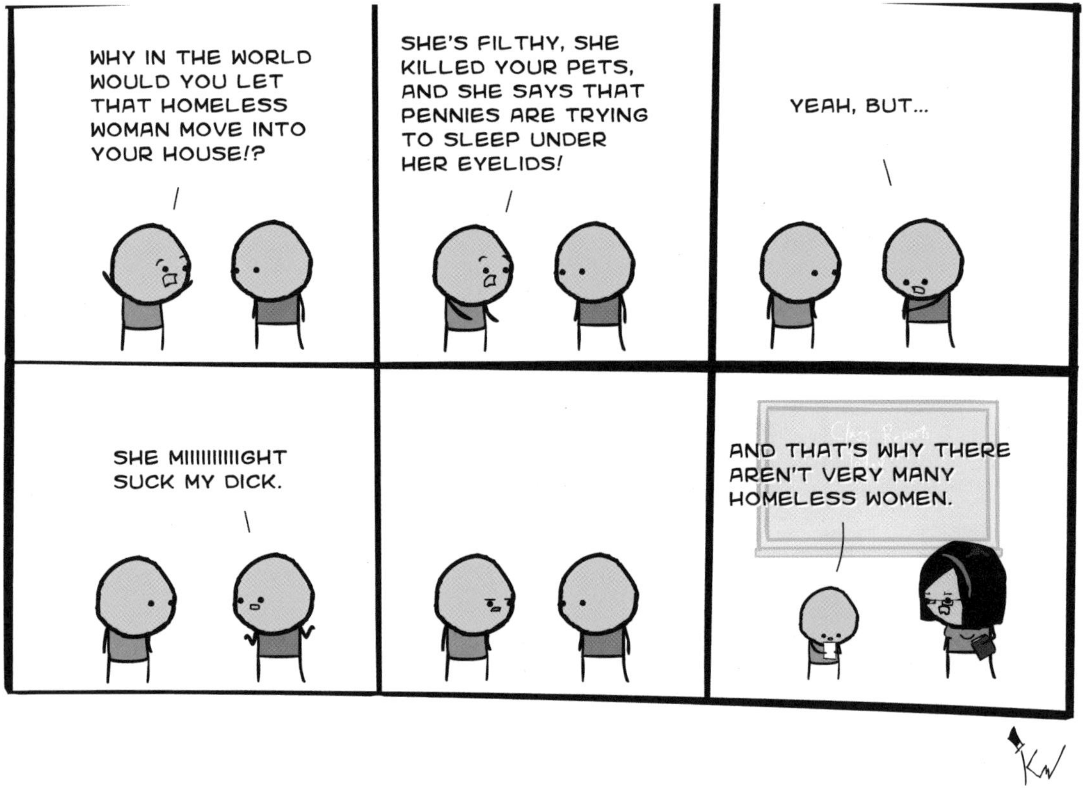
WHY IN THE WORLD WOULD YOU LET THAT HOMELESS WOMAN MOVE INTO YOUR HOUSE!?
SHE'S FILTHY, SHE KILLED YOUR PETS, AND SHE SAYS THAT PENNIES ARE TRYING TO SLEEP UNDER HER EYELIDS!
YEAH, BUT...
SHE MIIIIIIIIIIGHT SUCK MY DICK.
AND THAT'S WHY THERE AREN'T VERY MANY HOMELESS WOMEN.

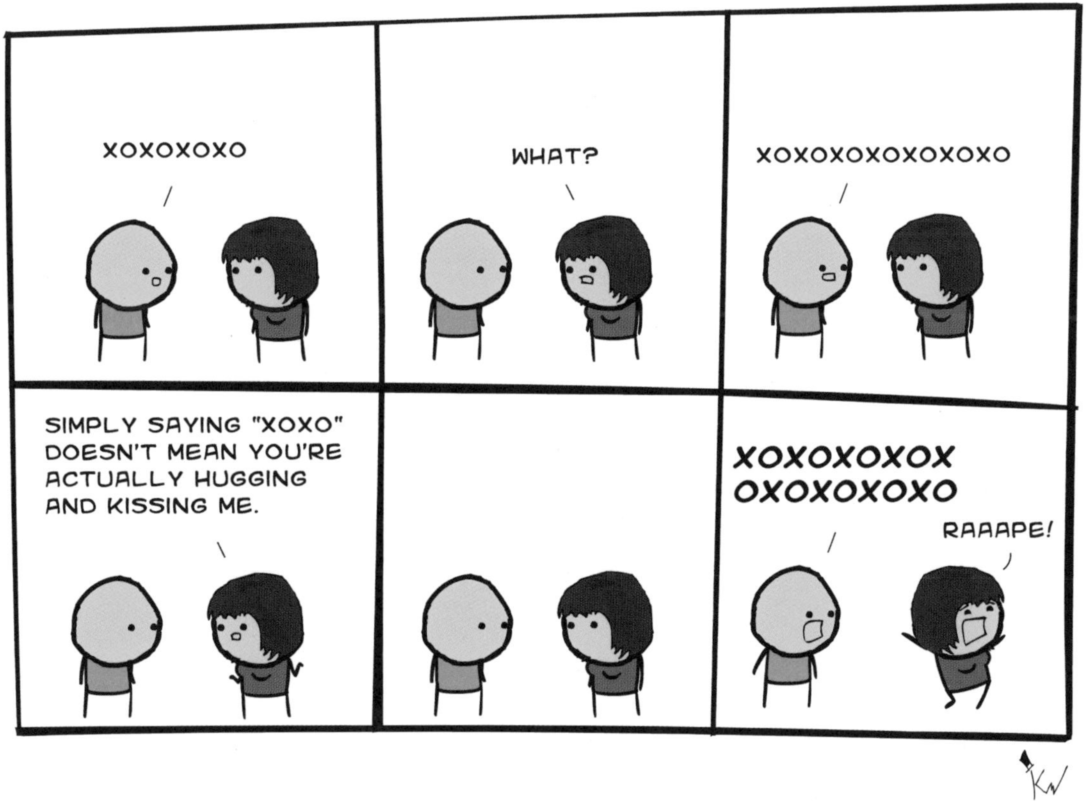
XOXOXOXO
WHAT?
XOXOXOXOXOXOXO
SIMPLY SAYING "XOXO" DOESN'T MEAN YOU'RE ACTUALLY HUGGING AND KISSING ME.
XOXOXOXOX OXOXOXOXO
RAAAPE!

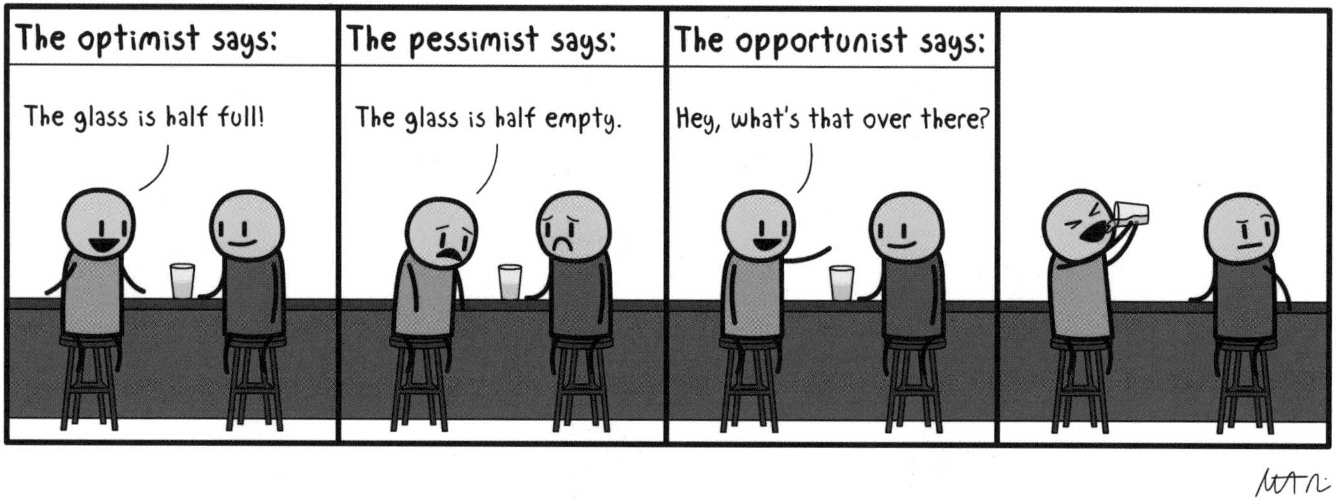
The optimist says:
The glass is half full!
The pessimist says:
The glass is half empty.
The opportunist says:
Hey, what's that over there?

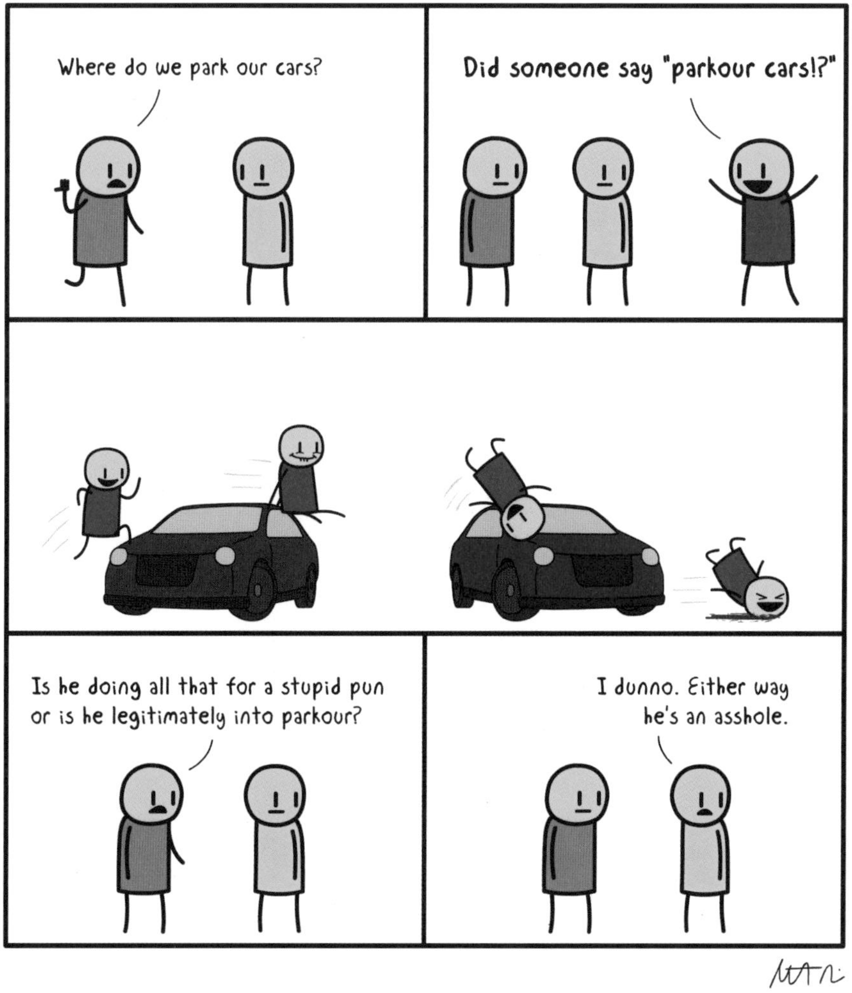
Where do we park our cars?
Did someone say "parkour cars!?"
Is he doing all that for a stupid pun or is he legitimately into parkour?
I dunno. Either way he's an asshole.

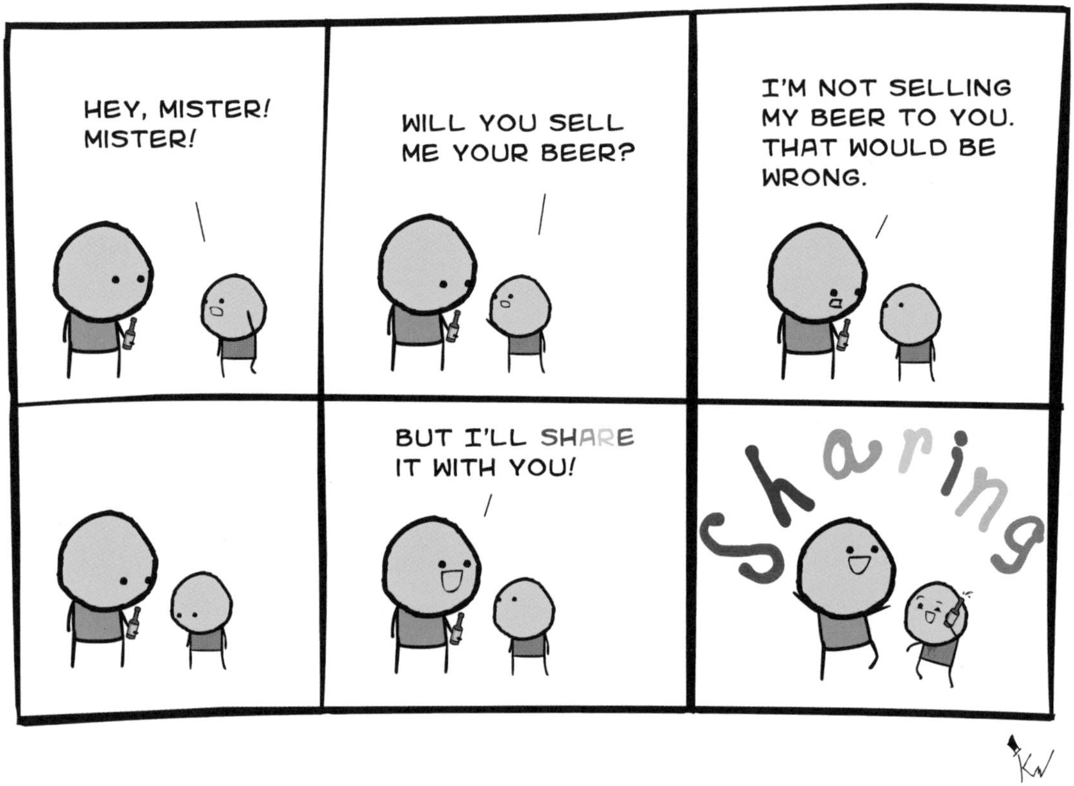
HEY, MISTER! MISTER!
WILL YOU SELL ME YOUR BEER?
I'M NOT SELLING MY BEER TO YOU. THAT WOULD BE WRONG.
BUT I'LL SHARE IT WITH YOU!
Sharing

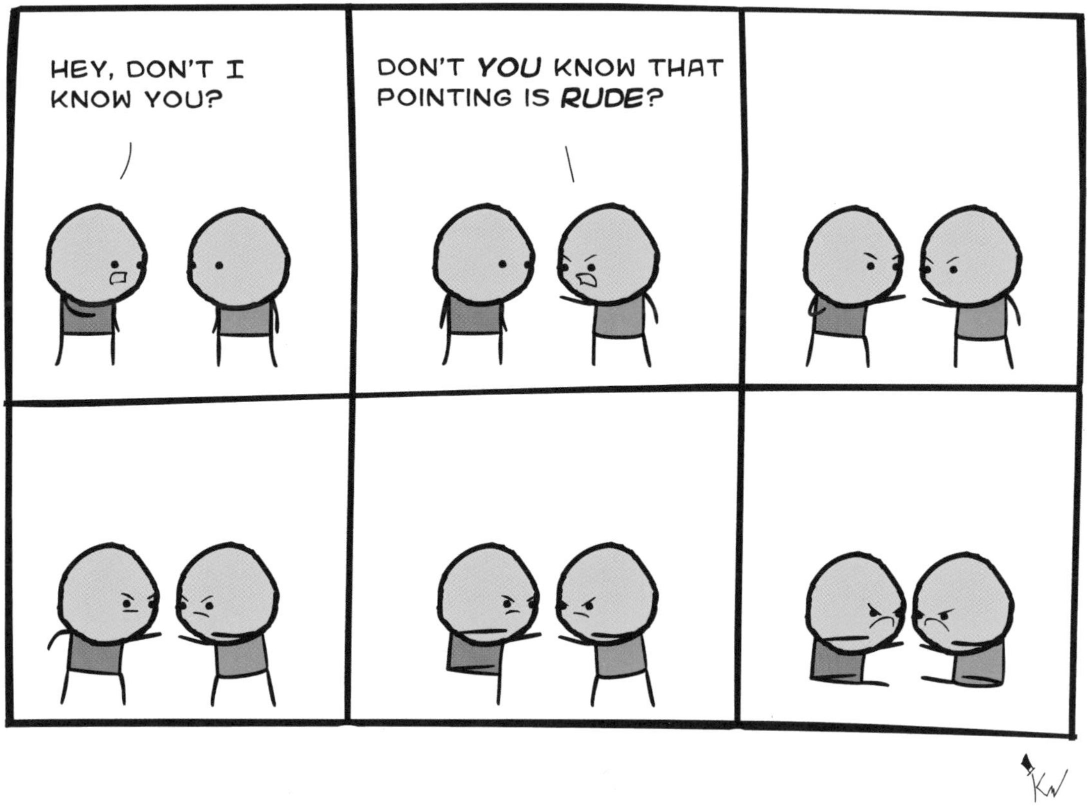
HEY, DON'T I KNOW YOU?
DON'T **YOU** KNOW THAT POINTING IS **RUDE**?

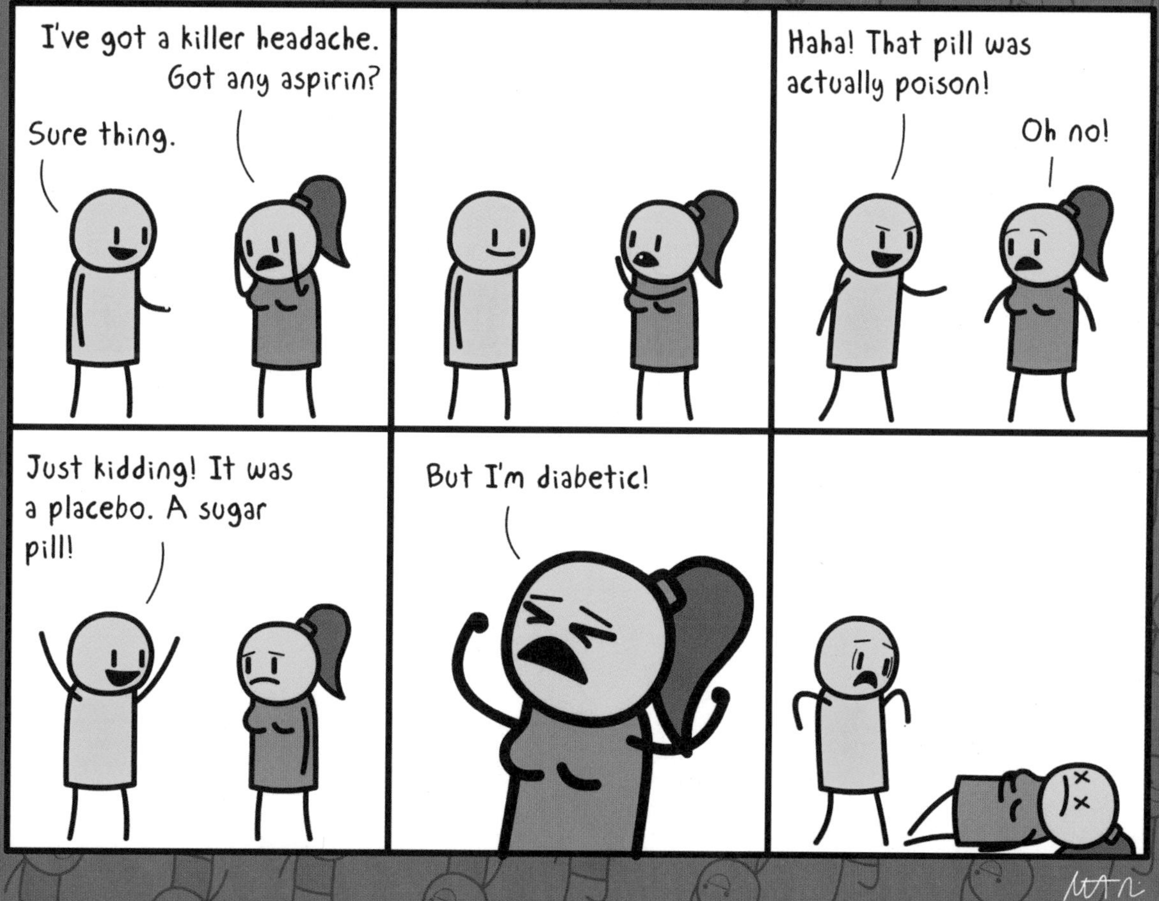
I've got a killer headache. Got any aspirin?
Sure thing.
Haha! That pill was actually poison!
Oh no!
Just kidding! It was a placebo. A sugar pill!
But I'm diabetic!

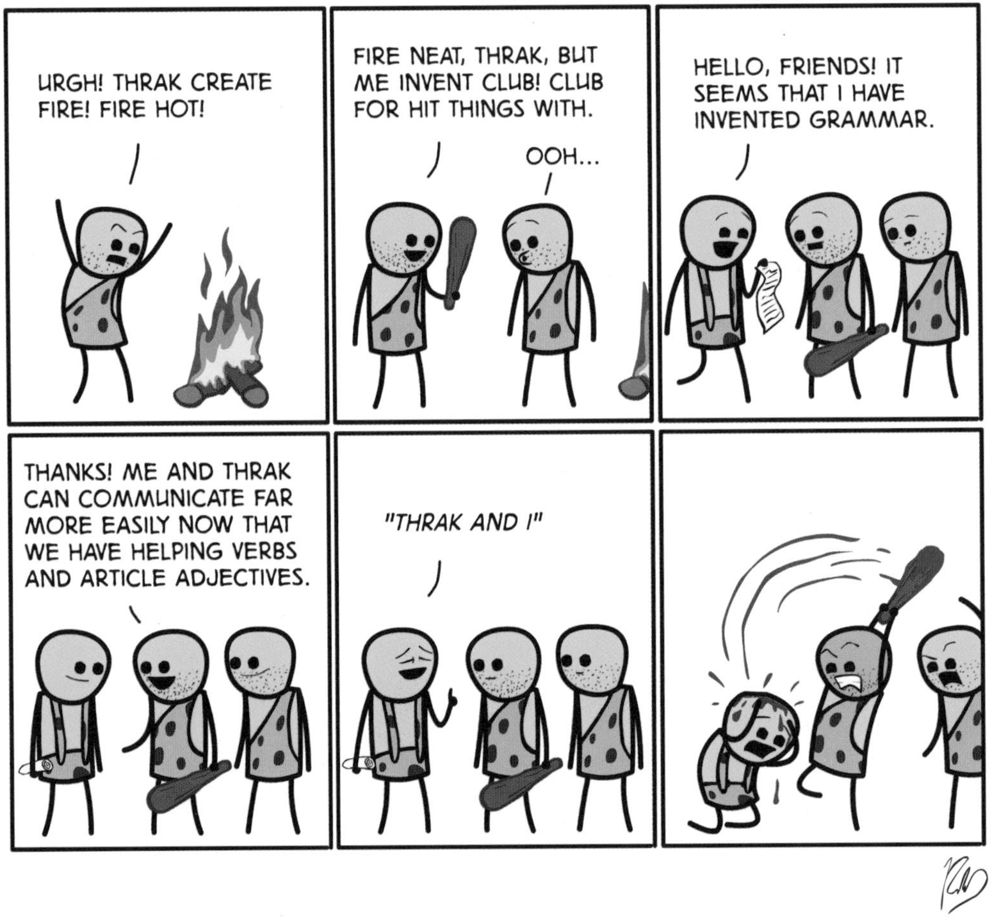
URGH! THRAK CREATE FIRE! FIRE HOT!
FIRE NEAT, THRAK, BUT ME INVENT CLUB! CLUB FOR HIT THINGS WITH.
OOH...
HELLO, FRIENDS! IT SEEMS THAT I HAVE INVENTED GRAMMAR.
THANKS! ME AND THRAK CAN COMMUNICATE FAR MORE EASILY NOW THAT WE HAVE HELPING VERBS AND ARTICLE ADJECTIVES.
"THRAK AND I"

BABY, I THINK I WANT TO TAKE OUR RELATIONSHIP TO THE NEXT LEVEL.
REALLY, CHARLES?
YEAH, THE NEXT LEVEL DOWN.
YOU WANNA JUST BE FRIENDS?
OOPS, NO. TWO LEVELS DOWN.

STROKES OF GENIUS

Einstein's introduction of the Theory of Relativity.

Nikola Tesla's heart attack in 1943.

Aristotle's first handjob.

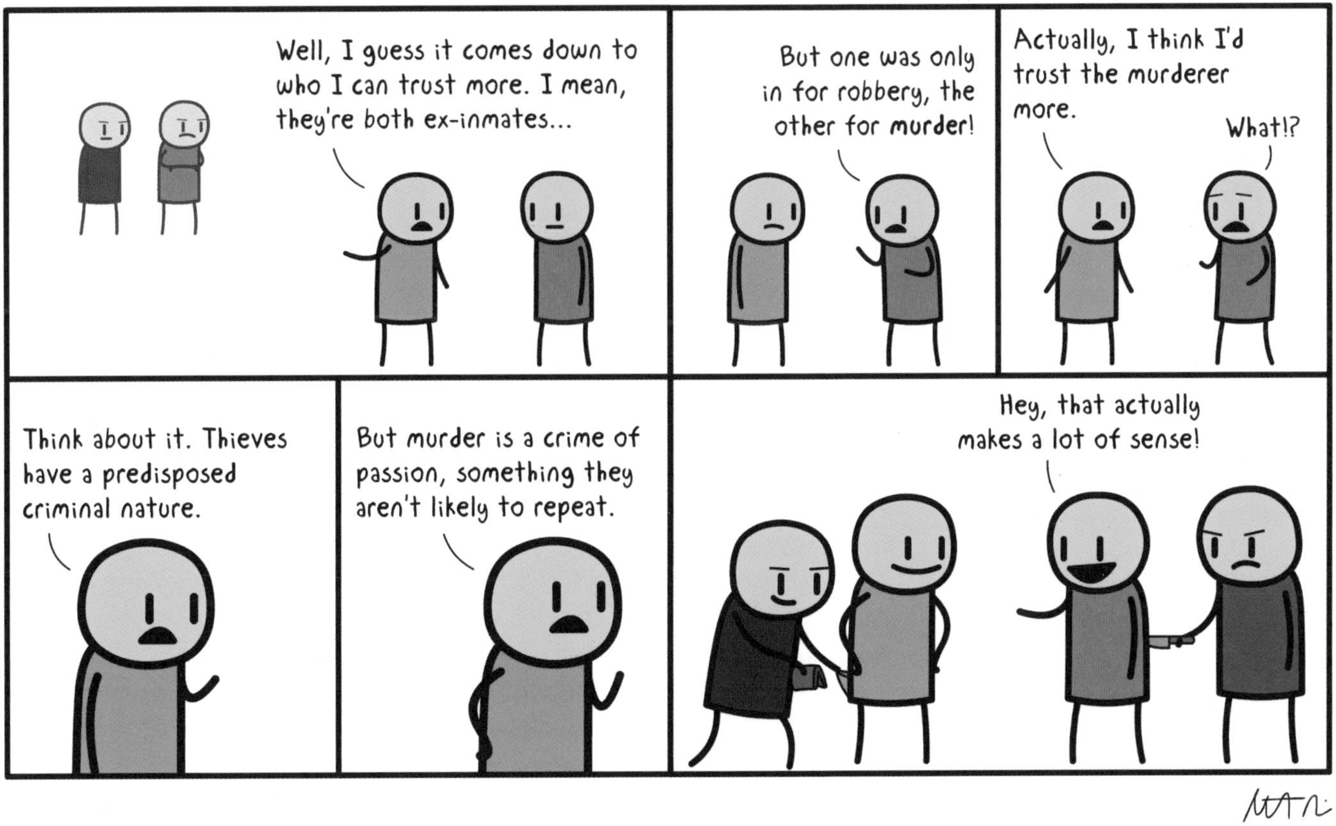
Well, I guess it comes down to who I can trust more. I mean, they're both ex-inmates...
But one was only in for robbery, the other for murder!
Actually, I think I'd trust the murderer more.
What!?
Think about it. Thieves have a predisposed criminal nature.
But murder is a crime of passion, something they aren't likely to repeat.
Hey, that actually makes a lot of sense!

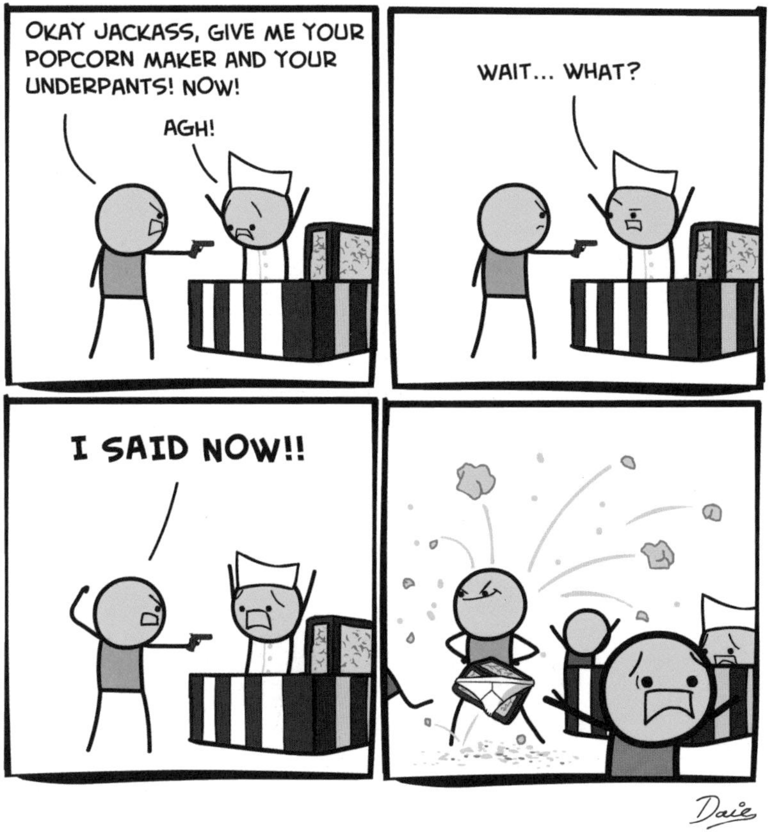
OKAY JACKASS, GIVE ME YOUR POPCORN MAKER AND YOUR UNDERPANTS! NOW!
AGH!
WAIT... WHAT?
I SAID NOW!!
Dave

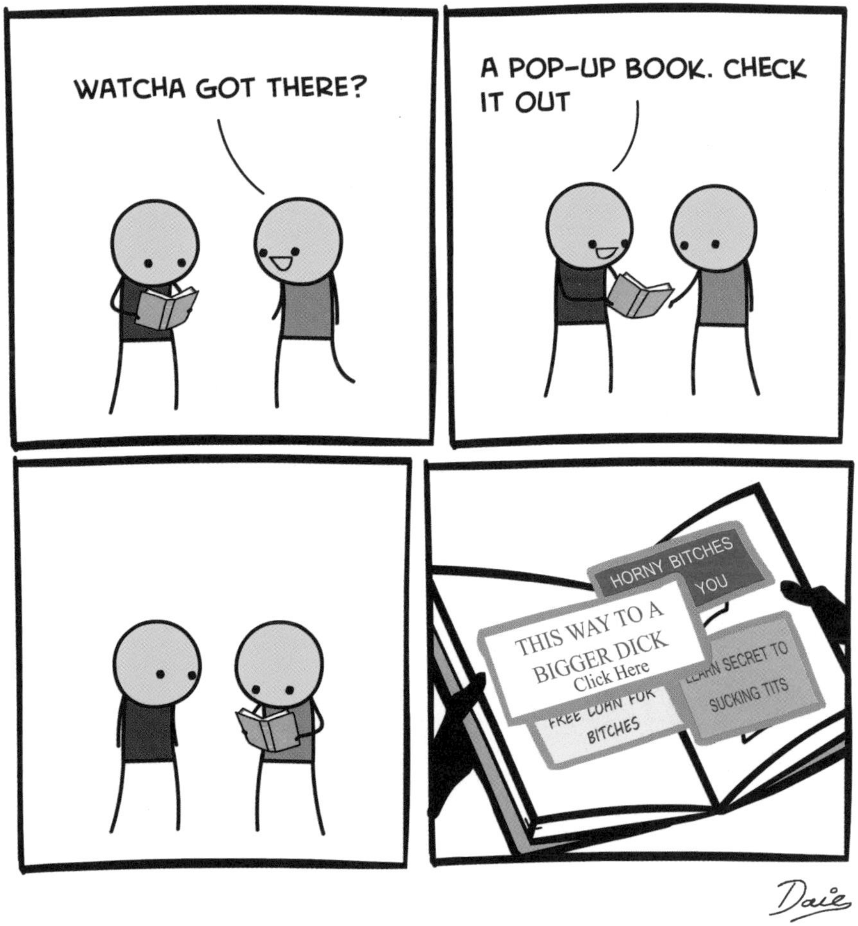
WATCHA GOT THERE?
A POP-UP BOOK. CHECK IT OUT
HORNY BITCHES
YOU
THIS WAY TO A BIGGER DICK
Click Here
SECRET TO
SUCKING TITS
BITCHES
Dave

The Titanic is sinking! Everyone to the lifeboats!
Bros before hoes!

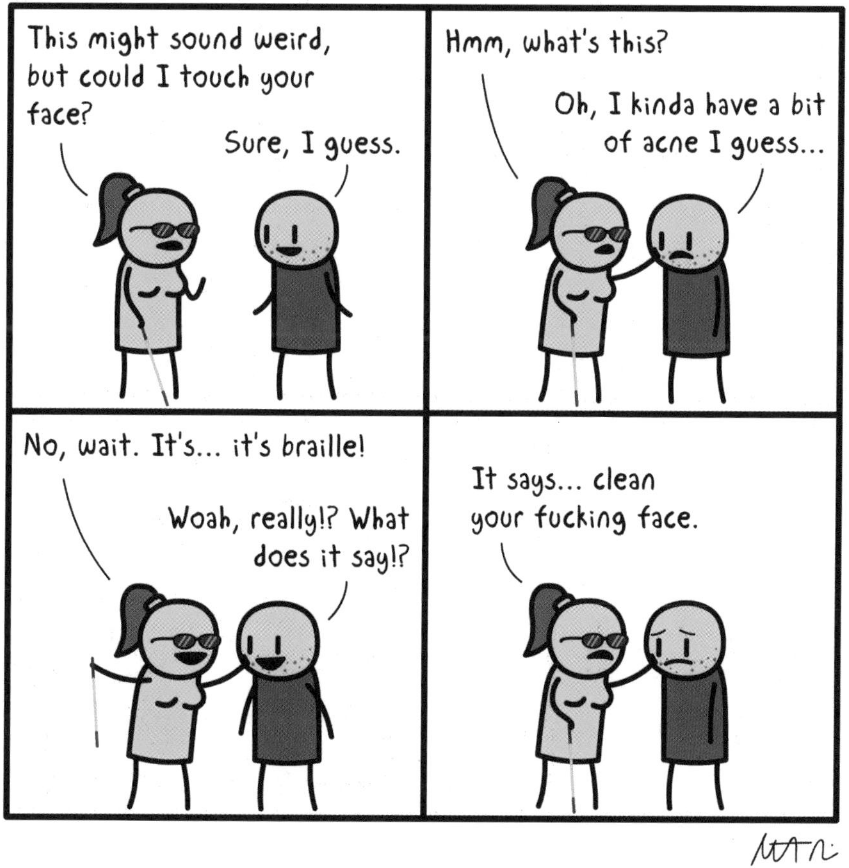
This might sound weird, but could I touch your face?
Sure, I guess.
Hmm, what's this?
Oh, I kinda have a bit of acne I guess...
No, wait. It's... it's braille!
Woah, really!? What does it say!?
It says... clean your fucking face.

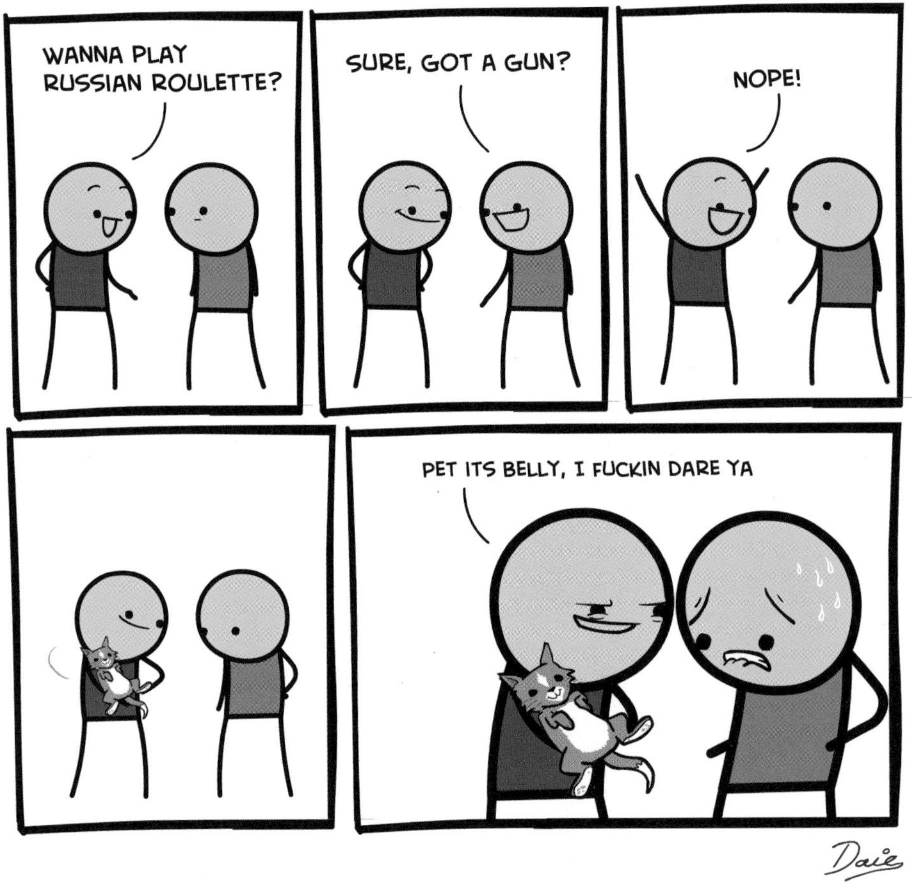
WANNA PLAY RUSSIAN ROULETTE?
SURE, GOT A GUN?
NOPE!
PET ITS BELLY, I FUCKIN DARE YA
Dave

UGH! WHY ARE THERE SO MANY MONSTERS IN THIS FUCKING DUNGEON?!
BECAUSE THEY LIVE THERE.

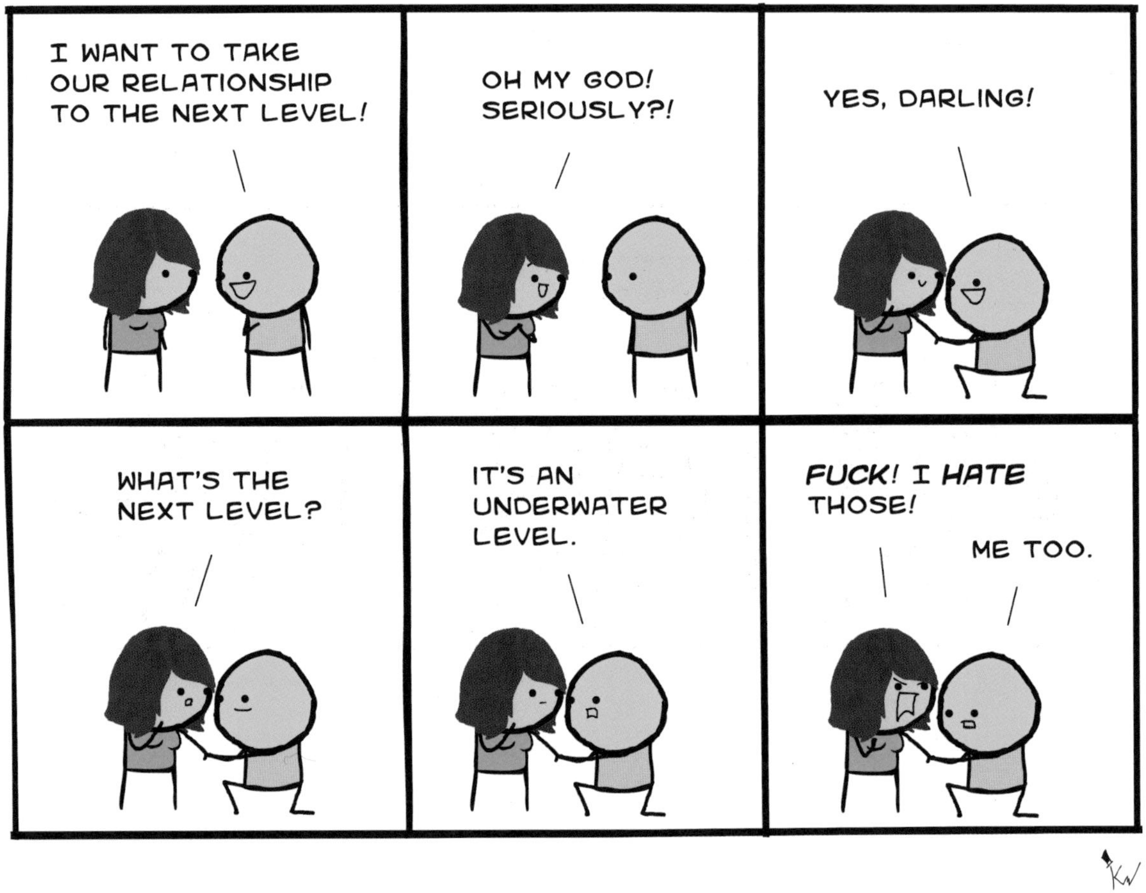
I WANT TO TAKE OUR RELATIONSHIP TO THE NEXT LEVEL!
OH MY GOD! SERIOUSLY?!
YES, DARLING!
WHAT'S THE NEXT LEVEL?
IT'S AN UNDERWATER LEVEL.
FUCK! I *HATE* THOSE!
ME TOO.

THE NEW ONES

30 BRAND-SPANKING-NEW

Never-Before-Seen Comics...

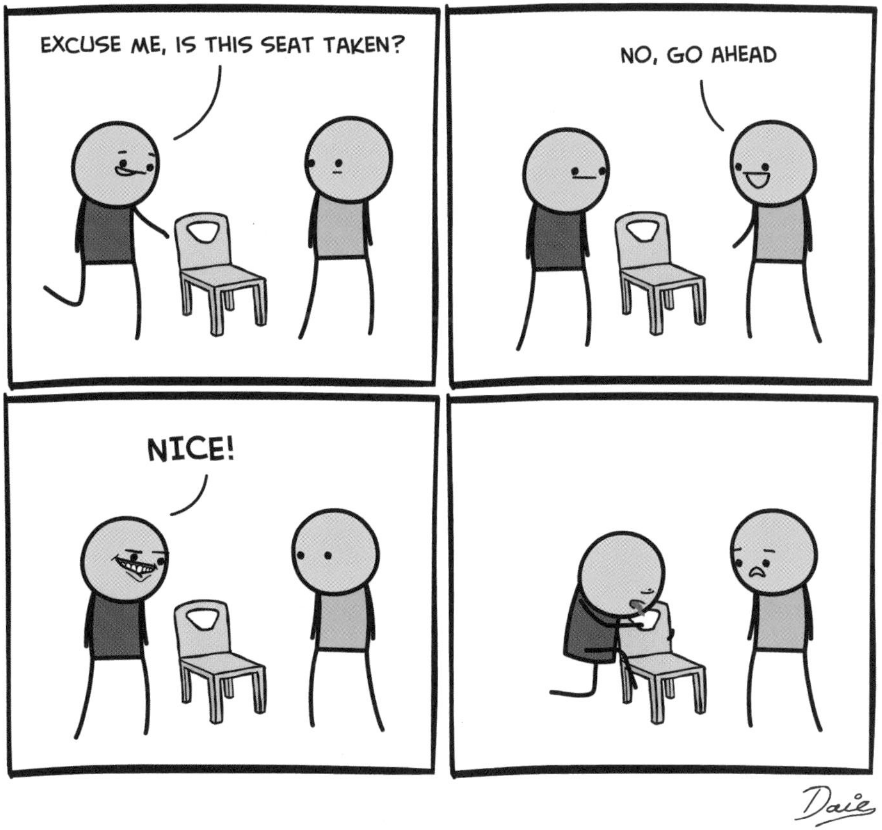
EXCUSE ME, IS THIS SEAT TAKEN?
NO, GO AHEAD
NICE!
Dave

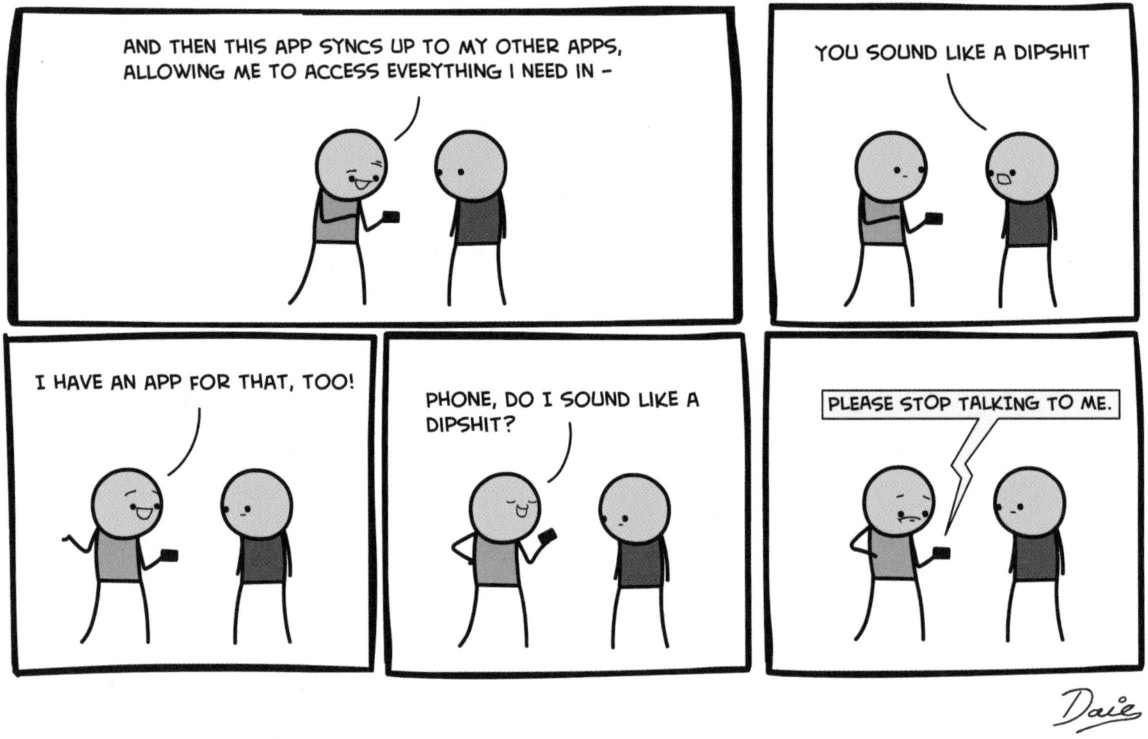
AND THEN THIS APP SYNCS UP TO MY OTHER APPS, ALLOWING ME TO ACCESS EVERYTHING I NEED IN –
YOU SOUND LIKE A DIPSHIT
I HAVE AN APP FOR THAT, TOO!
PHONE, DO I SOUND LIKE A DIPSHIT?
PLEASE STOP TALKING TO ME.
Dave

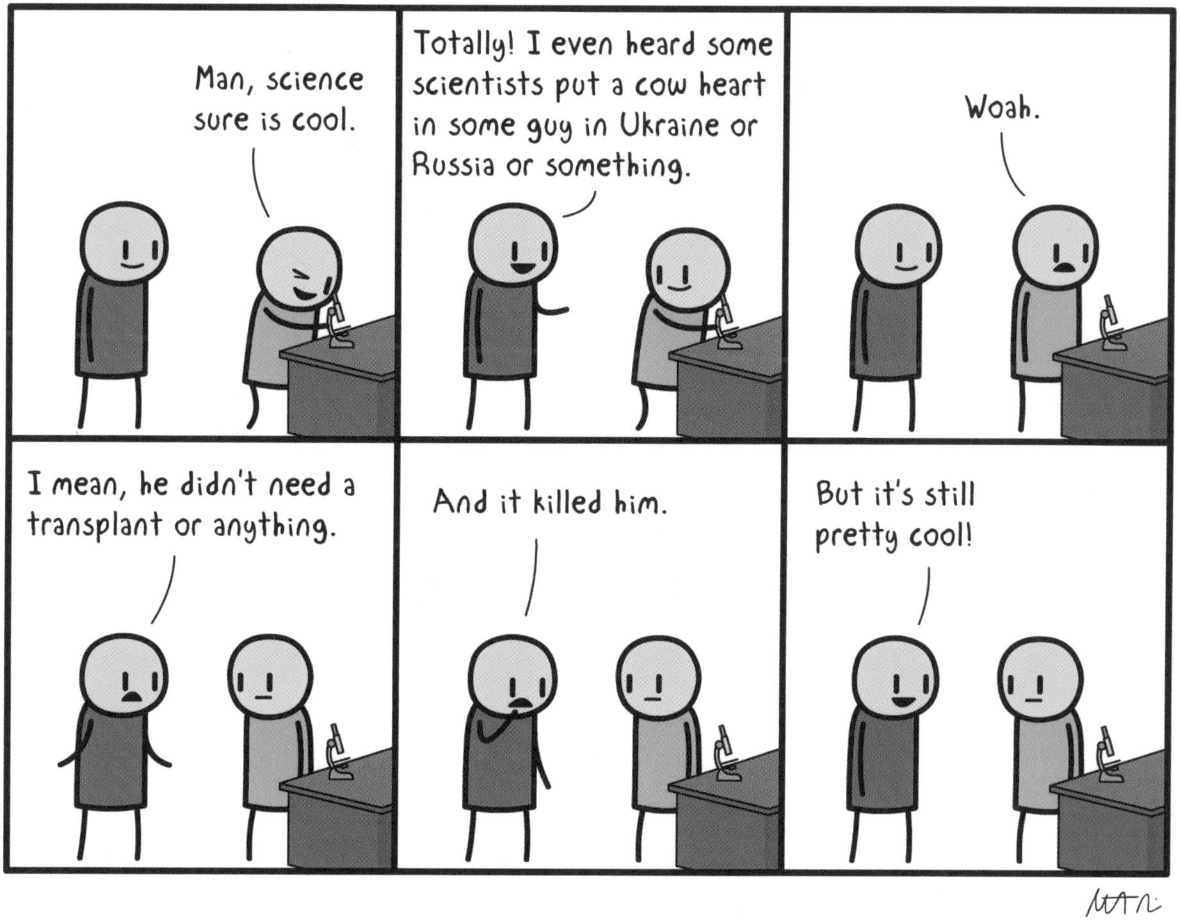
Man, science sure is cool.
Totally! I even heard some scientists put a cow heart in some guy in Ukraine or Russia or something.
Woah.
I mean, he didn't need a transplant or anything.
And it killed him.
But it's still pretty cool!

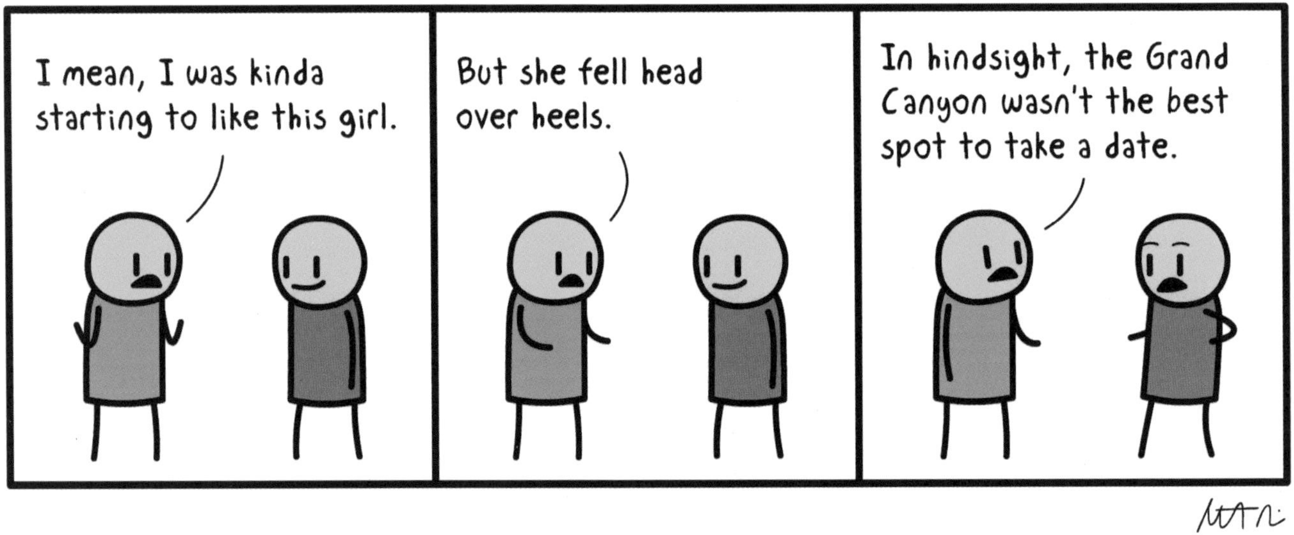
I mean, I was kinda starting to like this girl.
But she fell head over heels.
In hindsight, the Grand Canyon wasn't the best spot to take a date.

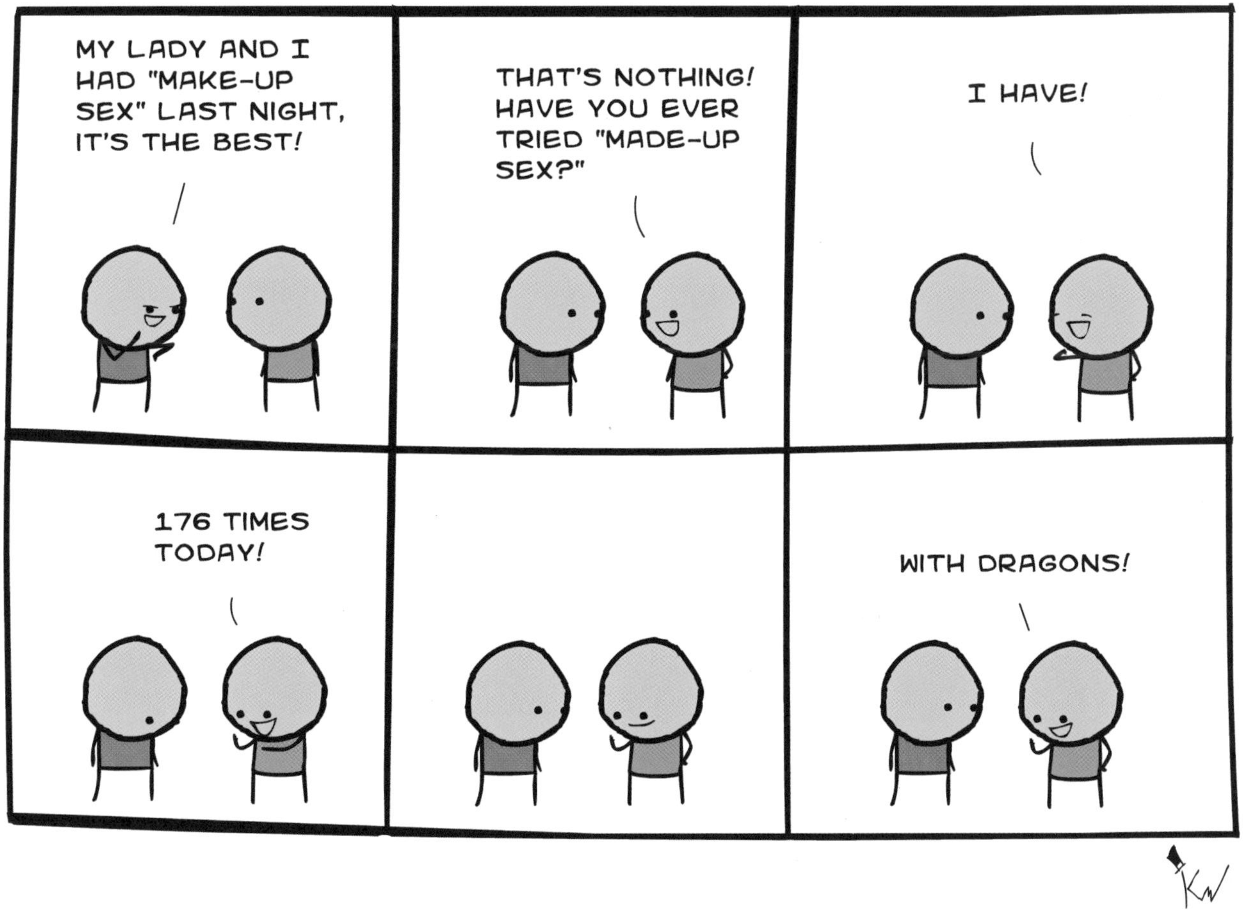
MY LADY AND I HAD "MAKE-UP SEX" LAST NIGHT, IT'S THE BEST!
THAT'S NOTHING! HAVE YOU EVER TRIED "MADE-UP SEX?"
I HAVE!
176 TIMES TODAY!
WITH DRAGONS!

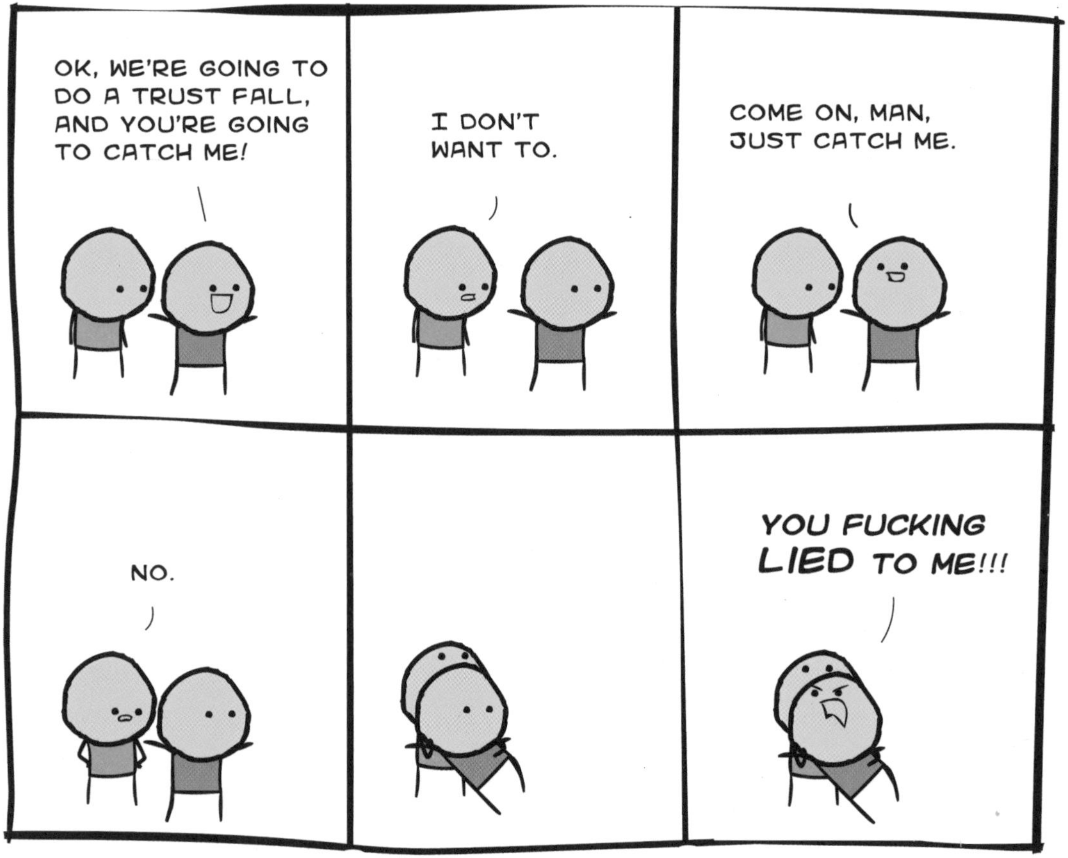
OK, WE'RE GOING TO DO A TRUST FALL, AND YOU'RE GOING TO CATCH ME!
I DON'T WANT TO.
COME ON, MAN, JUST CATCH ME.
NO.
YOU FUCKING LIED TO ME!!!
KW

HONEY, I CAN'T SLEEP.
HUH... WHY NOT?
I THINK IT'S BECAUSE OUR BED IS ON THE WALL.
OH, I GUESS YOU GET TO DECIDE WHERE THE FURNITURE GOES TOO!!

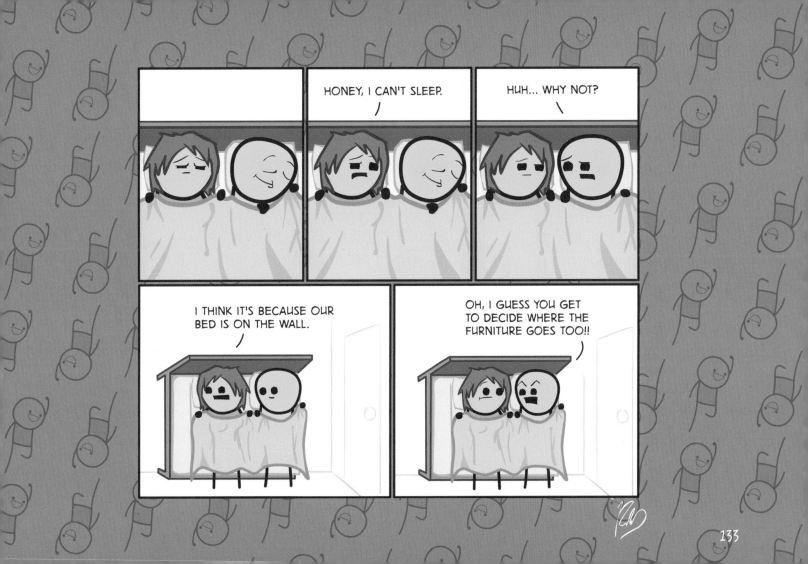

I DON'T UNDERSTAND. WHY DON'T YOU WANNA GO ON A SECOND DATE WITH ME?
BECAUSE WE NEVER WENT ON A FIRST DATE. YOU JUST STOOD BEHIND ME WHILE I WAS EATING DINNER WITH MY HUSBAND.
WOMEN.

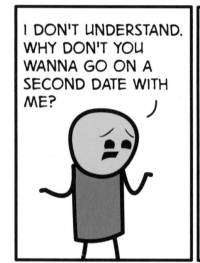

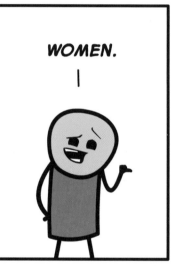

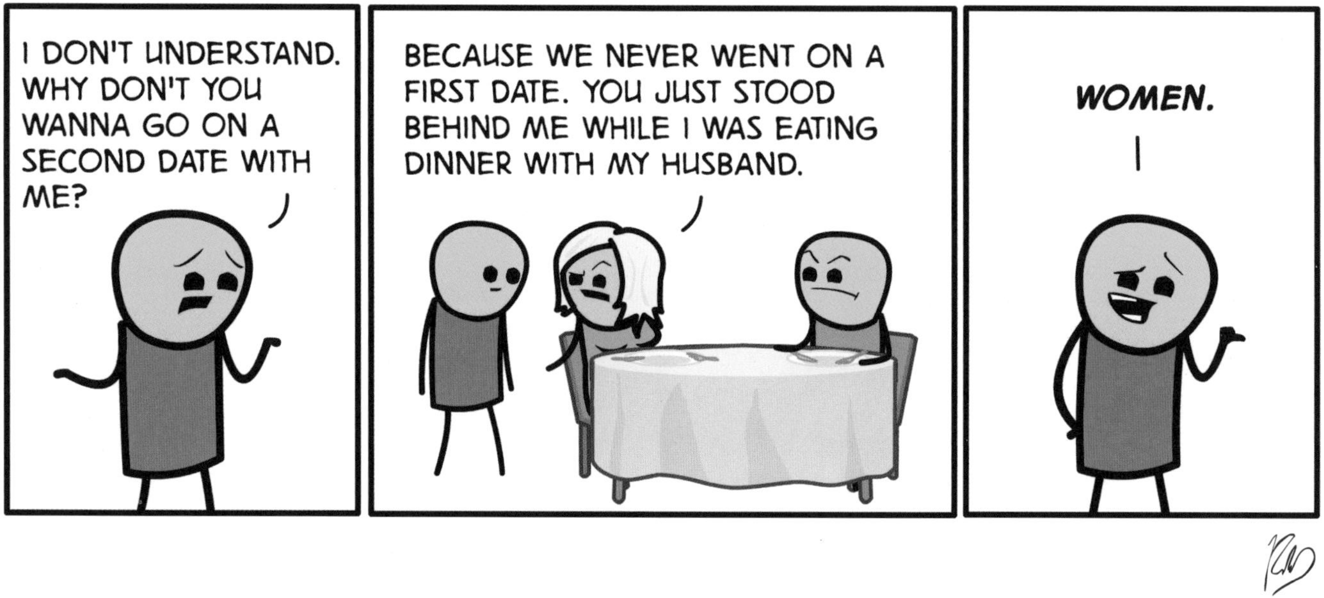

MOM, DAD! MEET MY NEW BOYFRIEND! WE'RE SO PERFECT TOGETHER, WE LIKE ALL THE SAME THINGS AND EVEN FINISH EACH OTHER'S...
FAAAAAAAAAAAAARRRRRRRR
RRRRRTTTTTTTTTTT*
Dave

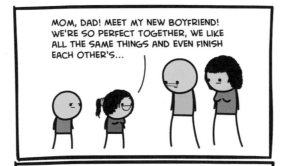

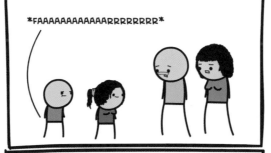

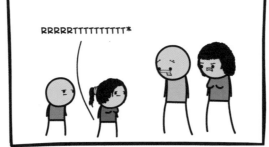

I JUST ATE 15000 FORTUNE COOKIES, AND ONE OF THEM CAME TRUE!
COOL! WHAT DID IT SAY?
You will get diabetes.
Dave

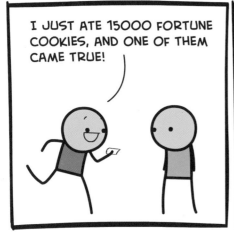

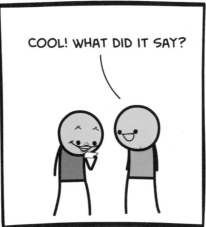

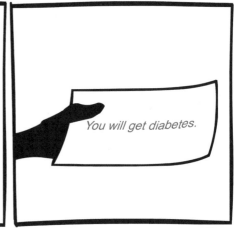

SHIT, WE'RE LOST!
WHAT ARE THE BARS LIKE ON YOUR PHONE?
IT'S NOT GIVING ME A GREAT RECEPTION.

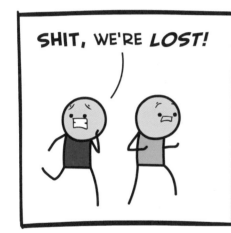

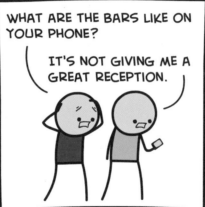

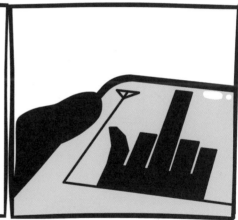

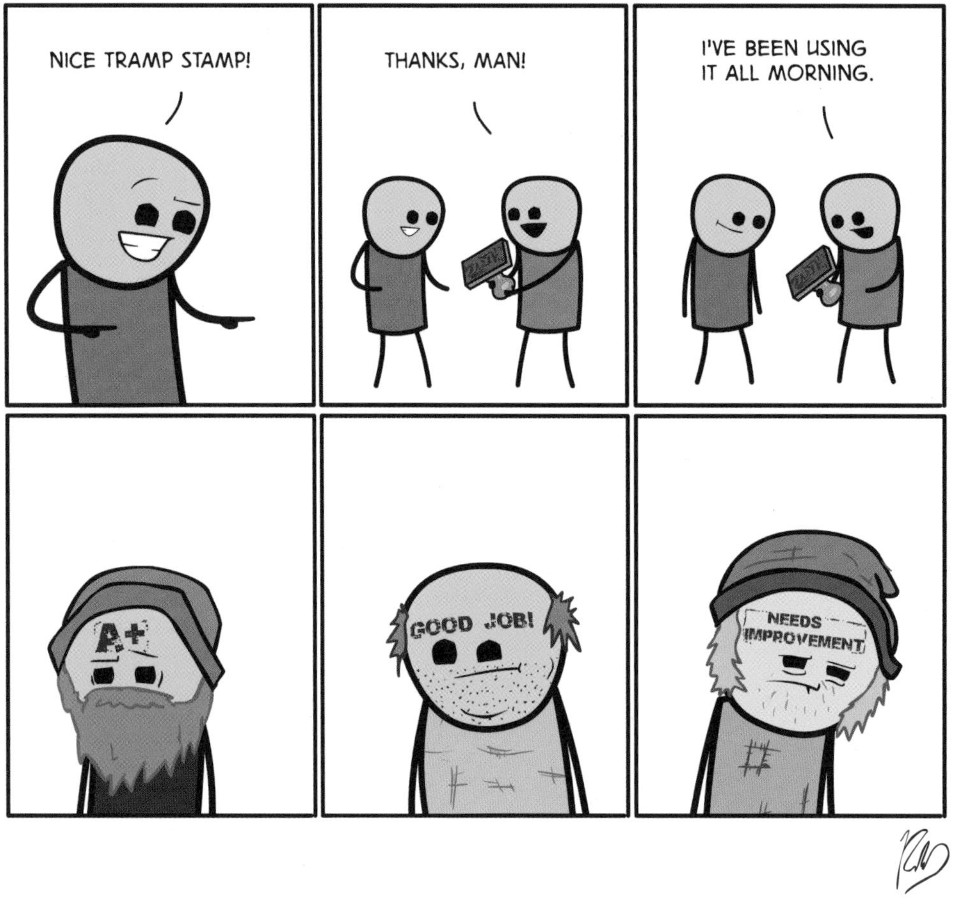
NICE TRAMP STAMP!
THANKS, MAN!
I'VE BEEN USING IT ALL MORNING.
A+
GOOD JOB!
NEEDS IMPROVEMENT

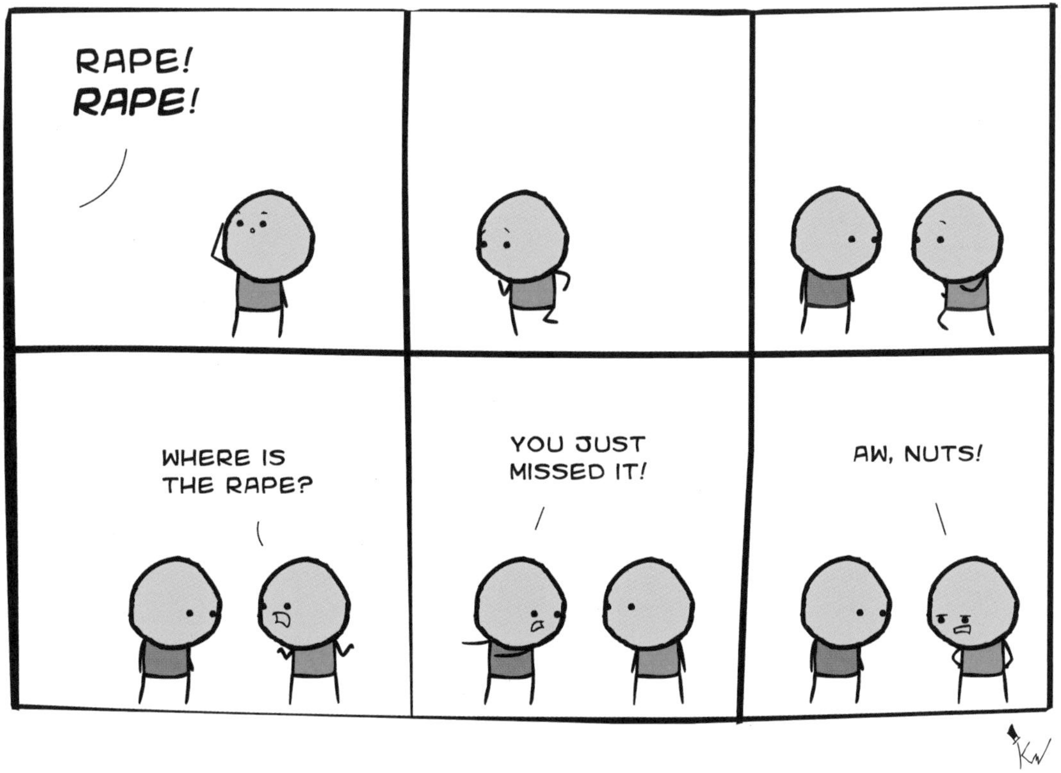
RAPE!
RAPE!
WHERE IS THE RAPE?
YOU JUST MISSED IT!
AW, NUTS!

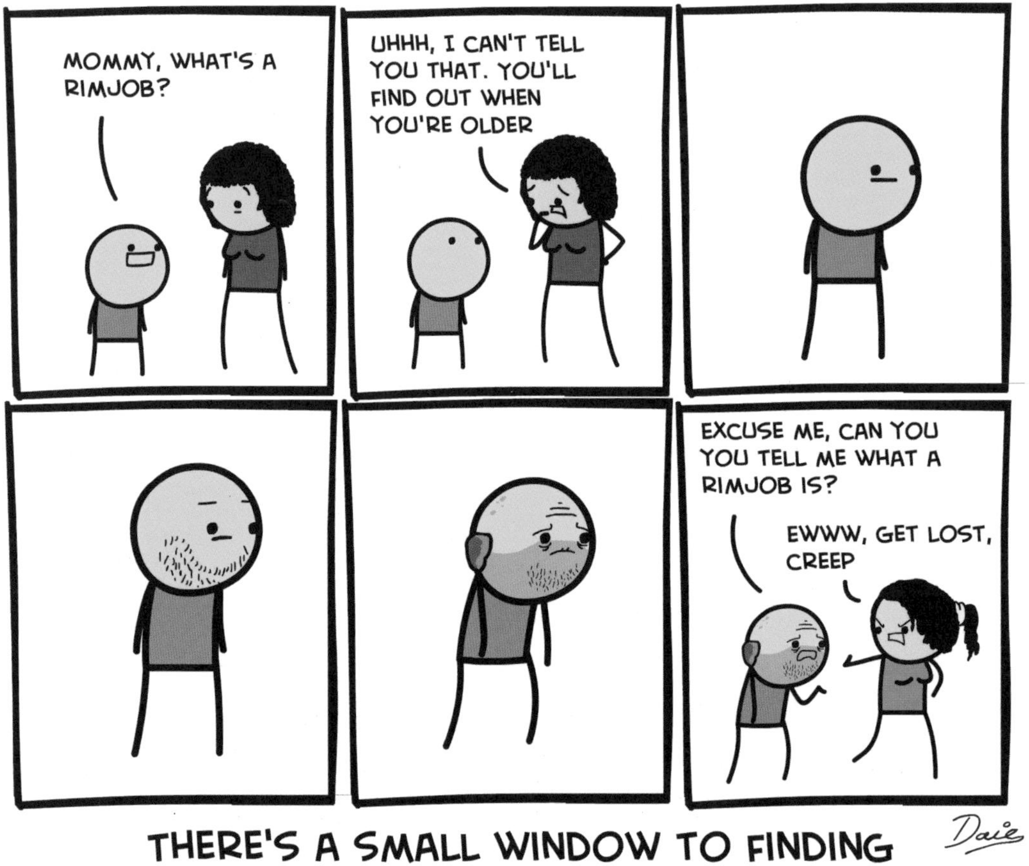
MOMMY, WHAT'S A RIMJOB?
UHHH, I CAN'T TELL YOU THAT. YOU'LL FIND OUT WHEN YOU'RE OLDER
EXCUSE ME, CAN YOU YOU TELL ME WHAT A RIMJOB IS?
EWWW, GET LOST, CREEP
Dave

THERE'S A SMALL WINDOW TO FINDING OUT WHAT A RIMJOB IS. TAKE IT.

HEY MAN, WANT SOME DRUGS?
I DON'T NEED YOUR DRUGS, FOR I'VE GOT JESUS
HEY MAN, WANT SOME DRUGS?
Dave

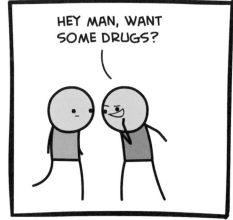

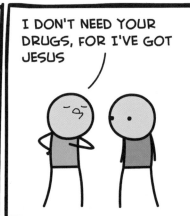

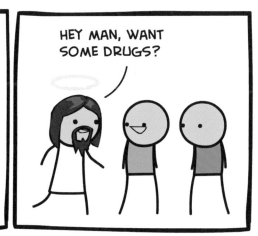

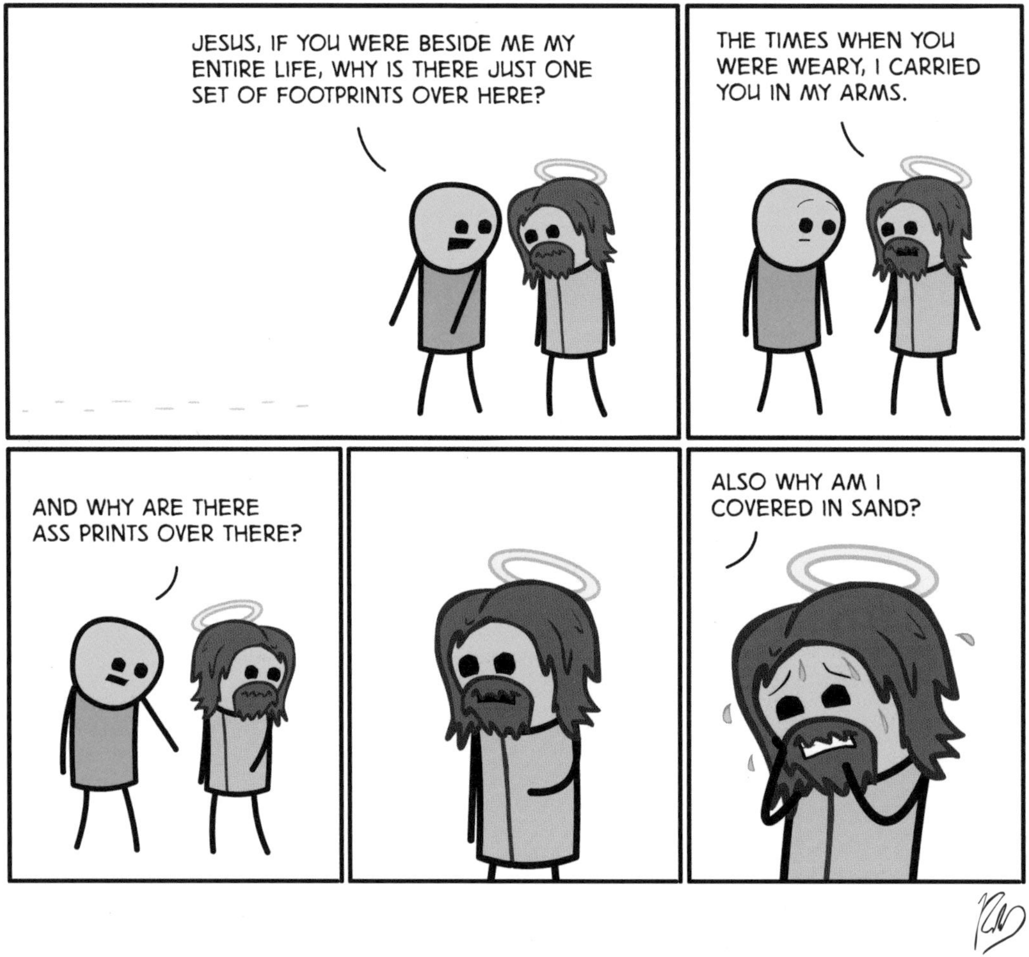
JESUS, IF YOU WERE BESIDE ME MY ENTIRE LIFE, WHY IS THERE JUST ONE SET OF FOOTPRINTS OVER HERE?
THE TIMES WHEN YOU WERE WEARY, I CARRIED YOU IN MY ARMS.
AND WHY ARE THERE ASS PRINTS OVER THERE?
ALSO WHY AM I COVERED IN SAND?

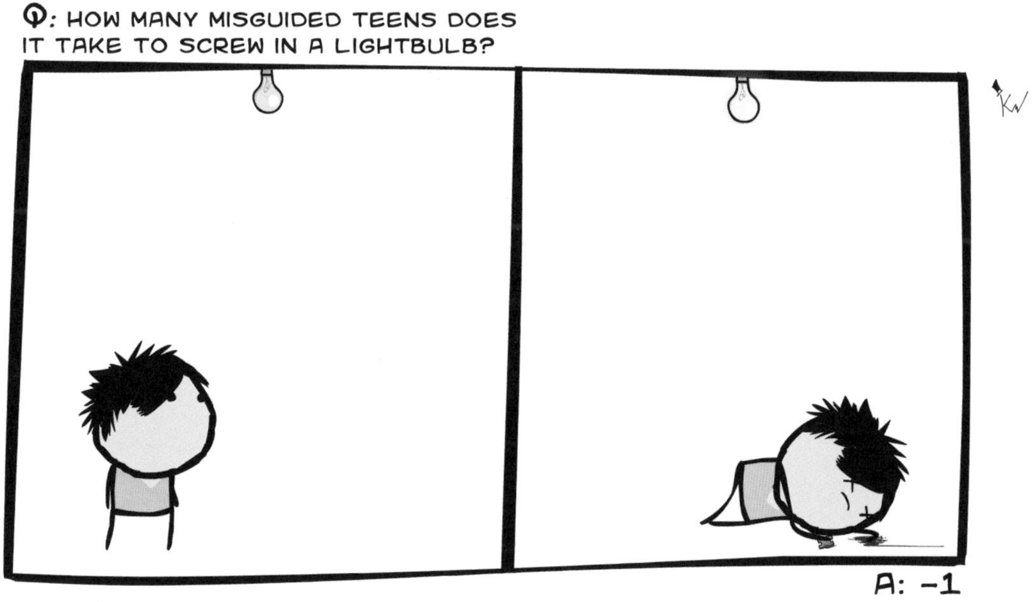
Q: HOW MANY MISGUIDED TEENS DOES IT TAKE TO SCREW IN A LIGHTBULB?
A: -1

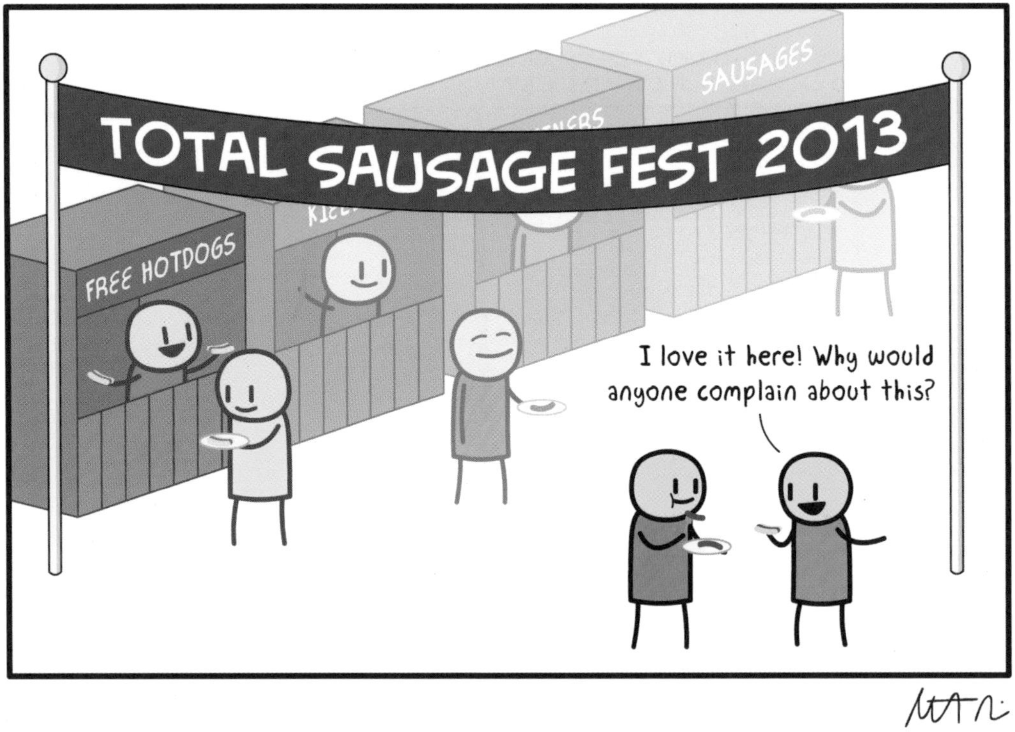
TOTAL SAUSAGE FEST 2013
FREE HOTDOGS
SAUSAGES
I love it here! Why would anyone complain about this?

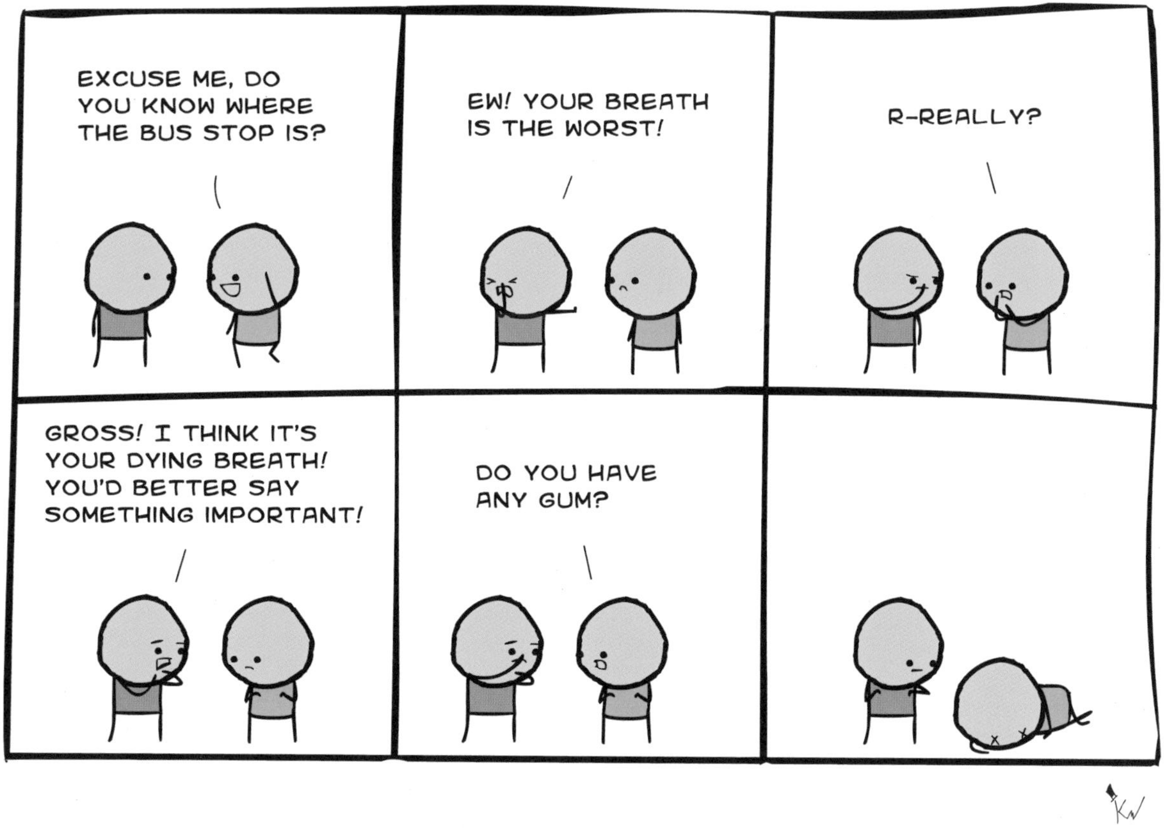

EXCUSE ME, DO YOU KNOW WHERE THE BUS STOP IS?
EW! YOUR BREATH IS THE WORST!
R-REALLY?
GROSS! I THINK IT'S YOUR DYING BREATH! YOU'D BETTER SAY SOMETHING IMPORTANT!
DO YOU HAVE ANY GUM?

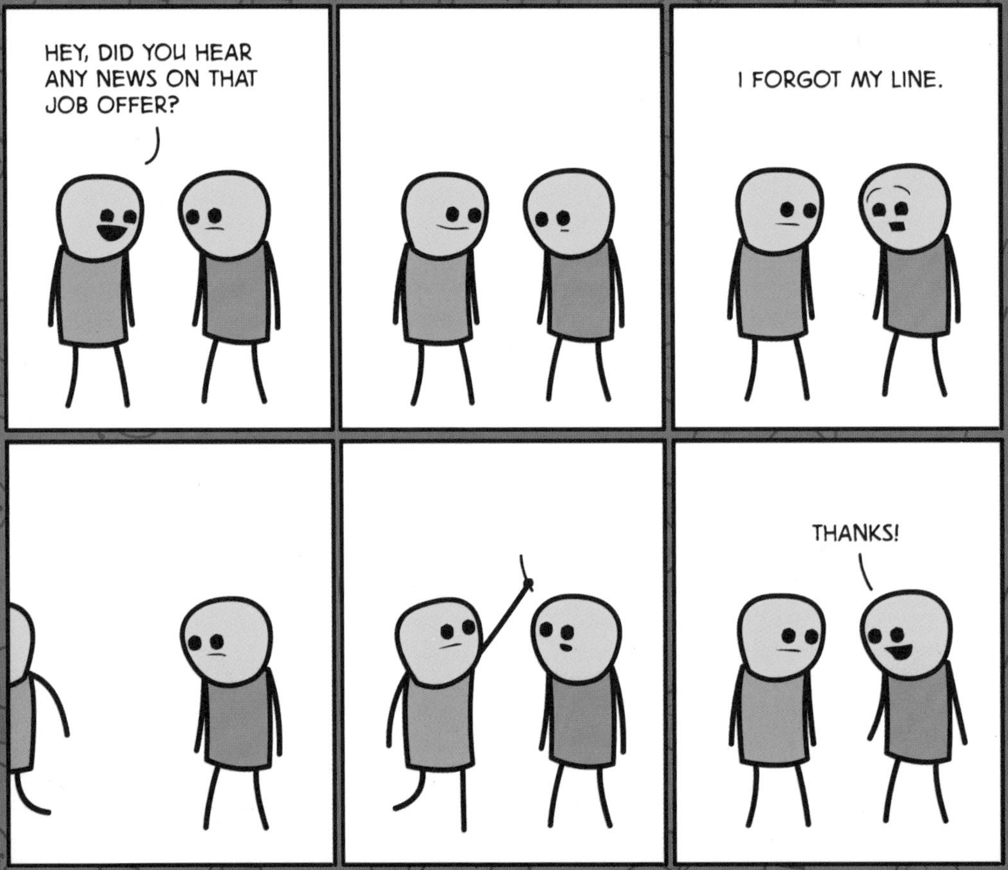
HEY, DID YOU HEAR ANY NEWS ON THAT JOB OFFER?
I FORGOT MY LINE.
THANKS!

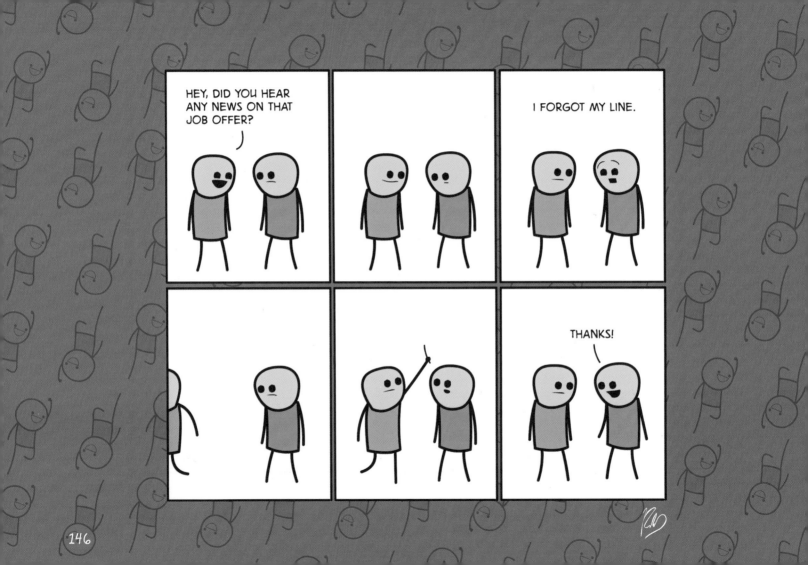

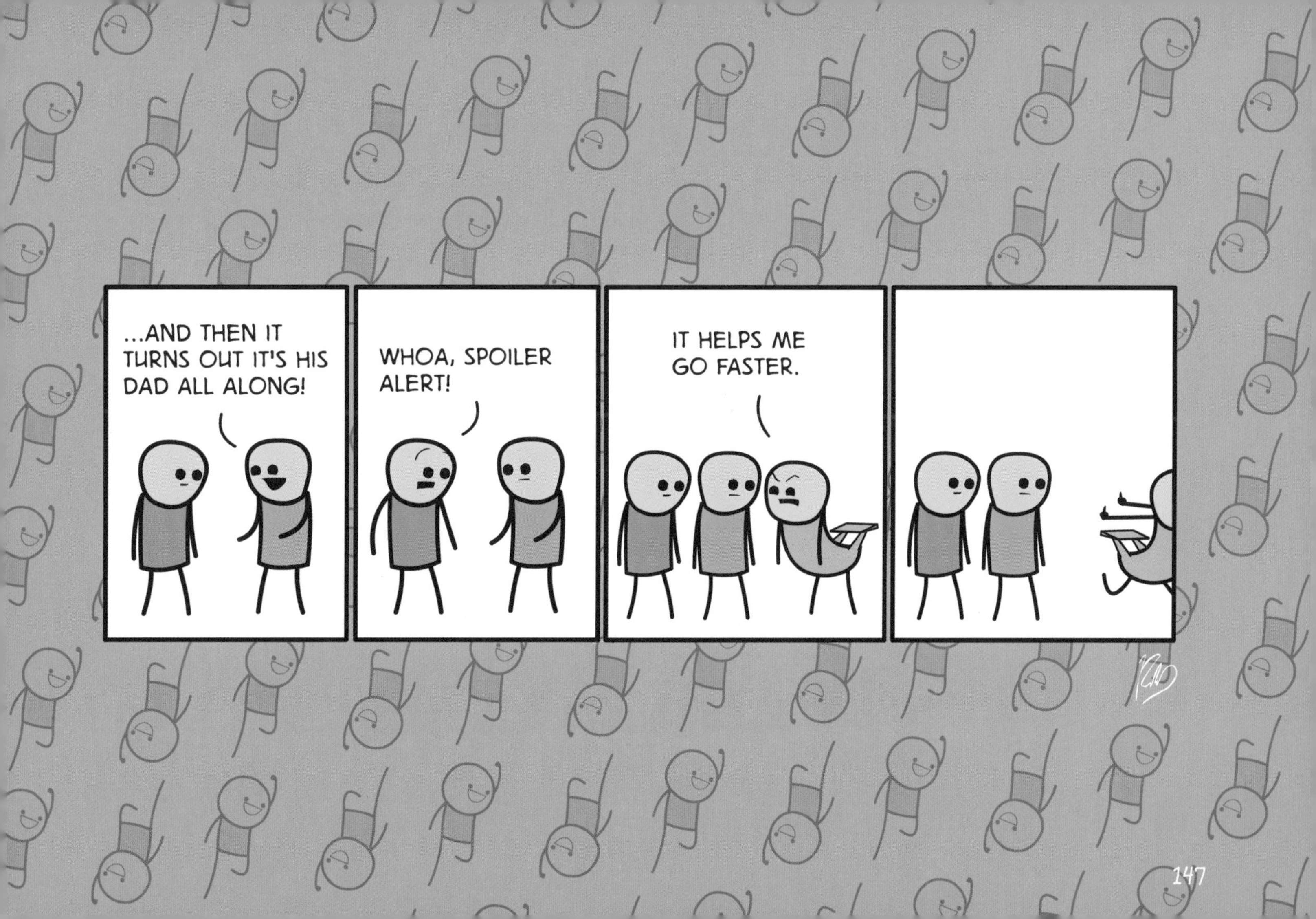
...AND THEN IT TURNS OUT IT'S HIS DAD ALL ALONG!
WHOA, SPOILER ALERT!
IT HELPS ME GO FASTER.

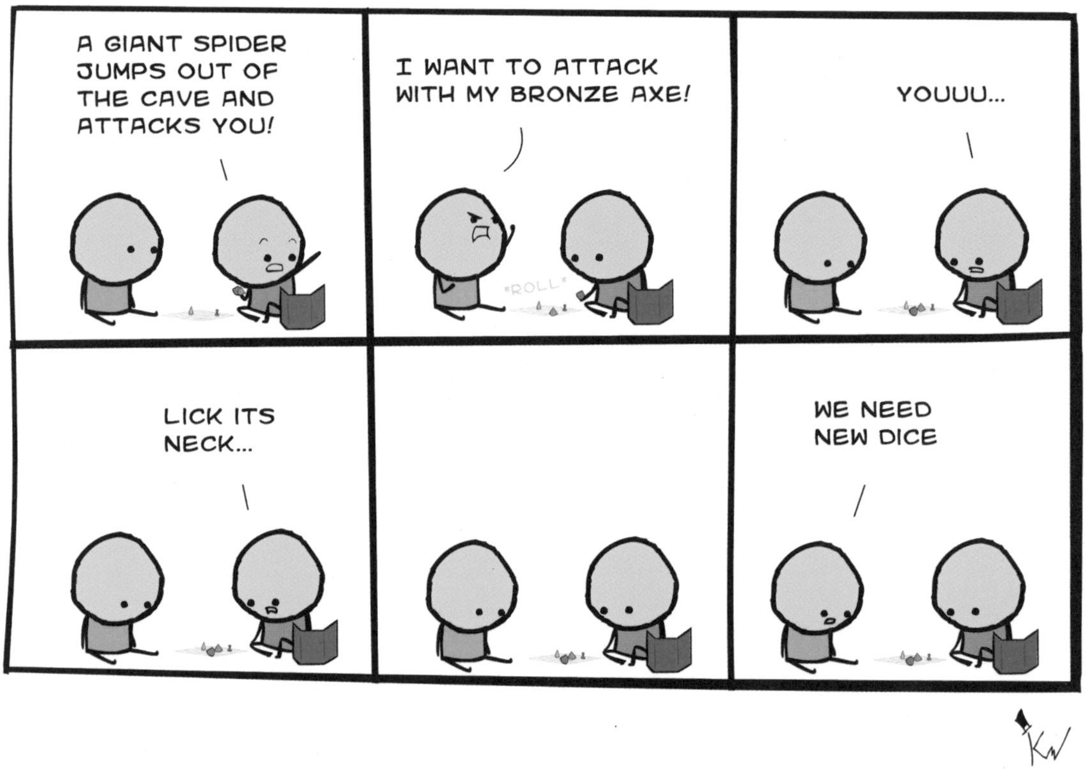
A GIANT SPIDER JUMPS OUT OF THE CAVE AND ATTACKS YOU!
I WANT TO ATTACK WITH MY BRONZE AXE!
ROLL
YOUUU...
LICK ITS NECK...
WE NEED NEW DICE

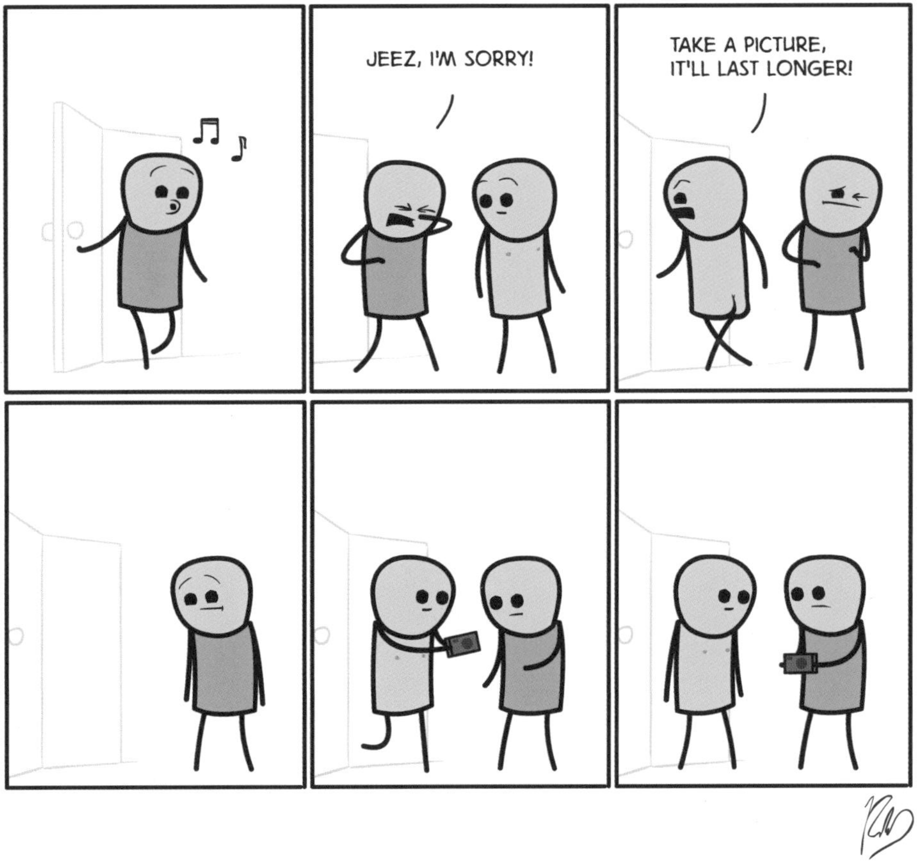
JEEZ, I'M SORRY!
TAKE A PICTURE, IT'LL LAST LONGER!

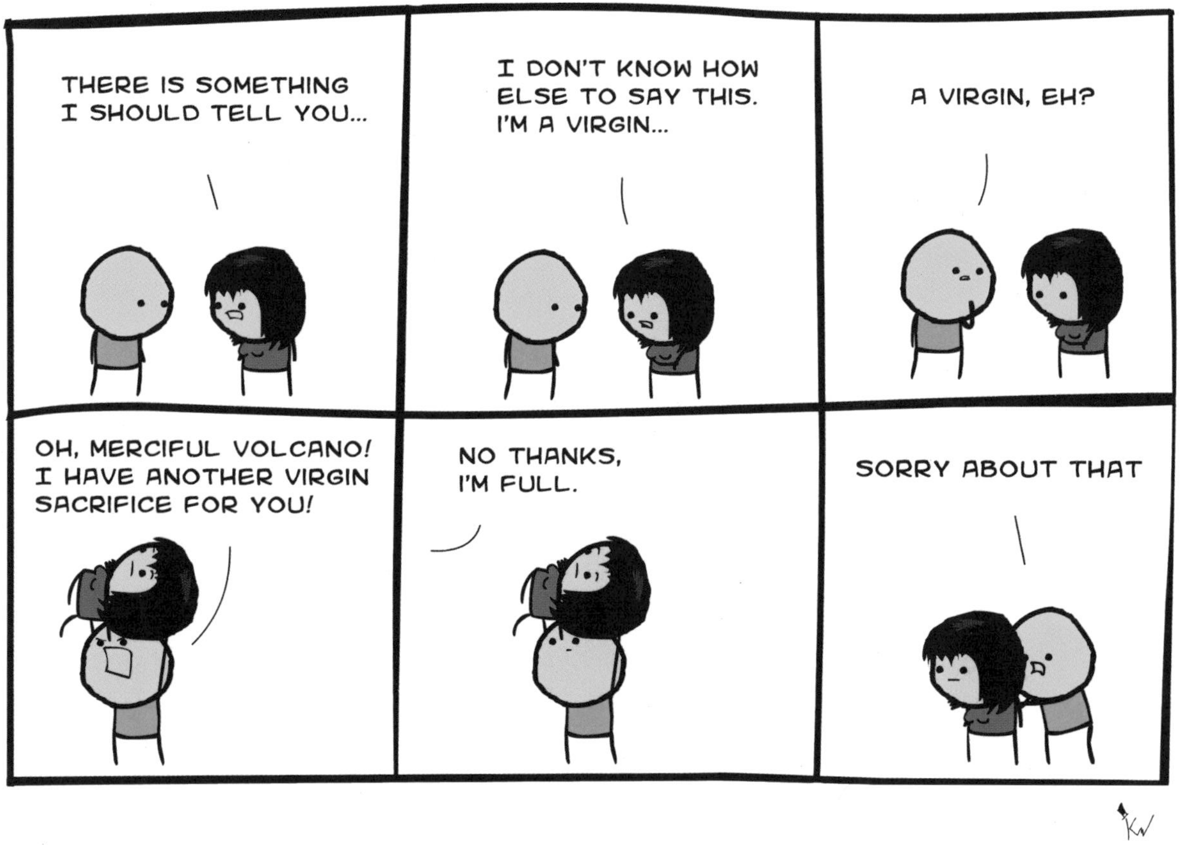
THERE IS SOMETHING I SHOULD TELL YOU...
I DON'T KNOW HOW ELSE TO SAY THIS. I'M A VIRGIN...
A VIRGIN, EH?
OH, MERCIFUL VOLCANO! I HAVE ANOTHER VIRGIN SACRIFICE FOR YOU!
NO THANKS, I'M FULL.
SORRY ABOUT THAT

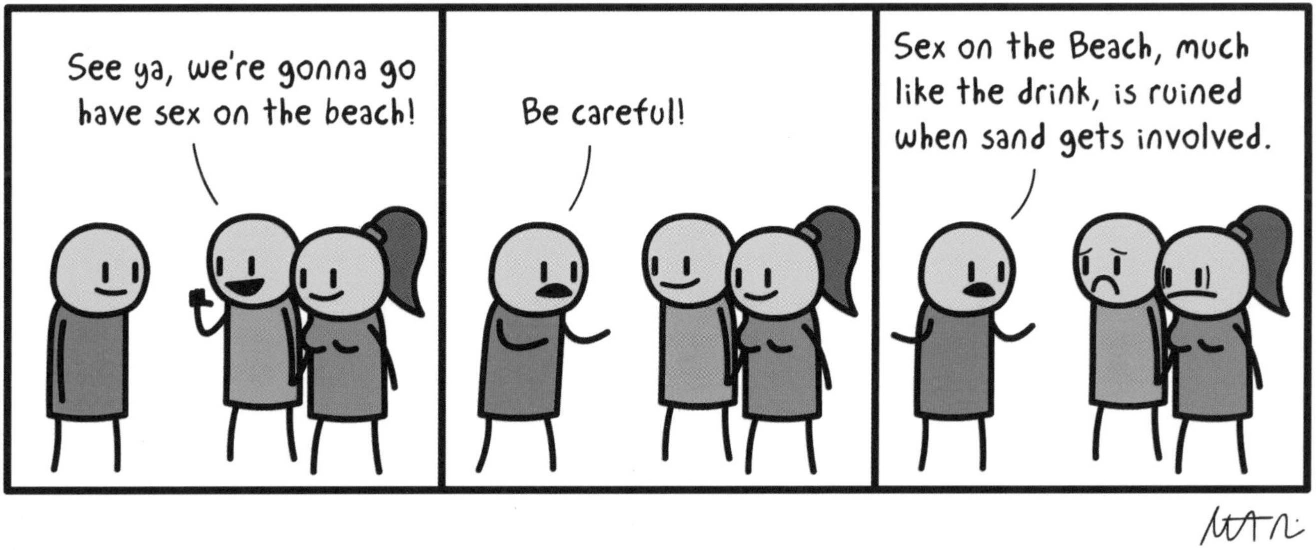
See ya, we're gonna go have sex on the beach!
Be careful!
Sex on the Beach, much like the drink, is ruined when sand gets involved.

PATENT OFFICE
Have I got the patent for you!
This is gonna make me rich!
You sure sound optimistic. What's your idea, sir?
Get this: lambskin condoms! A natural alternative to latex!
Interesting... but would lambskin really work?
Sure will! I screwed a dozen lambs and none of 'em got pregnant!

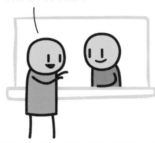

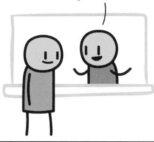

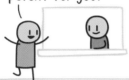

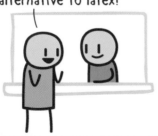

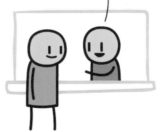

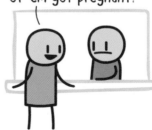

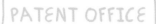

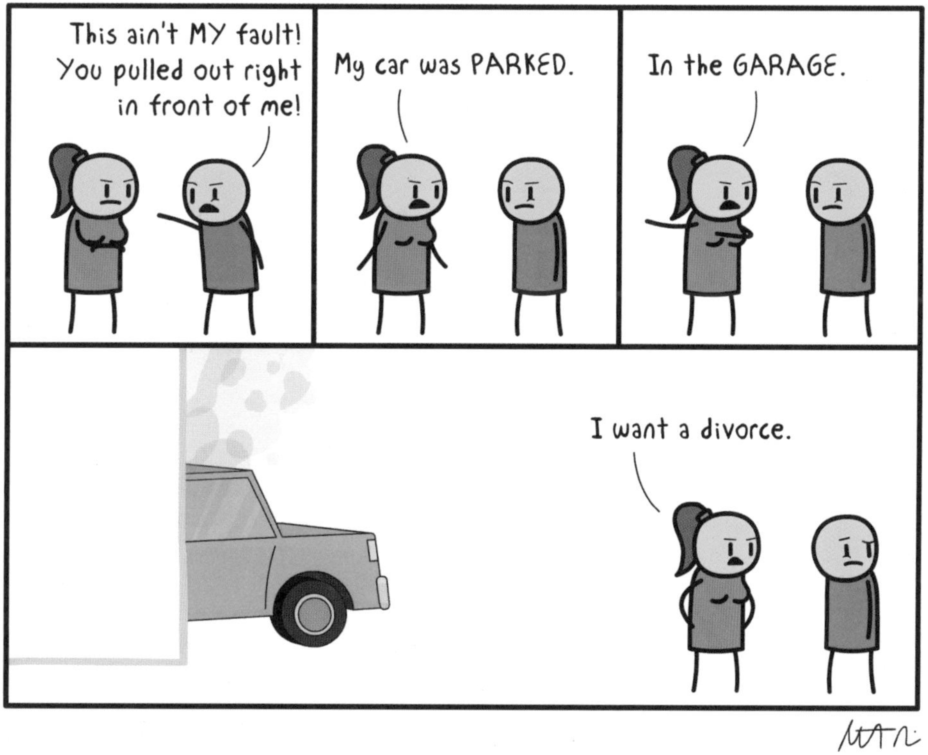
This ain't MY fault! You pulled out right in front of me!
My car was PARKED.
In the GARAGE.
I want a divorce.

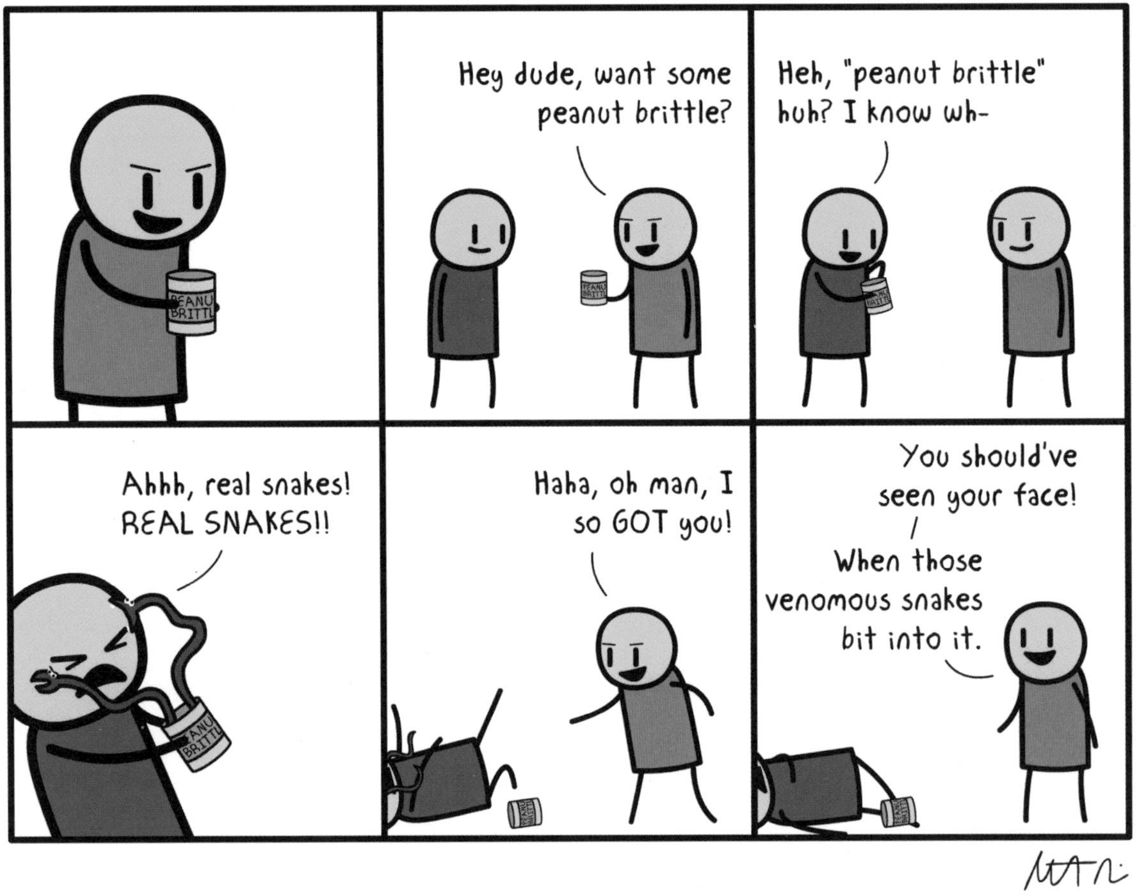
PEANU BRITTL
Hey dude, want some peanut brittle?
Heh, "peanut brittle" huh? I know wh-
Ahhh, real snakes! REAL SNAKES!!
Haha, oh man, I so GOT you!
You should've seen your face!
When those venomous snakes bit into it.

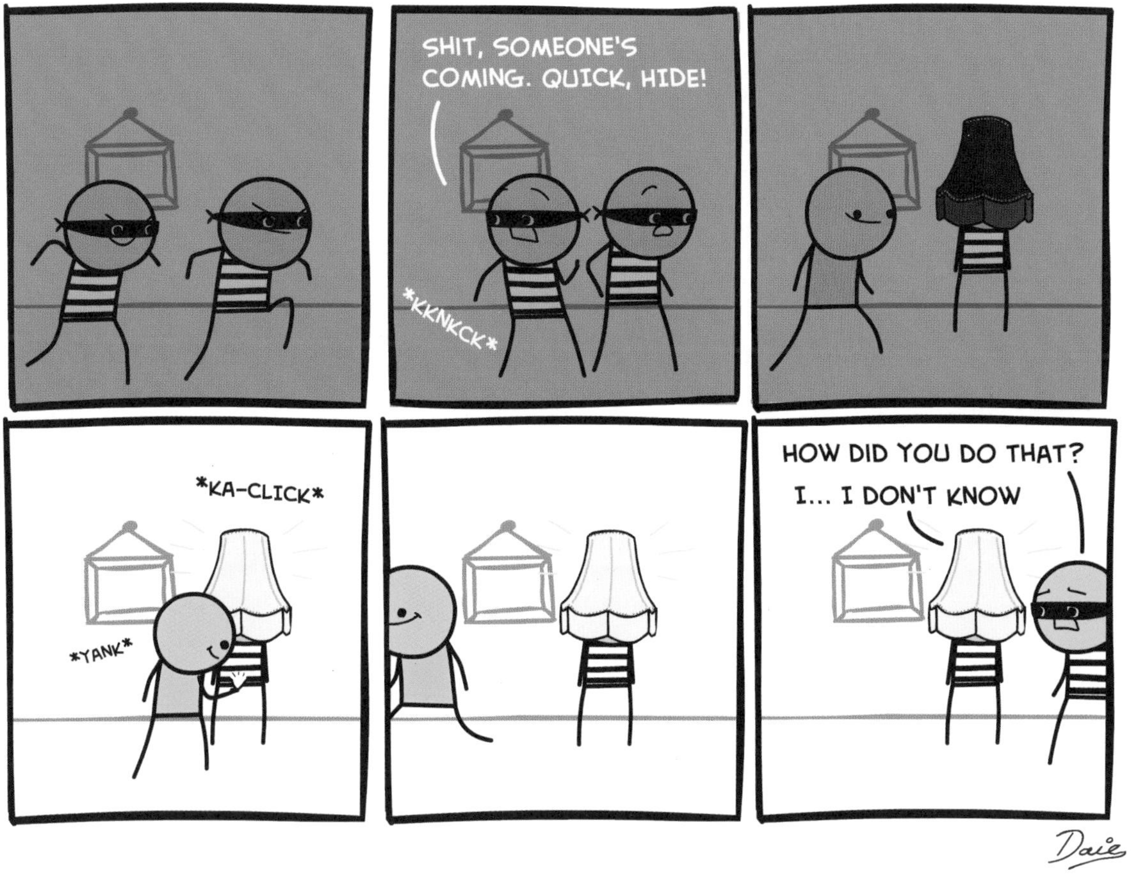
SHIT, SOMEONE'S COMING. QUICK, HIDE!
KKNKCK
KA-CLICK
YANK
HOW DID YOU DO THAT?
I... I DON'T KNOW
Dave

BURN IN HELL, FURRY!
VAIT, YOU MISHEARD! I SAID I'M A *FÜHRER*!
OH, THANK GOD.
I ALMOST *SHOT* YOU!

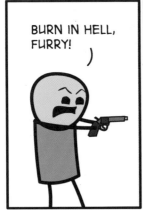

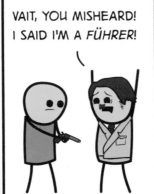

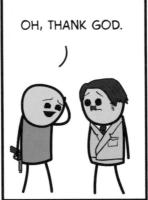

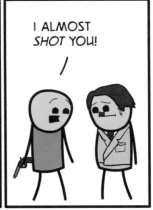

THE HOT DATE

A Chew Your Own Adventure

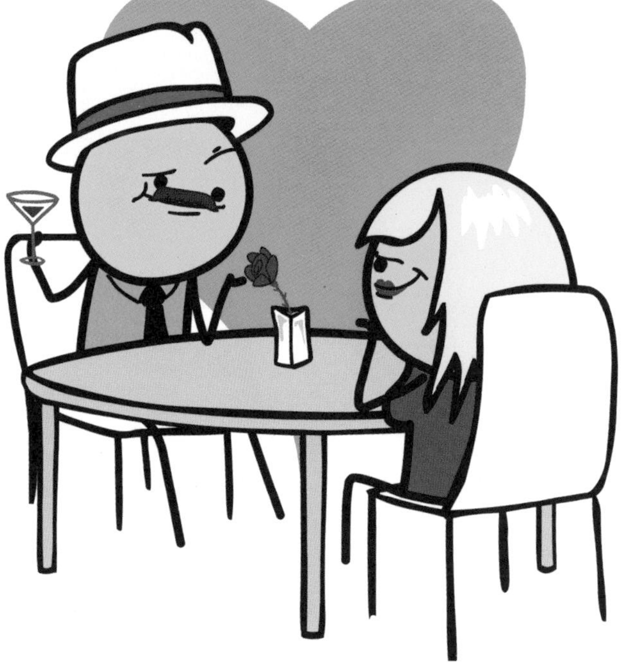

You've got a hot date coming over!

At least you hope so; you met her on the Internet. The same Internet that brought us cats and photos of women pooping on themselves. Obviously, you have mixed feelings, but this night can't go too wrong. Your mustache is waxed, you've got a feather in your cap, and potentially a sexy new string in your bow.

Speaking of caps, where is your cap? You can't have a hot date without a cool fedora. Do you go without it, or try to find it?

To look for your handsome headgear,
 turn to page 162

To ignore it and simply rely on your hunky head,
 turn to page 161

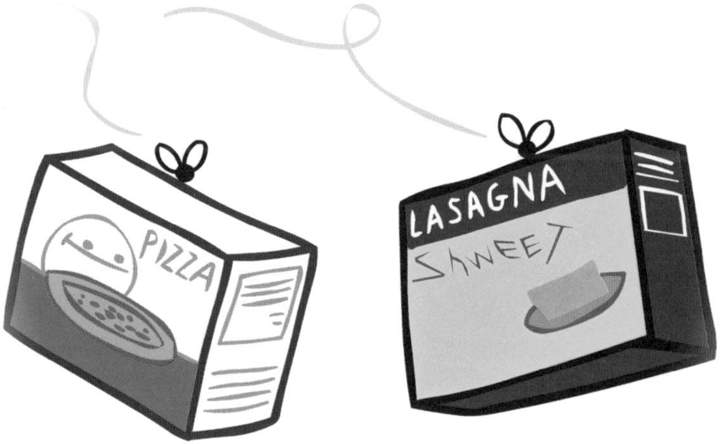
PIZZA
LASAGNA
SHWEET

Fedora-less, you limply walk toward the front door.

Your son suddenly jumps in front of you, giving you a spook. You really wish your ex-wife had custody of your shitty spawn.

"I'm fucking hungry!" he screams, screamily.

You realize putting food into Timmy's dumb mouth is the quickest way to get him into bed now so that you can get your date into bed later, if you know what you mean. And you do.

You swing open the pantry to see what you can throw together for Timmy. Several moths fly out, carrying two dinner options: a boxed lasagna or an instant pizza. Since you had moths for dinner yesterday, you should decide between the other two choices.

Timmy can't live on moths forever.

To opt for some delicious (and quick!) pizza,
turn to page 188

To fix up some authentic boxed lasagna,
turn to page 165

You search the hat rack, both of your wardrobes, and your head, but your hat is nowhere to be found! Frustrated, you walk out of your bedroom when you see your awful son, Timmy.

He's been an awful son ever since the divorce, and before as well. You forgot you had custody. Goddammit!

He waves his arms around, wearing your fedora, and says "Look at me! I'm a big dumb idiot!" You are not impressed with his impression. "More like un-impression," you say to him, smirking.

Timmy ignores your biting wit. "I'm hungry!" he says hungrily.

To beat the shit out of him,
turn to page 179

To flip him the bird and get ready for your saucy date,
turn to page 161

You crank the oven to 700. You throw the lasagna and meat sauce together into a collage of beef and noodles and throw it all into the oven.

Fifteen minutes go by while you twiddle your dick pensively. The lasagna is done, with mere seconds to spare.

You take a quick bite. It's crispy and savory. Mmmmm! Delighted, you serve it up for little Timmy.

"Whoa, Dad, you actually didn't fuck this up," he politely growls, like a fart on a ferris wheel.

It's the only compliment you've gotten from him in ten years. A small tear tickles your cheek. It is your tear. "Teehee!" says your tear. "It tickles!" you say as you weep.

Timmy chows down on a slice of lasagna, while you chow down on your watch with your eyes. Any moment now

your hot date will arrive, and you've successfully taken care of Timmy. The night is all yours now. You are the night. You are Batman. You are an Iron Chef and an Iron Man. A Batchef-Ironman. Yup. That's what you are.

You're roused from your superhero ruminations as the doorbell rings. It's showtime.

turn to page 194

163

You decide to boil the noodles first. "That makes sense!" you think in your brain. Water makes things soft, and these noodles are hard!

It's sharp intellect like that that'll win over your hopefully sexy date later tonight. And now you've got an interesting anecdote to impress her with!

Pleased with yourself, you look over at the other half of the equation: the packet of cheesy meat sauce. That should probably be cooked too. But how do you cook beefy cheese juice? You recall seeing a cooking show where they put things into a pot or something. Do you cook them together? Separate? You also have a microwave, which would be quick and painless.

To boil the meat with the noodles, turn to page 183

To sauté the meat, turn to page 174

To microwave the meat, turn to page 172

With little time to spare before your big date, you grab the lasagna box and rip it apart like a bear trying to read a newspaper. Way to show that lasagna box who's lasagna boss!

Out from the box falls a pouch of cheesy meat sauce and some dry noodles. You look back at the instructions only to realize you've mangled them beyond legibility because you can't open boxes like an evolved, human adult.

Too late, you realize you have no idea how to make lasagna. If only you could turn back time and not destroy the instructions. Or not have a child.

There are only two ingredients, so you swiftly deduce that you need to boil the noodles and cook the meat sauce. The question is, which do you do first?

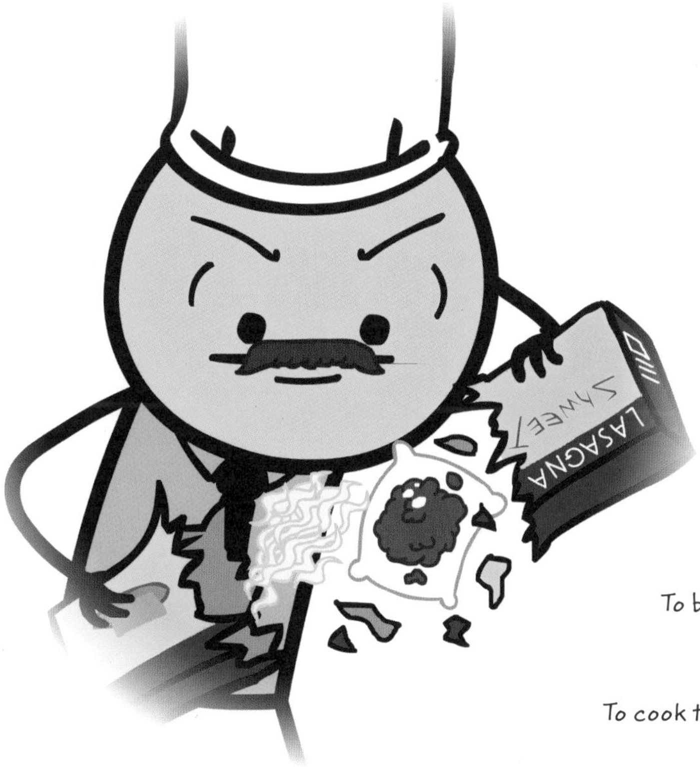
LASAGNA
Shweet

To boil the noodles first,
turn to page 164

To cook the meat sauce first,
turn to page 167

To opt for that pizza instead,
turn to page 188

"Son," you say hesitantly, carrying the oregano bottle into the other room. "Is this yours?"

"Fuck yeah it is. Quit bogartin' my stash, Daddy-o!"

He snatches the weed out of your hands. He then grabs a panflute and plays a song fit for a siren. A giant vulture swoops onto the window, carrying him to safety. That part doesn't really happen. Only in Timmy's head, because he's using druuuuugz.

Timmy's living his own life, and you've got no part in it. Dejected, you return to cooking your meat. The one thing in your life that isn't getting baked behind your back.

You've failed as a parent, but maybe you won't fail as a cook. With the meat sizzling, it's time to cook the noodles.

To boil the noodles, turn to page 170

To microwave the noodles, turn to page 172

To give up on Timmy and start a new life, turn to page 199

You slam dunk a hunk of meat chunk into the pan and get to business.

All is well, and for the first time in your life, you're starting to feel like you got this shit. You got lasagna down like a pro, yo. You're the mack daddy of macaroni. The King Weenie of linguini. The masta of pasta.

You're such a master chef now that you decide to spice it up even more. Screw boxed dinners, let's add some real ingenuity! Oregano, perhaps! Now you're cookin' up some good ideas, but where is the oregano? You've never used oregano in your life. You see a jar in the spice rack and what appears to be fresh oregano growing under the kitchen sink.

To use the fresh probably-oregano, turn to page 169

To use the jar of dried oregano, turn to page 168

You drop a dash of dried oregano into the sauce, only to be hit with a familiar odor. An odor you haven't smelled since college. That one time you walked past a college. While you were smoking that marijuana joint.

168

"This isn't oregano!" you whisper at the top of your lungs. "This is marijuana! Bermudagrass! The ol' giggly ganje! The green beans! The slappy jazz! Narcotics!"

After running out of euphemisms, you realize it's definitely not your marijuana. You moved past that shit ages ago and you're onto the hardcore stuff now, namely tasty lasagna. But if it's not your weed, that could only mean... Timmy! He must smoke uber-fat blunts and sit around being rad all day when you aren't home.

How could he be hiding this from you? Have you failed as a father? Also where's your oregano? Nothing about this adds up at all.

To confront Timmy about him doing drugs, turn to page 166

To get super-rad baked with him, turn to page 181

To ignore the whole situation and keep cooking, turn to page 170

To run away from all this and absolve yourself of responsibility, turn to page 199

You reach under the sink and grab two handfuls of what appears to be oregano. Adding it to your dish, you are immediately hit with a cloud of pungent vapors. It smells... delicious!

Having now departed from the recipe with fresh ingredients, you feel quite proud of your newfound culinary skills. You smile loudly.

You look over and see that you have an onion on the counter as well. Maybe if you add some onion to the meat sauce you'll get Timmy to finally admire and respect you. Everyone knows kids go ape-shit crazy for onions. Especially Timmy. You really hate onions, but Timmy REALLY loves them. Only because YOU really hate them, though.

How do you prepare it? Do you sauté the onions in a separate pan? Do you add them to the meat sauce? Or do you microwave them?

To cook the onions in a separate pan, turn to page 185

To cook the onions with the meat, turn to page 175

To throw everything in the microwave, turn to page 172

169

The meat now smells fragrant, like a delicious carrion flower. You gently thrust the noodles into a pot of boiling water.

"Boop bee-boop," says your phone. "Yay!" says you. You begin to rejoice.

You finish rejoicing. It's a text from your hopefully at least mildly attractive date! She'll be here in just 15 minutes!

With the noodles boiled, all that's left is baking the entire lasagna. That'll satisfy your miscreant of a son so you can get busy. You dig out a small piece of the lasagna instructions from the trash. It says to bake it for 30 minutes at 350 degrees. Fuuuuuuck!

But wait! After doing some incorrect math, you conclude that baking for 15 minutes at 750 degrees would accomplish the same thing! Maybe.

To live life in the fast lane, bake at 750 for 15 minutes and turn to page 163

To live life in the fastest lane, throw it in the microwave and turn to page 172

To live life on the service road and cook it at the recommended 350, turn to page 187

"Son, ever since the divorce I know I haven't always been there for you. And I know it's not easy seeing me date again," you say, pausing to think about that slight chance of awesome sex you'll have later, with your sexy date, maybe.

Timmy looks at you quietly, listening.

"But I just want you to know, I still love you, just as much, and I know your mom does, too. Even though we aren't as close as we used to be, I want you to know I still care about you very much. I think you're growing into a fine young man and I really want to spend more time with you. Just getting to know each other. I want to focus on being a better father."

Timmy stands there for a moment.

"Well, then maybe you should focus on those noodles, dickbrains," he jeers.

You look over and the pot of noodles is boiling over. You hastily grab the strainer, but it's too late. They're a sad, mushy pile of mush. A gooey appropriation of dinner. You hang your head in shame and hang your apron in the trashcan.

You've ruined the lasagna but there's still hope. Your choices are obvious: order in more lasagna, or give up on fatherhood and start a new life. Or punch your kid for being such a little shitbird.

To order in,
turn to page 177

To beat the hell out of little Timmy,
turn to page 179

To give up,
turn to page 184

You heave the food into the microwave because why not, right? God didn't invent microwaves for us to not use them. You hold your hands to your waist and throw a smug look in Timmy's direction. It misses him and leaves a smug mark on the wall. "This is how you cook when you've got a burly man brain, son. Now, let's get nuclear!"

"Beep boop boop!" you say to the microwave, slapping the buttons like a manta ray on a waterbed.

Despite your unorthodox hand slappings, the microwave timer is miraculously set for thirty seconds, like you wanted. You and Timmy eagerly watch it count down.

5... 4... 3... 2... 1...

The microwave violently explodes before you even have the chance to say, "That's not meant to happen." In fact, you can't even fire one last thought before every cell in your body is obliterated by the blast.

The End.

172

The microwave explodes in a fiery blast, obliterating your precious atoms, not to mention Timmy's tiny little boy atoms, your delicious dinner atoms, and the terrorists' atoms. A bright white light washes over you. It's warm and reminds you of your mother's womb. It's a very womby white light. It's a womb with a view.

The light fades, revealing a sole figure standing in front of you. He towers eight feet tall, draped in robes with a billowy white beard. This better not be your date. Or Satan.

"Are you Satan?" you ask.

"Nope. I'm God." says God, gaudily.

"Oh, okay." you say, realizing it really is God, "Satan would never say that."

"Thank you for killing those four terrorists. You lost your life but saved a bunch of people, I bet. Here's heaven." God says, motioning to a bunch of clouds. "Have fun, man."

"No problem, big G," you say. "Wait-four terrorists? I only killed three."

"That fourth, littler terrorist." God says.

"Oh, that was my son. He's no terrorist! He's just terrorble!" you quip.

You both laugh all-knowingly. God slaps you hard on the back and treats you to his beercan hat while Timmy burns in hell due to the mix-up.

The End.

You gently sauté the meat. So gently. So, so gently. Firm, but tender to its needs. You could fall asleep on its breast. Breasts... Date night! You check your watch. You still have twenty minutes.

You're awoken from your "saucy" daydream when you notice Timmy sneaking a peek through the doorway.

You realize this might be your chance to connect with your estranged and shitty son. You notice you have a whole pan full of beef that you could skillfully flip without the use of a spatula. What could be more fathersome (fath-awesome?) than tossing your meat in the kitchen?

Alternatively, you could say something deep and fatherly. Sometimes words can speak louder than rad meat flips. But not often.

To flip the meat,
turn to page 180

To give him some fatherly advice,
turn to page 171

In a moment of blind genius, you can't see, but you can think up great ideas. Suddenly, your moment is gone, and you can see again, but now you're dumb. Thank god.

You pour in some twice diced onions into the cheesy oregano-y saucy meat sauce. "This seems about right!" you say, and you would know. You're an all-star chef dad who can do no wrong, right?

You realize it's time to boil the noodles. You quickly check your watch. You can't quite make it out, so you check your watch again, but slower this time. You don't have long until your date shows up, and the noodles are still high and dry! How are you gonna prepare them?

To boil them like you know you should, turn to page 170

To microwave them for some goddamn reason, turn to page 172

Congratulations!

You've found the secret page, the page not connected to any other page. This means you're either really clever or really bad at turning pages!

Feels like purgatory, doesn't it? There's not much going on here, but you're welcome to stay a while. Towels are on the left, toilet roll on the right. Toilet's in the middle. Take a seat. Make a shit. Since you've found the secret page, here are some secrets about the Cyanide & Happiness crew...

Cyanide & Happiness is ghost-written by the writers of Marmaduke, so they can use all their —too out there— ideas.

By night, Dave runs a vast underground harem of immigrant women whom he forces to watch Netflix and give him a summary of everything.

The Purple-Shirted Eye-Stabber never washes his shirt or his knife.

The comics have actually looped back around since 2009, and no one has noticed.

Rob cried while writing every one of his comics. Kris cried while reading them.

Rob is a man's body trapped in a man's body Forever stuck in a dog knot.

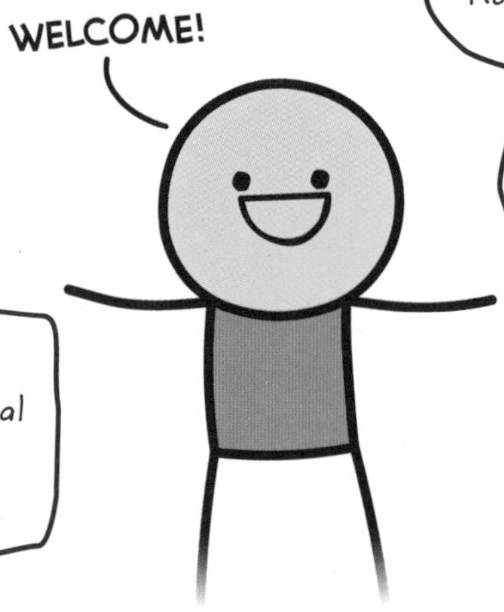
WELCOME!

Matt once slapped his mom for the last pancake. With the pancake. She's dead now.

Matt's first job was a rimjob. He paid twice as much for it.

Matt's hair is a toupee. Kris' facial hair is actually Matt's real hair.

Kris is actually a bug living inside his own brain.

Dave once borrowed Kris's legs and never gave them back.

You make a quick phone call to your local 24 hour lasagna emporium and order one lasagna, extra noodly. Twenty minutes later, the doorbell rings.

This smells amazing! Why did you even bother trying to cook? It's almost as if you didn't even have a choice in the matter. It was God's will that you blew ass at cooking! Thank you, God. Thank you, Will.

You slough the lasagna onto a fresh plate to impress Timmy. Look at that lasagna-sloughing prowess, he will say. Look at that plate. So fresh. So now. So slough. Maximum mealage.

Now that your shitty son is fed, it's time for your big date. You check your watch. It's 8:00 sharp, and you're even sharper. She should be here any minute now!

The doorbell rings.

turn to page 194

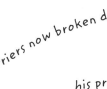

You refill the pipe and continue getting **mindblasted.** Your brain feels like a Super Nintendo full of toast. You and Timmy talk freely, your barriers now broken down by the smoky song of herb.

You tell him all about your problems and feelings, and he tells you about his problems and feelings, which are like your problems but not as important since he's just a kid. But you listen anyway. Since you're both on **whacky drugs,** most of your feelings are about how cool your hands are.

Suddenly, you smell something burning and not the good kind of burning like the green genie you're smoking. Something that smells Italian... meaty... your lasagna!

You run into the kitchen to see what's left of your meal. It's ruined! Burnt to a crisp! Cooked the hell up. It smells like Pompeii on a rainy day.

There's only one choice left: Order in some new lasagna. Or keep getting high. Two choices.

To order in, turn to page 177

To continue smoking, turn to page 181

Both fists akimbo, you corner your shitty
milktoast of a son and prepare to hail
down a storm of pain onto your child's
frowny brow. But all that rains down is a
light drizzle. Of tears. From your face.

Because unfortunately for you, his
mother's been sending him to bi-weekly
karate lessons. Since you couldn't
prepare him a dinner, Timmy serves a
three course meal of uppercuts to your
ass, sending you spinning through a
window.

It turns out Timmy's less of a milktoast
and more of a beerbeef. He's the new
man of the house.

You drop a quick text message to your
date saying you are not enough of a
man to date anyone and cry and bleed
yourself to sleep.

The End.

You strike a chef pose and rear back with your pan of meat sauce. Like an arthritic tennis player, you haggardly flip the pan upward, sending scalding hot meat high above the stove. It lingers in the air for a moment, seeming like an eternity. Here it comes, your big chance. Don't fuck it up!

You fuck it way the fuck up. The meat lands on the meat where your legs meet. Your dick. The beef is all over your pork. Way to go!

Your son looks you dead in the eye. Your third, third-degree burned eye. You force a smile while you fight back tears.

"Go sit on a spike and spin, Dad!" Timmy exclaims, throwing up two middle fingers and running off to find a new dad who can cook dinner without touching it with his dick.

Looks like your son won't be eating your meat. And neither will your prospective date.

You've boiled your loins instead of spoiling the spoils of your loins.

The End.

You grab a fistful of weed and walk into the other room.

"Son, let's smoke some marijuana weed. Some ganja beans. Some slappy jazz. Some swurvy herb. The Kansas campfire, I mean. The zany brain! The dandy handshake. Some silly dilly. The sticky twig. Some of that slimy crime," you say, knowingly.

"You mean pot?" Timmy replies.

"Is that what you kids call it now? I'll be sure to remember that." you say, not knowingly.

The two of you get super-rad bakesauced out of your minds. You both feel connected in a way you've never felt before, like two sides of a zipper on a nun's jumpsuit.

Timmy taps the pipe abruptly. A small bit of ash falls out. You are out of... what was it? Pot. But you aren't out of it! There's more in that jar in your hand.

Now, to make a choice.

To keep smoking,
turn to page 178

To keep smoking,
turn to page 178

Quick on your feet, you quickly get off your feet. You fall to the floor and roll and thrash around, not unlike a sausage in a sausage-race. Good job!

As you roll around in sausagey triumph, the terrorists shoot your son a glare. And then they shoot him a bullet. A dessert of bullet-flavored soufflet. Straight from the heart and into the brain.

You cry onto and around his body, creating a perfect outline around his body for the police to use later. "What have you done!?" you scream.

"We shot your son."

"Oh. Right," you say, noticing the brains everywhere.

"Now give us the device or we'll kill you, too," they yell, thrusting the gun into your pelvis. This is not the kind of pelvic thrusting you wanted to do tonight, but it seems like it's the best you'll get. You slowly thrust into the barrel of their gun, knowing this may be your last shot at some action.

"Stop being gross and give us the device!" they say.

To ask the terrorists what the device is, turn to page 196

To run away, hop in your car and start a new life, turn to page 186

To keep thrusting, turn to page 197

You dump the meat sauce directly into the boiling water. It swirls around and around, clouding the water with a delicious yellow-brown cloud of beefstuff. It looks like the ending of Jaws where the shark explodes everywhere, except with a cheese-filled cow exploding instead of a shark, which is not as cool.

"Mmm, that sure looks tasty doesn't it?" you say, nodding to Timmy.

"That looks like someone took a diarrhea in a hot tub," Timmy says. You say "Thanks" before you realize this isn't a compliment. Boy, you sure look stupid. You are a sad parody of a father and a chef.

"I thought you were hungry. I'm making a delicious meal for you," you bleat, bleatedly.

"I'd rather go to war," Timmy says as he solemnly walks out of the house, off to die fighting in some war-torn hellhole where he can find better food.

The End.

You've finally lost it. Your noodles are ruined, and your own noodle's gone crazy. You plop the noodles on your head and shout, "LOOK AT ME! I'M KURT COBAIN!" before pantsing yourself and climbing onto the roof.

"I'm the fucking emperor of the universe!" you scream at the top of your lungs as you jump face first into the pavement.

Your son watches patiently as you die a slow bleedy death. He does not object.

Your son goes on in life to achieve a major in bio-medical sciences, where he gains an internship into a multi-billion dollar weapons corporation. He invents a serum that revives dead people.

He doesn't use it on you.

The End.

Confident in your cooking skills, you drizzle peanut oil into a second pan and chuck in the diced onions. The oil drizzle sizzles. Fo' rizzle.

Timmy comes sprinting into the room.

"I FUCKING LOVE ONIONS!" he belts, grabbing a handful from the pan and stuffing them into his mouth.

You smile, pleased at your son. Your smile and son are short-lived, though. Timmy falls on the linoleum floor and starts convulsing.

"Oh no, he's loving onions to death!" you scream. Then you remember, he's allergic to peanuts. The same peanuts that are used to make peanut oil, which is why it's called that.

You prepare his tombstone engraving: "Here lies Timmy. He died doing what he loved. Onions." Paramedics arrive at the scene and comment on your lack of taste in preparing your son's tombstone. You, in turn, criticize them for arriving well after you buried him. Some paramedics!

They dig him up and shovel him into the ambulance. They pronounce him dead before they even start the engine back up, so they shovel him back into his grave.

You've missed your sizzlin' hot date, but there is another date coming up. A court date. Because you let your son die.

The End.

185

Forget your date, forget your kid, forget cooking. You're a free man. What you wanna do is LIVE, baby. Feel the wind in your hair, the rain on your cheeks, some boobies with your hands.

You run out yelling "Freebird!" hop into your convertible and peel out of the driveway. As you drive away, your son, with his last dying effort, grabs a gun from one of the terrorists and shoots you in the back of the face, exploding the top of your head in a really cool burst of blood and brain bits.

Probably one of the coolest brain explosions you'd ever see if you weren't the one exploding. Such is life.

The End.

turn to page 198 for the epilogue.

You set the oven to 350 and the timer for 30 minutes. A chandelier falls on your head. You die. **The End.**

OH SNAP!

You grab the pizza out of the pantry, carefully read the instructions, and slide it into the oven just like you plan to slide your "pizza" into your date's "oven" later tonight (a.k.a. having sex).

Eleven minutes pass like they ain't nothin'. You offer little Timmy a slice of the action, the action being pizza. Not the other action: the possible sex with your possibly hot date, possibly.

Timmy looks at his slice of pizza and says, "What the fuck is this?" You take a moment to realize that this wasn't a rhetorical question. Timmy hates your pizza, but why?

"But why?" you ask. Timmy points to the copious amounts of green mold covering the pizza. "Why don't you take a pizza advice and never cook again!" he sickly burns. You hear a lone moth yell, "Oh snap!" in the distance.

Frozen pizza is supposed to go in the freezer, you realize, also recalling you just ate a whole slice yourself. You spend the rest of the night crying and shitting yourself to sleep.

The End.

These terrorists chose the wrong dad to mess with. Not today. Not after all the shit you've dealt with. You've got a potentially-female date soon! Time to send these terrorists straight to an early terrorist grave.

Since you've learned how to fight through videogames, you decide to throw a banana at them and then drive them over with your go-kart. You don't have a go-kart, though. Or a banana.

You walk towards them, flailing your arms in big circles like a domestic abuser on a Saturday night. They deflect your swings like a well-prepared spouse. You try to spit wasps at them but realize you don't have any wasps in your mouth. You'll have to fix that later. But for now, you spit your teeth at them instead.

You proceed to punch your own eye to make it black and intimidating, much like a panda. The terrorists remark "Ha, that idiot punched himself!" and you carefully explain that it was intentional, in order to save face. But not your own.

They punch you inside your mouth. You stand there, feeling confused and awkward. You look a fool with your big black eyes and no teeth. If this is what a panda looks like, no wonder they're endangered.

To stand there pitifully,
turn to page 195

For a quick laugh,
turn to page 6 through 157
(the pages all the comics are on)

189

This is your moment of truth. You puff out your chest and wave your arms around to look more intimidating. Scouts taught you to make loud noises while showing your teeth. You feel like a big, scary kite. You look like an idiot. You smell like a kite.

In your moment of triumph, the terrorists give your son a dessert of bullet-flavored ice cream, straight from the gun. Timmy's brains explode all over your floral wallpaper, vastly improving it. You stand there in shock.

"What have you done!?" you scream whathaveyoudonedly.

The terrorists seem as shocked as you are.

"Whoa, I'm sorry. In our culture, the way you waved your arms is the sign for 'kill my son, please.' Now give us the device, or I'm afraid we'll have to kill you, too."

"I don't know about any DEvice, but I can give you some ADvice!" you smirk, "Always cook the meaty cheese sauce first when you're preparing a-"

"Shut up," they counter-advise, thrusting the gun into your mouth. "The device. Now."

To ask the terrorists what the fucking device is,
turn to page 196

To run off to your convertible and start a new life,
turn to page 186

They yell at you again. "I said give us th-"

Before they can finish, you go limp and slop onto the floor in front of the assailants.

You crack an eye open to see what happens next. One of the terrorists waddles over and prods you with his gun. He turns back to his buddies. "This guy's dead, I think."

"He's been dead to me for years," your son adds.

"I like your moxy, kid," the head terrorist says. "Wanna join our rag-tag team o' terror?"

"K." Timmy responds over-enthusiastically.

They seal the deal by high fiving REALLY well then bro-bumping with vigor. Their guns go off like champagne bottles, and they raise their guns to their mouths and take a sip of crisp smoke. "It's a good day to be a terrorist!" The ferocious foursome walks off into the sunset, a good day's work done.

Too scared to go on your date, you decide to take your lasagna to bed with you and finish it by yourself. This isn't the night you were expecting, but it's the night you deserve. A night to yourself.

The End.

You don't want to be a party pooper, but you do have a date coming. Terrorists and dead son be damned! You've been through enough tonight. This isn't the kind of action you wanted! The terrorists got their device, now it's time for a special lady to get yours.

"Buzz off, you big mean terror-heads," you say, pushing them aside. "I've got a pretty lady to woo."

The terrorists laugh. What's so funny? You check your fly, and it isn't down.

"What's so funny, huh?" you huh.

The terrorists politely explain that they were, in fact, your sexy date all along. The whole blind date was a ploy for them to retrieve the device. You all have a big hearty laugh over the situation. Online dating, right folks?

"Say, you guys are alright. Why let this delicious pasta go to waste?" you say, gesturing towards your noodly dish.

"Sounds infidelicious!" they enthusiastically enthuse.

To sit down and have a relaxing dinner,
turn to page 193

Your new friends sit down for a nice fancy feast. Over lukewarm lasagna, you all discuss the whacky occurrences of the evening, and everyone gets to know each other a bit more.

"Hold on a sec," one of the terrorists says, leaving and then returning with a twelve pack of ice cold beer.

"Right on!" you say, busting open a cold one.

"Good golly! This is tip-top chow!" one of the terrorists says britishly. "Did you make this lasagna yourself?"

"Sure did!" you exclaim, proudly.

"I would kill for the recipe!" he replies. You laugh nervously, while they laugh regularly.

You pass the lasagna around again; everyone seems happy and content. You're proud of yourself for the first time in your life. You break out the video camera to record this touching moment, a glorious memory that'll stick with you forever.

As the camera pans over Timmy's corpse, you take a moment to realize that while you might've lost a son, despite everything, you've gained a family.

You Win.

Your date must be here! You snap your fedora onto your head and suavely slither over to the door. You sensually reach for the knob, absorbing the anticipation before you see your sexy-ass date bitch. After all you've been through, you hope she's at least a woman. This night's been bad enough!

BAM!

Three burly men with guns kick the door in, knocking you flat on your back.

"Holy whack-a-moley! Terrorists!" yells Timmy.

He's right. They are terrorists. You're a little disappointed that they're not at least sexy-ass date terrorists. They're the bad kind of terrorists. Suddenly, you feel terrorized, which is EXACTLY WHAT THEY WANT.

"Give us the device!" the terrorists yell terroristly, raising their guns to you.

To stand there dumbfounded,
turn to page 195

To fight your way out of this mess like a true patriot action hero,
turn to page 189

To use the microwave,
turn to page 173

You stand there, disoriented and confused. The terrorists suddenly grab Timmy away from his dinner and shove a gun into his lasagna-filled mouth.

"Ah luff thith lathagnya," Timmy says, "But not thith gun."

"Give us the device!!" the terrorists spit at you.

"Say it, don't spray it!" you spray back, two-fold.

"I'll spray your sons brains all over this shit-tastic one bedroom apartment!" they terrorize. That was pretty clever wordplay for a bunch of terrorists, so you know they're serious. Also, you're going to move into a nicer house one of these days.

You have to do something, or little Timmy will be taken out of this world the same way he was brought in: at gunpoint. Maybe if you get out of this alive, you can tell us more about that story. C'mon, dude, don't leave us hanging. You need to survive. Wait! Survival

tactics! You suddenly recall your Cub Scout training from so many years ago. There are no trees nearby to climb or hug, so you realize you only have three ways to get out of this.

To play dead,
turn to page 191

To wave your arms and appear larger, turn to page 190

To stop drop and roll,
turn to page 182

"What fucking device?!" you fucking say.

"That one!" they say, pointedly. They point at the microwave that you've never used.

"My food-heater box thing?" you ask.

"That's no whatever you just called it. It's a bomb that was sent to you by mistake. We've been searching for it for ages, so we can do our big terrorist plot."

"Cool, I never use it anyway," you say, giving them the microwave.

"Thanks!" they exclaim. "Say, what is that heavenly whifferific dish you've cooked up?"

You realize they're talking about your lasagna. Our lasagna. Timmy's lasagna. Poor, poor Timmy.

Regardless of your hungry, unwanted guests and your dead son, you do have a date tonight. Are you gonna let these terrorists and one kid dying get in the way of some sweet action? You consider ordering more take-out lasagna to keep the terrorists at bay before realizing that doesn't make sense.

To tell the terrorists to go fuck themselves because you've got a date, turn to page 192

To forget your date and invite the terrorists to dinner instead, turn to page 193

You continue to hump the loaded gun like an animal in heat, unable to resist its charm.

"Stop it! Cut that out! Eww eww eww!!" the terrorist harps.

You whinney.

The terrorists are in no mood. The terrorist wielding the gun wraps his finger around the trigger and squeezes, shooting a load of lead in your unblowed load.

Now you've lost more than a son. You've lost millions of future sons. You'll never be a dad again, which is probably for the best given everything that's happened tonight.

The End.

The terrorists, equally amazed at your son's marksmanship and at your total lack of accountability as a father, vow to nurse Timmy back to health. They know they can give him the life you never could.

Meanwhile, the rest of your brain-exploded body drives off into the sunset, finally free of possessions, fatherhood, responsibility, and the top half of your head. Not to mention control of the vehicle. You miss the sunset and crash through a 16th century guillotine, decapitating what's left of your irresponsible excuse for a head.

Your headless body flies out of the car and goes on to become a successful Vegas magician. The car went on to join the Navy and was never heard from again. The terrorists went on to become even better terrorists, thanks to the sterling efforts of your boy, a feat for which he was awarded ten medals.

The End.

Forget your date, forget your kid, forget cooking. You're a free man. What you wanna do is LIVE, baby. Feel the wind in your hair, the rain on your cheeks, some boobies with your hands.

You run out yelling "Freebird!" and hop into your convertible and peel out of the driveway. The world is your god damn oyster.

You're a man. Your own man. A man's man. Whatever you wanna be. No longer a man of the house, you're a man of the world now! Spread those oats like you've got breakfast to share.

Maybe you'll hit Vegas! Become the next Elvis. Drive up the West Coast with the sun in your mirror and your hand in your pants. Go see New York. The big city. That's what they call it in New York.

You can hit up Cuidad Juarez. Or the outback. Atlantis. Margaritaville. The whole world is at your fingertips!

You drive off into the sunset, finally free of possessions, fatherhood, responsibility, and love.

The End.